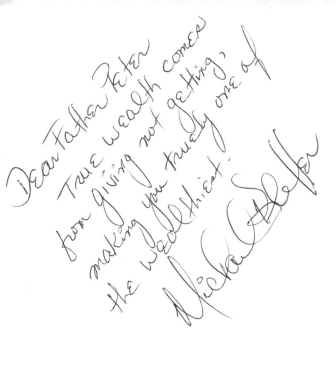

Dear Father Peter

True wealth comes
from giving not getting,
making you truely one of
the wealthiest.

Michael Steffen

The
Wealthy
1 0 0

The
Wealthy
1 0 0

*From Benjamin Franklin
to Bill Gates—
A Ranking of the
Richest Americans,
Past and Present*

Michael Klepper and Robert Gunther

A Citadel Press Book
Published by Carol Publishing Group

A Citadel Press Book

Published by Carol Publishing Group

Citadel Press is a registered trademark of Carol Communications, Inc.

Editorial, sales and distribution, rights and permissions inquiries should be addressed to Carol Publishing Group, 120 Enterprise Avenue, Secaucus, N.J. 07094

In Canada: Canadian Manda Group, One Atlantic Avenue, Suite 105, Toronto, Ontario M6K 3E7

Carol Publishing Group books may be purchased in bulk at special discounts for sales promotion, fund-raising, or educational purposes. Special editions can be created to specifications. For details, contact Special Sales Department, Carol Publishing Group, 120 Enterprise Avenue, Secaucus, N.J. 07094.

Manufactured in the United States of America

10 9 8 7 6 5 4 3 2 1

Library of Congress Cataloging-in-Publication Data

Klepper, Michael M.
    The wealthy 100 : from Benjamin Franklin to Bill Gates—a ranking of the richest Americans, past and present / Michael Klepper and Robert Gunther.
        p.   cm.
    "A Citadel Press book."
    ISBN 0-8065-1800-6 (hard)
    1. Millionaires—United States—Biography.   2. Capitalists and financiers—United States—Biography.   I. Gunther, Robert E., 1960–
. II. Title
HG172.A2K58   1996
332'.092'273—dc20   95-50109
                                                                 CIP

To my wife, Cindie, for her encouragement, assistance, and support throughout this project, and my sons, Anders and Pelle. They are all the riches I will ever need.

—R.E.G.

To my father, who epitomizes the American Dream. No, he's not one of the 100 wealthiest Americans of all time. He came to this country as a teenager who didn't speak any English and who had meager resources. But, by virtue of his energies and drive, he elevated himself to become a successful entrepreneur and investor, and, above all, a successful father, who instilled in me the values of caring, sharing, and winning. Thanks, Dad.

—M.M.K.

CONTENTS

HOW RICH WERE THEY?

This chart lists each of the Wealthy 100 by rank and shows total wealth at the time of the person's death or, if the person is still alive, as of 1995. Relative wealth is expressed as a ratio of the person's total wealth to the U.S. Gross National Product (GNP) at the time of the person's death (or in 1995 if the person is still alive). For example, when John D. Rockefeller died in 1937, his wealth of $1.4 billion equaled 1/65th of the nation's GNP.

Rank	Name	Birth	Death	Wealth (Thousands)	Ratio (Wealth ÷ GNP)
1.	John D. Rockefeller	1839	1937	$1,400,000	65
2.	Cornelius Vanderbilt	1794	1877	$105,000	87
3.	John Jacob Astor	1763	1848	$20,000	107
4.	Stephen Girard	1750	1831	$7,500	150
5.	Andrew Carnegie	1835	1919	$475,000	166
6.	A. T. Stewart	1803	1876	$50,000	178
7.	Frederick Weyerhaeuser	1834	1914	$200,000	182
8.	Jay Gould	1836	1892	$77,000	185
9.	Stephen Van Rensselaer	1764	1839	$10,000	194
10.	Marshall Field	1834	1906	$140,000	205
11.	Henry Ford	1863	1947	$1,000,000	231
12.	Andrew W. Mellon	1855	1937	$350,000	258
13.	Richard B. Mellon	1858	1933	$350,000	258
14.	Sam M. Walton	1918	1992	$22,000,000	275
15.	James G. Fair	1831	1894	$45,000	280
16.	William Weightman	1813	1904	$80,000	286
17.	Moses Taylor	1806	1882	$40,000	286
18.	Russell Sage	1816	1906	$100,000	287
19.	John I. Blair	1802	1899	$60,000	289
20.	Cyrus Curtis	1850	1933	$174,000	320

(continued)

Rank	Name	Birth	Death	Wealth (Thousands)	Ratio (Wealth ÷ GNP)
21.	Edward Henry Harriman	1848	1909	$100,000	322
22.	Henry H. Rogers	1840	1909	$100,000	322
23.	J. P. Morgan	1837	1913	$119,000	328
24.	Col. Oliver Payne	1839	1917	$178,000	337
25.	Henry C. Frick	1849	1919	$225,000	351
26.	Collis Potter Huntington	1821	1900	$50,000	374
27.	Peter A. Widener	1834	1915	$100,000	387
28.	James Cair Flood	1826	1888	$30,000	405
29.	Nicholas Longworth	1782	1863	$15,000	411
30.	Philip Danforth Armour	1832	1901	$50,000	413
31.	Bill Gates	1955	—	$15,000,000	425
32.	Mark Hopkins	1813	1878	$20,000	446
33.	Edward Clark	1810	1882	$25,000	458
34.	Leland Stanford	1824	1893	$30,000	462
35.	William Rockefeller	1841	1922	$150,000	493
36.	Hetty Green	1834	1916	$100,000	498
37.	James J. Hill	1838	1916	$100,000	498
38.	Elias Hasket Derby	1739	1799	$800	515
39.	Warren Buffett	1930	—	$12,000,000	532
40.	Claus Spreckels	1828	1908	$50,000	554
41.	George Peabody	1795	1869	$16,000	556
42.	Charles Crocker	1822	1888	$20,000	608
43.	William Andrews Clark	1839	1925	$150,000	609
44.	George Eastman	1854	1932	$95,000	611
45.	Charles Tiffany	1812	1902	$35,000	616
46.	Thomas Fortune Ryan	1851	1928	$155,000	633
47.	Edward Stephen Harkness	1874	1940	$155,000	643
48.	Henry M. Flagler	1830	1913	$60,000	651
49.	James Buchanan Duke	1856	1925	$140,000	652
50.	Israel Thorndike	1755	1832	$1,800	674
51.	William S. O'Brien	1825	1878	$12,000	696
52.	Isaac Merritt Singer	1811	1875	$13,000	709
53.	George Hearst	1820	1891	$19,000	712
54.	John Hancock	1736	1793	$350	714
55.	John W. Garrett	1820	1884	$15,000	715
56.	John W. Mackay	1831	1902	$30,000	718
57.	Julius Rosenwald	1862	1932	$80,000	726
58.	George F. Baker	1840	1931	$100,000	758
59.	George Washington	1732	1799	$530	777
60.	Anthony N. Brady	1834	1913	$50,000	781

(continued)

Rank	Name	Birth	Death	Wealth (Thousands)	Ratio (Wealth ÷ GNP)
61.	Adolphus Busch	1839	1913	$50,000	781
62.	John T. Dorrance	1873	1930	$115,000	786
63.	George Pullman	1831	1897	$17,500	835
64.	Robert Wood Johnson, Jr.	1893	1968	$1,000,000	864
65.	Horace E. Dodge	1868	1920	$100,000	889
66.	John F. Dodge	1864	1920	$100,000	889
67.	J. Paul Getty	1892	1976	$2,000,000	893
68.	William Aspinwall	1807	1875	$4,000	913
69.	Johns Hopkins	1795	1873	$10,000	944
70.	John Werner Kluge	1914	–	$6,700,000	952
71.	Samuel Colt	1814	1862	$5,000	966
72.	James Stillman	1850	1918	$77,000	989
73.	William Collins Whitney	1841	1904	$23,000	993
74.	William Thaw	1818	1889	$12,000	1040
75.	Paul G. Allen	1953	–	$6,100,000	1046
76.	Cyrus McCormick	1809	1884	$10,000	1072
77.	Arthur Vining Davis	1867	1962	$400,000	1103
78.	Thomas H. Perkins	1764	1854	$3,000	1116
79.	Joseph Pulitzer	1847	1911	$30,000	1142
80.	Daniel Willis James	1832	1907	$26,000	1169
81.	Howard Hughes	1905	1976	$1,500,000	1190
82.	Frank W. Woolworth	1852	1919	$6,500	1214
83.	John McDonogh	1779	1850	$2,000	1278
84.	Samuel Slater	1768	1835	$1,200	1312
85.	August Belmont	1816	1890	$10,000	1313
86.	Benjamin Franklin	1706	1790	$150	1320
87.	Sumner Murray Redstone	1923	–	$4,800,000	1329
88.	Capt. Robert Dollar	1844	1932	$40,000	1451
89.	Richard Warren Sears	1863	1914	$25,000	1457
90.	H. L. Hunt	1889	1974	$1,000,000	1474
91.	Jay Van Andel	1924	–	$4,300,000	1483
92.	Richard M. DeVos	1926	–	$4,300,000	1483
93.	Henry Phipps	1839	1930	$60,000	1506
94.	Lawrence J. Ellison	1944	–	$4,300,000	1519
95.	Ronald Owen Perelman	1943	–	$4,300,000	1519
96.	Peter Chardon Brooks	1767	1849	$1,300	1646
97.	Charles W. Post	1854	1914	$22,000	1656
98.	Samuel I. Newhouse	1895	1979	$1,500,000	1681
99.	William Wrigley, Jr.	1861	1932	$34,000	1707
100.	David Packard	1912	1996	$3,700,000	1724

PREFACE

It is the American Dream. An unknown cabin boy from France, Stephen Girard traded and financed his way to becoming the richest man in America. A poor flute salesman, John Jacob Astor then topped Girard's fortune by dominating the American fur trade and New York real estate. A farmer's son, Cornelius Vanderbilt rode the steamships and rails to unparalleled wealth. Henry Ford left the farm to tinker with engines into his late thirties, failed in two attempts to start a car company, and then built a billion dollar business. The son of a snake oil salesman, John D. Rockefeller found an oil that truly brought him fame and fortune. A store owner from the backwoods town of Bentonville, Arkansas, Sam Walton grew to dominate retailing and become a billionaire many times over. A college dropout who started a small software company, Bill Gates outsmarted the largest computer company in the world to become the nation's richest man.

In every age, there are a few who rise to the very top. Some claw their way up viciously. Others use their wits. Some use backroom deals and politics. Some inherit great wealth and make it bigger. Who are these wealthiest Americans?

This is the story of the 100 Americans who, ranked comparatively to the wealth of the nation at the time, had the largest fortunes in the history of the United States. Beginning with the Revolution, we have compared the individual fortunes to the gross national product (GNP), both in current dollars. Thus, John D. Rockefeller's oil fortune of over $1 billion, in relative terms, overshadows the $15 billion Microsoft empire of Bill Gates decades later. And George Washington's $500,000 estate gives him a place above multibillionaire H. Ross Perot, who doesn't make the list at all. More details about the creation of the list appear in the next section.

These 100 profiles offer broad-brush portraits of America's business barons—from the privateers of the American Revolution to the profiteers of the computer revolution. This is a story of contrast and paradoxes. It is the story not only of great greed and miserliness, but also of great philanthropy. It tells of the rise from unspeakable poverty to uncountable wealth. *The Wealthy 100* is about the power of dreams and the value of dogged persistence in the face of setbacks and obstacles. It is the story of the growth of the nation—from steamships, to railroads, to petroleum, to software.

The idea that wealth and success are open to all has always been at the heart of the American experience. It was the dream of riches that drove Columbus to the shores of the new continent. It was a dispute over freedom of trade as much as it was the ideals of democracy that sparked the Revolution itself. It was the vision of streets paved with gold that propelled thousands of poor immigrants into New York Harbor. As Frenchman Alexis de Tocqueville once remarked, "I know of no country, indeed, where the love of money had taken a stronger hold on the affections of men."

The American Dream held that anyone with enough energy and talent could come to America, work hard, and become comfortable, or perhaps even a millionaire. These are the stories of some Americans who did.

A land built upon contempt for the aristocracy, America created a new aristocracy—not of title, but of wealth. In America, perhaps more than anywhere else, money became the measure of the man. As author Ferdinand Lundberg comments, "Citizens may be equals at the polls, where little is decided; but they are not equals at the bank tellers' wickets, where much is decided."

At the time of the European expansion on the new continent, fortunes of $1 million were unheard of. The term millionaire was reportedly coined in 1740, only shortly before the birth of American democracy. The term *billionaire* didn't follow until 1861, and was quickly attached to the names of John D. Rockefeller and others.

We have long been fascinated with wealth. A list of New York's wealthies compiled by Moses Yale Beach in 1847 turned up more than two dozen millionaires in the nation's wealthiest city. A similar survey in Philadelphia in 1845 found nine millionaires in that city. By the early 1900s, people in Chicago contended that there were as many millionaires in the town as there had been voters in 1840. By 1954, *Fortune* magazine estimated that there were about 250 Americans who had created fortunes of more than $50 million. A study in 1972 concluded that there were 133,400 million-aires in the United States. By 1992, there were an estimated 3.2 million households with more than $1 million in investable assets. Three million millionaires. In 1995, *Forbes* listed more than 100 individuals with fortunes of more than $1 billion.

The transgressions of the wealthy, over the years, have been amply detailed in Gustavus Myers's *History of the Great American Fortunes* and Matthew Josephson's *Robber Barons.* During a commemoration of the two hundreth birthday of Cornelius Vanderbilt, Edward Koch, then mayor of New York City, acknowledged that many of America's richest were scoundrels. He said that these Americans, in building the nation, "took more than their share of its wealth." But, he pointed out, they also showed a powerful vision that drove the nation's progress. "Contrast these people with those of today," he said. "Where are our titans? I don't see the vision that created America that existed when these men were in positions of power. Now let me say I do not want their corrupt, authoritarian displays of power to be reborn today. But I wouldn't mind their vision. Indeed, we need their vision."

Like frontiersmen, they lived in an unsettled country, and they made up their own rules as they went along. Judged by the current standards of business, many of their actions appear ruthless and savage, but their deeds reflect the uncivilized nature of the nation as much as their character.

In America, the way to wealth is, at least in principle, open to all. If the following profiles show anything, they reveal the ability of creative individuals to change their lives and the future course of the nation. These individuals weren't always the smartest or most creative. They didn't always come up with ideas that made them wealthy. Quite a few started out dirt poor. They found opportunities. They pursued a vision, which often was more important than the money itself. In the words of Sam Walton, they just "got after it and stayed after it."

Their stories are intriguing, sometimes shocking, but never dull. They demonstrate the drive and vision that built the nation. In the pages that follow, we explore the winding roads that often led these men to their fortunes, their trials and triumphs, and their own thoughts on what made them successful.

These stories show there are at least one hundred different ways to build an American fortune. Henry Phipps found his next door in the person of a poor immigrant boy named Andrew Carnegie. For Edward Clark, Singer Sewing Machine founder, fate knocked on his door when he was forty in the form of the flamboyant Isaac Singer. For Richard Sears, opportunity arrived in the form of an unclaimed shipment of watches. Cereal king Charles Post stumbled on the source of his fortune while recovering in a sanitarium—run by a Dr. Kellogg. Sometimes, it was the bond between brothers—Richard and Andrew Mellon, Horace and John Dodge—who worked side by side that helped create large fortunes. Cyrus McCormick found his wealth in an invention his father could never quite get to work, and then he spent years trying to convince farmers to use his reaper. Once, when he was bankrupt, the bank took everything McCormick owned except the reaper; they didn't consider it to be of any value. These 100 found opportunities that no one thought were valuable, and they made them valuable.

Every age and every individual has unique opportunities. But only a few are perceptive enough to recognize them and determined, or lucky enough, to make them work. These 100 stories leave us with the challenge: What are our opportunities, and what will it take to build the next great American fortune? Future fortunes will not come from land or railroads, or steamships or automobiles. There will be new sources of progress and of wealth. While many of the paths these Americans followed to riches are closed, their stories point the way to new fortunes waiting to be won.

How This List Was Developed

Putting together a list like this was like looking for needles in the vast haystack of history. We sifted through estimates of the wealth of hundreds of individuals to come up with the list of 100. Many wealthy individuals dropped off the bottom of the list, including John Ludwig, Walter Annenberg, the Mars family, Harvey Firestone, Armand Hammer, Donald Trump, Alfred P. Sloan, John Wanamaker, Roy Cullen, H. Ross Perot, John D. MacArthur, Ray Kroc, Katharine Graham, the Gallo brothers, Nathan and Isidor Strauss, Richard King and Robert Kleberg, Edwin Land, Louis Swift, and Will K. Kellogg.

Estimates were considered at the time of death, whenever possible, beginning with individuals who died after the founding of the nation in 1776. Estimates of wealth can vary widely, and we often sought several sources for a given individual to make a determination. For the most part, the estimates are conservative. For living members of the list, estimates (most from *Forbes* or *Fortune*) were compared with the GNP at the time of the estimate. Philanthropy is added back into the totals, when possible. Otherwise, Andrew Carnegie and others might fall off the list simply because of their generosity.

Lost fortunes, on the other hand, are cause for dismissal. For this reason, Jay Cooke, Daniel Drew, Charles Schwab, Robert Morris, and a few others drop off the list. As J. P. Morgan once said, "Even a fool can make a million dollars, but it takes a sage to hold on to it."

Family wealth is not considered, removing the fortunes of the DuPonts and the Guggenheims, which are shared among so many family members that they do not make the list. Individual wealth that is distributed to children, in trusts for example, is included, whenever possible, in totals for the individual who earned it.

There also is a bias against inherited wealth. The list could have been more heavily populated with Astors, Vanderbilts, Rockefellers, and others, because they started with so much and didn't disperse it widely. The passage of a fortune from one generation to the next is fairly uninteresting and much more difficult to assess.

This is a history of public fortunes. Neither of us is a business historian, and we did not attempt to ferret out little known fortunes from the dark recesses of American history. There are a few members of this list who are not household names, but most have their names prominently imprinted on the companies and charitable institutions that are at the foundation of American life. Since the mid 1800s, there have been many others who have picked over history, looking for wealthy individuals—although there has never been a comprehensive list across the entire span of U.S. history. These partial lists gave us an excellent starting point. It is impossible for a list of this scope to be comprehensive or exhaustive, despite our best efforts.

The value of individual estates, in many cases, is subject to speculation. Beneath the apparent precision of the numbers on the list and the rankings, there are a variety of judgment calls about sources and estimates. We have used information about wills, whenever possible. But John D. Rockefeller, easily a billionaire, died with a scant $26 million in his official personal estate. Where did all that money go? He had squirreled it away in trusts and foundations. Andrew Mellon, worth hundreds of millions, left an estate of only $27 million on paper. Henry Ford transferred all but a few of his holdings into the Ford Foundation. Howard Hughes gave Hughes Aircraft to a medical foundation, which he alone controlled, leaving him well shy of $1 billion at his death. In addition to the deliberate moves of the wealthy to hide their cash, there are also shifts in the market value of their holdings that can build or erode a fortune overnight. As billionaire J. Paul Getty once commented, "If you can count your money, you don't have a billion dollars."

Finally, there is no elegant way to compare wealth across the entire history of the nation. The GNP is a crude instrument, particularly in the early years, but it is probably as good as any other measure available. The Consumer Price Index doesn't extend back as far, and has problems of its own, because true buying power doesn't translate well across time. The GNP, for all its flaws, gives us a list in which fortunes from 1795 can be placed next to fortunes of 1995, and the many wealthy individuals of virtually every period—from George Washington, to John D. Rockefeller, to Bill Gates—can find a place on the list.

ACKNOWLEDGMENTS

While the mistakes herein are ours alone, any accurate information contained in this volume reflects the dedication and careful study of individual biographers and previous investigators of wealth, a sampling of whom are noted in the bibliography. Leading the way, particularly in modern times, is the staff of the *Forbes 400*, who have made the determination of wealth as close to a science as it can get, since they began their rankings in 1982. They also produced several retrospective investigations of wealth (which, unfortunately, did not come to our attention until late in the process, but served to confirm and extend our own observations). Before the *Forbes* lists, *Fortune* produced lists of multimillionaires in November 1957 and May 1968.

In earlier times, there is the pioneering Moses Yale Beach, who developed several lists of wealthy New Yorkers in the 1800s, and there were also millionaire lists by the *Tribune* in 1892 and the *World Almanac* in 1902. The *New York Times* published an article on the wealthiest Americans in 1907. B. C. Forbes, the founder of *Forbes* magazine, produced a one-time list in 1918, which only came to the attention of the modern *Forbes* staff after they had published their first list in 1982. In addition to the formal lists, a book by Joseph J. Thorndike, Jr. on *The Very Rich: A History of Wealth* offered many fruitful leads and fascinating stories about the wealthy in America. John Ingham's *Biographical Dictionary of American Business Leaders*, and his more recent *Contemporary Business Leaders: A Biographical Dictionary* (with Lynne B. Feldman), contributed greatly to many of these profiles.

We owe a debt of gratitude to Joshua Altman, who diligently researched biographical information in the New York libraries, adding many colorful details to the portraits of the Wealthy 100. His creative and indefatigable efforts in hunting down obscure information contributed greatly to this book. Thanks to Valerie Vogel for tracking down photos of all 100, and thanks to Jonathan Berland, who began the process of finding the names and fortunes of the wealthiest Americans. Without the help of these researchers, this project never would have come together.

Mary Tavon, who served as the guardian angel of our first book *I'd Rather Die Than Give a Speech*, again provided guidance, comments, and encouragement throughout the process of developing this work.

Finally, our sincere thanks to our editor Hillel Black for his patience, persistence, and skill in urging us to higher levels, to Carrie Nichols Cantor and the staff of Carol Publishing Group, and to our agent, Ivy Fisher Stone, for the cultivation of this idea from a conversation over lunch into a finished book.

The
Wealthy
1 0 0

1

John D. Rockefeller

(1839–1937)

The Oil King

Est. wealth: $1.4 billion or more

America's first billionaire, John Davison Rockefeller rose from modest origins to build the most powerful and notorious company in the history of the nation. Before it was brought down by government trustbusters, his Standard Oil Company *was* the oil industry in the United States, and Rockefeller was the dominant force in American industry. His name became synonymous with wealth, and his family became a fixture in American business, philanthropy, and politics.

Everything about Rockefeller said that he was strictly business. He was an intense, lanky man with cold, piercing eyes, yet he possessed a polished and courtly manner—like an iron fist within a velvet glove. When other young men were keeping diaries of their lives, the young Rockefeller kept a ledger book, tracking the progress of his life in columns of dollars and cents. The cost of flowers and an engagement ring recorded the courtship of his future wife.

Rockefeller had an extraordinary talent for making money. As his older sister Lucy once said, "When it's raining porridge, you'll

3

always find John's bowl right side up." Rockefeller, himself, had a more self-righteous explanation for his riches, saying, "God gave me my money." Whether it came from good luck or divine right—or just blind ambition—before his death, he had given away half a billion dollars and still had hundreds of millions left over, at least $900 million, perhaps more.

Rockefeller was born on a farm in Hartford Mills, New York, in 1839. His father, "Doctor Bill" Rockefeller, made a comfortable living from a different kind of oil—snake oil. When the elder Rockefeller wasn't out peddling his phony cancer cure, he also made an unorthodox contribution to the development of his children. "I cheat my boys every chance I get," he would boast. "I want to make 'em sharp." Rockefeller received a different kind of education from his mother, a strict and religious Baptist, who taught her children the values of order and piety. Rockefeller took these lessons to heart. He was a hard worker, disciplined, and devoutly religious. Because of his serious and austere nature, associates called him "the deacon," but there was still more than a trace of his father's spirit in Rockefeller's approach to business.

In 1853, Rockefeller moved with his family to Cleveland. Two years later, at the age of sixteen, he started out as a clerk at Hewitt and Tuttle, a shipping and real estate company in Cleveland. He earned about sixty cents per day. Rockefeller ran errands and collected rents. With a talent for numbers, he rose to the position of bookkeeper.

It was his first and last job. He would never work for someone else again. After three years there, Rockefeller left to become a junior partner with merchant Maurice B. Clark. The nineteen-year-old Rockefeller had saved $800 and borrowed another $1,000 from his father—at 10 percent interest. The Clark & Rockefeller commission house dealt in hay, grain, meats, and other goods. In 1859, the discovery of oil in western Pennsylvania set off an explosion of drilling and refining in the region. Rockefeller and partners built a refinery near Cleveland in 1863.

At that point, oil was still a small sideline, but Rockefeller was prosperous enough in the grain business that he could think about settling down. He married Laura Celestina Spelman, whom he had known since high school. Like her husband, "Cettie," a schoolteacher, was devoutly religious and a shrewd thinker. Rockefeller once said, "Without her keen advice, I would be a poor man."

Rockefeller turned his full attention to dominating the oil business. The emerging industry was fragmented and inefficient at the time, providing ample opportunities for Rockefeller to exercise his disciplined management and iron hand. He hired his own wagons to cut hauling costs, and he built his own barrels for oil, reducing the cost from $2.50 each to just 96 cents per barrel. He kept pushing for more efficiency. Once when Rockefeller inspected a barrel making plant, he found that employees were using forty drops of solder to make a barrel. He suggested they try thirty-eight. It turned out they needed thirty-nine. One drop of solder in an oil empire. Rockefeller commented that the difference could save a fortune.

With a successful refinery, Rockefeller and his partners then began building his empire. In 1870, when Rockefeller was just thirty-one, he and his partners established Standard Oil. With his close friend and business partner, Henry Flagler, Rockefeller set about collecting all the diverse refineries in the nation into his dominant oil trust. When he couldn't buy out competitors, he would force them out of business.

Rockefeller teamed up with railroads to develop a system of "drawbacks." Under this system, Standard Oil received reduced rates for shipping as well as a surcharge on the shipping of competitors' products. The railroads carried his oil at ten cents per barrel and his competitors' at thirty-five cents per barrel, paying back Rockefeller the additional twenty-five cents. Rockefeller's rivals couldn't afford to compete. He gave them the choice of either joining with him or going under. Most added their companies to Standard Oil in exchange for stock. Rockefeller's own younger brother, Frank, was one of these rivals. After refusing to give in to John D.'s demands, Frank was crushed by Standard Oil, leaving him bitter for the rest of his life. John's other brother, William, had the sense to join in the business, and he became a multimillionaire.

Through cloak-and-dagger backroom deals and bribes to politicians, Rockefeller and his partners brought almost all of the major refiners in the nation under the Standard banner. In 1880, just one decade after it was officially founded, Standard Oil controlled 95 percent of the oil production in the nation.

Then, Rockefeller's empire began to unravel. The Sherman Antitrust Act, designed to crush the big corporate monopolies, was passed in 1890, and within two years, Standard Oil was declared illegal. Rockefeller and his partners evaded the decision through interlocking directorates until 1911, when Standard Oil was broken into thirty-four separate companies. Many of these companies are still major players in the oil industry, including Chevron, Amoco, Mobil, and Exxon. Although the names had changed, Rockefeller continued to own portions of all of them.

Rockefeller was declared the richest man in the history of the world. A small cottage industry was kept busy speculating on his fortune and comparing his wealth to kings of the past. As George F. Redmond wrote in *Financial Giants of America,* "Solomon, the Pharaohs, Cleopatra, Monte Cristo and Croesus himself and all the personages of the centuries past are outclassed by this modern Croesus." (Croesus was the Lydian king from the 6th century B.C. who gave the modern equivalent of more than $300 million in gifts to the temple at Delphi.) The Rockefeller name became synonymous with wealth. The phrase "rich as a Rockefeller" came into parlance. A seafood dish was dubbed Oysters Rockefeller because of its unsurpassed "richness."

Rockefeller didn't flaunt his riches in the style of the free-spending Goulds or other Fifth Avenue millionaires in New York, but he lived very comfortably. He had a seven hundred-acre country estate on the outskirts of Cleveland as well as homes in New York, Florida, Maine, and a private golf course in New Jersey. His favorite was his Pocantico Hills estate near the Sleepy Hollow area in New York.

In addition to the bitter government antitrust actions, Rockefeller's image was tarnished by sordid accounts of Standard Oil's backroom dealings described by Ida Tarbell and other muckrakers. In the early 1900s, there were heated debates from the pulpit and in the national press about whether religious charities should accept the "tainted money" of Rockefeller. (Most ultimately overcame their scruples.)

Rockefeller was not troubled by twinges of conscience. He felt he had won his wealth fair and square, and that he had benefitted the industry by making it more efficient. He also prided himself on his generosity. Rockefeller had always considered himself a Christian businessman and had tithed 10 percent of his income to the church since he was a child. By 1905, that tithe approached $100 million.

Rockefeller was, however, troubled by his bad press, and he hired a publicist to help improve his image and to retell the story of Standard Oil. One publicity stunt that caught his fancy was the idea of giving away shiny dimes wherever he went. He distributed more than 30,000 of these lucky dimes in his lifetime.

Starting in 1897, he had already turned over the business of Standard Oil to his able partners and devoted his full attention to giving away his money. He made possible the founding of the University of Chicago in 1892. He established the Rockefeller Institute for Medical Research (later renamed Rockefeller University) in 1901, the General Education Board a year later, and the Rockefeller Foundation in 1913.

Despite his carefully cultivated public image that portrayed his generosity, he remained strict and austere. His groundskeeper at his Pocantico estate was given a $5 Christmas bonus, only to find he was docked the same amount of pay for taking off the holiday. Rockefeller was known to have cried on just two occasions. The first was the death of his wife in 1915. The second was when it was reported (inaccurately) that his childhood home was being hauled off to Coney Island as a spectacle. He routinely retired to his private office for two hours every morning to conduct stock transactions over the phone.

Rockefeller outlived the controversy over Standard Oil. By the time he died in 1937, at the age of ninety-eight, he was remembered as much for his philanthropy as for his treachery in business. A withered and wizened old gentleman, he was revered for his business success and benefactions by a generation that had grown up after the scandals of Standard Oil had passed.

Giving away the Rockefeller fortune turned out to be a lost cause. As Rockefeller's advisor Frederick Gates once cautioned him, "Your fortune is rolling up, rolling up like an avalanche!" When Rockefeller died, he had given away more than half a billion and still left more than $460 million to his only son, John D. Rockefeller, Jr. The younger Rockefeller once said his "chief mission in life is giving away money." Along with more than half a billion dollars in gifts, he also restored Colonial Williamsburg and donated the $9 million site for the United Nations building in New York. He also added the towering Rockefeller Center to the New York City skyline to house the emerging communications industry. He still left more than $240 million to his six children.

The five grandsons in the third generation of Rockefellers continued the tradition of philanthropy and struck out into politics. The most prominent was Nelson Rockefeller, a liberal Republican governor of New York from 1959 to 1973 and three-time contender for

U.S. president, assisted in his endeavors by $20 million in family funds. In 1974, he was appointed by Gerald Ford to serve as vice president after both President Nixon and Vice President Agnew resigned during the Watergate scandal. John D. Jr.'s youngest son, David Rockefeller, served as CEO of Chase Manhattan Bank between 1969 and 1980. In 1995, *Forbes* listed David and two other Rockefeller descendants among the 400 richest Americans. The magazine estimated the total value of John D. Sr.'s family fortune at $6.2 billion.

As biographers Peter Collier and David Horowitz commented, "Rockefeller's name and power would be carried into the future by a dynasty without peer as an enduring institution of American life." John D. Rockefeller had stoked the engines of American business. He had built the Empire State Building of corporations. Although its size might be eclipsed by later arrivals, its power and influence never would. It would remain a symbol of the best and worst of an unequaled era of American business expansion. Rockefeller towers over those who preceded him, and those who followed. He was, and is, the richest American in the history of the nation.

Prominent but Poor

Christopher Columbus

(1451–1506)

DIDN'T EVEN EARN FREQUENT FLIER MILES

On his third voyage to the New World, Christopher Columbus wrote to his benefactors in Spain: "Your Highnesses have an Other World here, by which our holy faith can be so greatly advanced and from which such great wealth can be drawn." While many people did, in fact, draw great wealth from the continent, Columbus was not one of them. He was an excellent sailor, and he negotiated for governorship of the lands he discovered and a large share of the trade, but his fortunes turned sour after a near revolt by colonists in Santo Domingo. Columbus was imprisoned. After release from jail and an unsuccessful fourth voyage, he died virtually penniless.

2

Cornelius Vanderbilt
(1794–1877)
A Captain of Enterprise
Est. wealth: $105 million

A six-foot-two, foulmouthed Dutch sailor, Cornelius Vanderbilt piloted his way from a humble farmhouse on Staten Island to become the wealthiest man of his time. He was as forceful and as fiery as the steam boilers that powered his boats. Starting with a $100 barge, he drove forward to build an empire in steamboats and railroads—and an estate estimated at $105 million.

Cornelius Vanderbilt was born on May 27, 1794, on his family farm on Staten Island, the fourth of nine children. Vanderbilt earned the nickname "the Commodore" as a young man, piloting passengers and produce around New York Harbor in his father's boat, a heavy two-masted barge called a "periauger." While other young men were studying reading and arithmetic, Vanderbilt dropped out of school at age eleven to begin a lifelong study of the channels and currents around New York.

A month before his sixteenth birthday, he told his mother he was planning to run away to become a sailor. She knew he really wanted his own boat, so she made him a proposition: Plow and plant a rocky eight-acre field on the Vanderbilt farm, and she would lend him $100 to buy the boat. It was a nearly impossible task, but Vanderbilt was undaunted. On his sixteenth birthday, he was the proud owner of a small barge named the *Swiftsure*. He ferried passengers across the harbor for 18 cents a trip. By the end of the year, he had paid back his mother's loan and contributed another $1,000 to the family besides.

Nothing could interfere with Vanderbilt's desire to build his business. During the War of 1812, he made his way through a British blockade of New York Harbor to ferry supplies to six army garrisons around the harbor. At the age of nineteen, Cornelius took a few moments away from his work to marry his neighbor and cousin, Sophia Johnson, a woman who was every bit as driven and hardworking as her husband. The morning after their wedding, Cornelius was back at the docks picking up passengers. By the age of twenty-three, Vanderbilt owned several boats and had saved about $9,000.

Then steamships came along. At first, Vanderbilt scorned the new spark spewing contraptions, but when they began to take away his harbor business, he decided he needed to learn the steamship business. In 1818, he sold his boats and began working as a steamboat captain for Thomas Gibbons, a Georgia plantation owner. For the next decade, Vanderbilt learned everything he could about steamships, running a steam ferry from New York, down the Raritan River, to New Brunswick, New Jersey. Sophia supported the family by running a wayside inn at the steamboat landing, in addition to caring for the first of their thirteen children. (Meanwhile, the tightfisted Vanderbilt was stashing away all his earnings.)

Not content with the Raritan route, Vanderbilt soon began making steamship runs across New York Bay to the Battery. There was just one small problem: The run was illegal. The New York legislature had given a monopoly for steam travel in New York waters to Robert Fulton and Robert Livingston. Vanderbilt, undercutting his rivals' rates, dashed back and forth between New Jersey and New York with constables in hot pursuit. Amused passengers enjoyed both the excitement of the chase, and the $2 savings of the Vanderbilt run.

Vanderbilt always managed to elude his pursuers, sometimes hiding in a secret closet he had constructed on the ship. Once an officer almost collared him at a New York dock, but was shocked when Vanderbilt ordered the boat to pull away. The officer, afraid of being carried out of his jurisdiction, jumped back onto the dock. The game of cat and mouse continued until the U.S. Supreme Court declared the monopoly on New York steamship travel unconstitutional, opening up the harbor again.

By 1829, at the age of thirty-five, Vanderbilt had grown Gibbon's shipping business from a struggling one-boat operation to a successful seven-ship fleet. Through his own work, and his wife's inn, they had built a fortune of $30,000, which the Commodore used to strike out on his own again. He set up a New York–Philadelphia steamboat route and cut his prices so deep that his rivals soon paid him handsomely to stay off the route. (This pattern of undercutting rivals and then extorting a fee for leaving the market would become the modus operandi for Vanderbilt in his early days.)

Vanderbilt then moved his operations to the Hudson River. There he launched an even more ruthless price war against the powerful Hudson River Steamboat Association. Vanderbilt cut his rates on the run from New York City to Albany from $3 to $1, then to 10 cents, and finally he offered free passage. Even with higher rates for food onboard, he was losing money. But his larger rivals, with more passengers and more ships, were losing even more money. They finally agreed to pay him $100,000, and an additional $5,000 per year, if he would just leave the Hudson River for the next ten years. Vanderbilt took the money and his ships and set up routes to the north in Boston, Hartford, and Providence, and to the south in Washington, Charleston, and Havana. By the time he reached his mid-forties, between the money he was making *not* running boats in New York and Philadelphia, and the money he was making operating his fleet of more than one hundred steamboats in other places, his fortune had grown to several million dollars.

But his millions couldn't buy for him a place in New York society. On the few occasions when he managed to obtain an invitation to dine with New York's elite, he shocked his hostesses by swearing like a sailor, spitting tobacco juice on the carpet, and pinching the behinds of young serving women. Shunned by polite New York society, he built a beautiful mansion on Staten Island.

Ten years later, he came back to Manhattan, building a four-story townhouse at 10 Washington Place in order to be closer to his business. He didn't have much time for society, anyway. His sole focus was on making money.

In 1851, at the age of fifty-seven, Vanderbilt watched the prospectors stream out of New York to the Gold Rush in California. Most of these travelers went by the Pacific Mail Line across the Isthmus of Panama, which had a monopoly on the Panama route. But Vanderbilt wasn't about to be shut out of such a lucrative opportunity. He pored over maps of Central America and found a new route across Nicaragua that would cut 500 miles and two days off the journey. His steamboats took passengers from New York to the east coast of Nicaragua, up the San Juan River, and across 100-mile-long Lake Nicaragua. Then, stagecoaches took them the twelve miles from the lake to the Pacific, where a second set of ocean steamers completed the trip to California. With neither a pickax nor a pan, Vanderbilt earned $1 million a year from the gold rush. By the mid-1850s, he had become the leading American steamship owner.

In 1853, with more than $11 million in the bank, the sixty-year-old Vanderbilt decided it was time to take a vacation. Even so, it was a busman's holiday. He built *The North Star*, a 270-foot steam yacht that was the first oceangoing steamship ever commissioned for a private citizen. The $500,000 ship was royally appointed with velvet furniture, ten staterooms, and a marble-walled dining room. With his family and friends aboard, he took the grand tour of Europe. As he headed out of New York Harbor and past the small farmhouse on Staten Island where he had grown up, he ordered a military salute to his eighty-six-year-old mother, who had lent him the money for his first boat nearly half a century before.

When Vanderbilt returned from his journey, he found that the agents he had entrusted to run his Nicaraguan line had double-crossed him and taken over the route. The fierce Vanderbilt penned a quick letter to his former agents:

> *Gentlemen:*
> *You have undertaken to cheat me. I will not sue you, for the law takes too long. I will ruin you.*
>
> *Sincerely yours,*
> *C. Vanderbilt*

He then proceeded to follow through on his threat. He established a competing line across Panama and slashed prices dramatically. His rivals capitulated within a year. Not only that, but the next year all the other lines running through Panama, shaken by the rate wars, paid Vanderbilt $40,000 per month *not* to operate the Nicaraguan line.

During the Civil War, Vanderbilt sold his fleet of steamships to the Union. After the showdown between the *Merrimack* and the *Monitor*, Vanderbilt gave the Union forces his best steamship, the *Vanderbilt*, and it was sent out to chase the *Merrimack*. At the close of the war, he received a gold medal from Congress for his support during the war.

When he was nearly seventy, the Commodore struck out in an entirely new direction—railroads. After he was nearly killed in a train derailment in his forties, the Commodore swore he would never get involved with railroads. But he changed his mind when he saw the money to be made there. Some thought the sailor was out of his element and would lose the fortune he had spent his life creating. He proved them wrong, demonstrating the same shrewd and ruthless competitive spirit that had made him the dominant force on the water.

Vanderbilt first bought control of the railroad line running along the Hudson River from New York to Albany, where it connected to the New York Central. During the winter, Vanderbilt's line took Central passengers between Albany and New York, but during the summer, the Central ran its own steamboats down the Hudson, bypassing Vanderbilt's line. Vanderbilt didn't care for this arrangement, so he decided to tighten the screws on the Central. He stopped his trains two miles short of Albany, stranding passengers across the Hudson from the Central. With its passengers cut off from New York City, the Central eventually capitulated to Vanderbilt, giving him control of the Central. Eventually, Vanderbilt would control a four-hundred-mile track stretching from the New York seaboard to the Great Lakes.

The Central's largest rival on the East-West route was the Erie. Vanderbilt next tried to seize control of that railroad, launching a fierce financial battle against Daniel Drew, Jim Fisk, and Jay Gould for control of the line. Vanderbilt lost the fight, but the Erie was driven so close to bankruptcy by the stock watering and financial manipulations during the struggle that it was no longer much of a threat to the Central. Through his railroad investments,

Vanderbilt added another $90 million to the more than $11 million he had amassed in steamships.

The Commodore was a notorious tightwad. He used to carry his cigars around in the pocket of his frock coat rather than a cigar case so he wouldn't be obliged to offer them to others. Mark Twain once published an open letter to him in a monthly magazine, calling upon him to "Go, oh please go, and do one worthy act. Go, boldly, grandly, nobly, and give four dollars to some public charity. It will break your heart, no doubt . . . "

The founder of the Vanderbilt fortune lived rather frugally, considering his wealth. His Washington Square townhouse, for example, cost only $55,000, a pittance compared to his fortune. A year after his world tour in *The North Star*, he sold the half-million-dollar yacht at a profit. (Late in life, Vanderbilt did give $1 million to Central University in Nashville, Tennessee, the institution which now bears his name.)

Vanderbilt's family, which inherited his fortune, was a disappointment to him. As he once told a friend, "I have a large family and none of them were brought up to do anything." He didn't care much about his eight daughters, and his three sons seemed to be nothing but trouble. His youngest, George, a West Point graduate who appeared to be the most promising, died at age twenty-five. His middle son, Cornelius, was an epileptic free-wheeling gambler and hustler, whom his father twice committed to the Bloomingdale Insane Asylum and later set up with a fruit farm in Hartford. By the age of thirty-eight, young Cornelius was $80,000 in debt and forced to declare bankruptcy.

The Commodore didn't expect much more from his eldest son, William Henry. He called his son a "sucker," a "stupid blockhead," and other choice epithets from his richly varied sailor's vocabulary. The rough Commodore, considering his son a weak-willed dolt, lost no opportunity to humiliate him. Once when the thirty-three-year-old William was smoking a cigar on the deck of a ship, the Commodore said:

"Billy, I wish you would quit that smoking habit of yours. I'll give you $10,000 if you do."

"You need not give me money, father," the dutiful son responded. "Your wish is sufficient." He threw the cigar over the rail.

Then the Commodore pulled a Havana cigar from the pocket of his frock coat, rolled it around luxuriously in his hands, and lit it, blowing the smoke into his startled son's face.

William turned out to be a pleasant surprise to his father. The Commodore had set the young man up on a seventy-acre farm on Staten Island and thought he would be lucky to keep his family alive. But William made his farm a success, expanding it to 350 acres. He then brought the Staten Island Railway back from the brink of ruin. When William was forty-three, his father at last accepted that he had one son worthy of inviting into the family business.

"Bumbling Billy" turned out to be a shrewd businessman, making as much money in the eight years after his father's death in 1877 as his father had made in a lifetime. He is best remembered for his remark to a newspaper reporter on the elimination of a Chicago train route that was losing money.

"Don't you run it for the public benefit?" asked the reporter.

Vanderbilt replied, "The public be damned. I am working for my stockholders. If the public want the train, why don't they pay for it?"

His "public be damned" comment is all that was remembered of the conversation, which naturally did not endear the man to the American public. But Vanderbilt had about as much need for public adoration as he had for a million dollars.

He was once quoted as saying, "I wouldn't walk across the street to make a million dollars." No wonder. His income from holdings was estimated at more than $10 million per year, or $1,200 per hour.

Despite his public persona, William had a softer heart than his father. For example, the elder Vanderbilt had taken Ulysses S. Grant's swords, medals, and real estate as security for a $150,000 loan the former president had never repaid. After his father's death, the kindhearted William returned them to Grant's widow without asking for the money back.

William, who inherited $90 million from his father, began to find ways to spend his huge fortune. William launched the Vanderbilt mansion-building tradition with the creation of the Twin Mansions, completed in 1882. The $3 million Renaissance mansions, one for Vanderbilt and the other for two of his married daughters, were unprecedented in splendor. Each mansion contained forty-seven rooms, which were rapidly filled with suits of armor, frescos, chandeliers, stained glass, and an art collection worth more than $1 million. The $3 million project, which spanned an entire city block, kept more than 700 workmen employed for more than two years, including sixty Italian sculptors carving fancy cornices and columns. *Harper's Weekly* called the mansions "the Taj Mahal of New York."

William's descendants carried on the tradition with a fortune of about $200 million that he left to them at his death in 1885. His sons, William Kissam and Cornelius, built neighboring mansions in Newport—the Marble House and The Breakers—at a cost of about $10 million each. Their brother, George Washington Vanderbilt built the famous Biltmore mansion in North Carolina. Mrs. William Kissam is credited with building one of the most beautiful of the Fifth Avenue mansions, modeled after the Château de Blois in France. The mansion, opened with an elaborate costume ball in 1883, finally allowed the Vanderbilts to gain admission into New York's elite "Four Hundred." More than 1,200 guests attended the ball, including the queen of New York's high society, Mrs. Caroline Schermerhorn Astor. The Knickerbockers, who had snubbed the rough-mannered Commodore, now embraced his more polished heirs with open arms.

The Commodore's great-great-granddaughter was Gloria Vanderbilt, artist, actress, and fashion designer. Although she was called "the world's most expensive tot" when she was born in 1924, the Vanderbilt name was perhaps the most valuable part of her inheritance. Her father, Reginald Claypoole Vanderbilt, had squandered all of his fortune except the $5 million held in trust for his children. Her mother, also named Gloria, had tried unsuccessfully to manufacture dresses, cosmetics, and perfumes but failed to make the business a success during the Great Depression. The younger Gloria, more successful than her mother, added the Vanderbilt name to stationery, jeans, china, and scarves.

In all, ten Vanderbilt mansions had risen in stately splendor on Fifth Avenue, the crown jewels in the diadem of America's high society. But within thirty years of the Commodore's death, not one of the fast spending Vanderbilts remained among the ranks of the richest Americans. Within seventy years, the last of the mansions on Fifth Avenue fell to the wrecking ball. When 120 of his descendants met at Vanderbilt University for the first family reunion in 1973, there was not one millionaire among them.

All in the Family

THE DU PONTS AND GUGGENHEIMS

Where are the du Ponts and Guggenheims, two of the most wealthy and prominent families in America? While they may wield great power as families, their individual fortunes fall short of what it takes to make the list of the 100 richest Americans.

In 1925, Ferdinand Lundberg estimated the value of du Pont and Guggenheim fortunes using a multiple of taxable income to estimate the true size of the fortune. He put the du Pont fortune at $240 million to $1 billion, but it was divided among twenty family members, giving a conservative estimate of an average of $12 million each. The Guggenheims were worth nearly $200 million, divided among six of them, resulting in individual fortunes averaging just over $30 million.

The du Ponts continue to be the richer of the two, and several du Ponts appear on the 1995 *Forbes* 400 list (but not at the top). The family gunpowder plant and chemical business flourished but remained dispersed in family hands. Even the powerful Pierre S. du Pont II, who brought much of the company under his control in 1915, left a fortune conservatively estimated at $175 million shortly before his death in 1954, leaving him shy of the total needed for the bottom of the list. By 1995, the fortune Pierre had left to his family was estimated by *Forbes* to exceed $10 billion, but was spread among many, many family members.

The family's mining fortune, from the outset, was evenly divided among all Meyer Guggenheim's seven sons. So while the family wealth grew to more than $200 million, so did the number of family members who had claim to it. To make matters more complicated, the Guggenheim family also held the record for divorces per capita among American families of wealth.

Simon Guggenheim, believed to be the richest of the brothers, died in 1941 with a fortune that was perhaps as much as $50 million. Founder Meyer Guggenheim's wealth at his death in 1905 was estimated at just $2.25 million. When *Fortune* surveyed people with $50 million in 1957, it didn't spot one Guggenheim on the list. Noting the family's absence, Richard Austin Smith commented, "Not that they are now living in straitened circumstances, but simply that their individual fortunes have fallen below the $50 million level."

3

John Jacob Astor

(1763–1848)

From Seven Flutes to an Empire in Fur and Real Estate

Est. wealth: $20–$25 million

John Jacob Astor grew rich by making the fur fly. He initially made his fortune as one of the largest and most successful fur traders, who "clothed the city people of two continents for thirty years against wintry weather." Then Astor invested in New York real estate just as the city began to become the leading business center in the United States, buying up choice properties like so many pelts. He amassed the largest and most enduring fortune in the history of the nation and founded a family dynasty that would dominate and define America's elite.

When Moses Yale Beach compiled his list of the wealthiest residents of New York in 1847, Astor towered above the rest. Others had a million dollars or two at most, but Astor weighed in at $20 million. As Gustavus Myers wrote, "In all the length and breadth of the United States, there was no man whose fortune was within even approachable distance of his."

John Jacob Astor, five-foot-nine with a square and stout build, started with almost nothing except the German accent that remained with him throughout his life. Son of a poor butcher, the seventeen-year-old Astor headed out from the town of Waldorf in the Black Forest region of Germany in 1799 to seek his fortune. His first stop was London, where he worked with his brother, who made musical instruments. After the signing of the Treaty of Paris in the fall of 1783, Astor headed to the United States, arriving in Baltimore at the age of twenty. His total wealth at that time: $25 and seven flutes from his brother.

During his trip across the Atlantic, Astor listened with great interest as a fellow traveler discussed his experiences in fur trading with the Indians. After a brief stint selling his flutes in New York, where another of his brothers worked as a butcher, Astor went to work for a New York furrier. In 1786, Astor established his own shop in New York, where he sold musical instruments and furs. In the same year, he married Sarah Todd, of the well-to-do Breevoorts family, who also had a keen sense for business. It wasn't long before Astor was selling his own furs, along with musical instruments, on both sides of the Atlantic. By 1793, Astor was shipping over 100,000 beaver skins per year, along with thousands of other pelts. He personally traveled on buying trips to Mackinaw and other outposts. His expansion was assisted by the Jay Treaty, a trade agreement between the United States and Canada that allowed Astor to import furs directly from Montreal.

By 1800, Astor was worth about $250,000, owned one ship, and had become one of the leading fur traders in the nation. A year later, he moved from his modest dwelling to a fine mansion on the corner of Broadway and Vesey Street, which later became the Astor House hotel.

Astor's determination and craftiness was demonstrated in the way he managed to circumvent government restrictions. During a U.S. embargo on shipping to China, President Jefferson received a request to allow a Chinese mandarin to return home to see his family after the death of his grandfather. Jefferson willingly granted the old man's petition. The "mandarin"—a Chinese deck hand who was dressed in silks for the occasion—just happened to travel on Astor's ship, *The Beaver*, and was accompanied by a full cargo of otter skins and cochineal. The ship returned with a valuable cargo of Chinese teas.

To control the western fur trade, Astor established the American Fur Company in 1808, taking advantage of the new opportunities for trading created by the Louisiana Purchase. The company established new trading outposts on the Great Lakes and the Rockies. With a small staff, Astor relied primarily on independent trappers. But he would generously advance money to these trappers for their expeditions into the wilderness. These independent trappers became so indebted to Astor that they were forced to trade exclusively with the American Fur Company.

Astor then pushed on to the West Coast, where he envisioned a huge fur trading empire in the Northwest, from which he would ship furs out to China and Europe. The race between Astor and Canadian rivals to gain control over fur trading in the region was immortalized by Washington Irving in his book *Astoria*. In 1811, Astor's Pacific Fur Company founded the town of Astoria at the mouth of the Columbia River in present-day Oregon. It was the first American settlement west of the Rocky Mountains. Astor planned to use the Pacific outpost as a collection point for a network of trading posts throughout the Northwest. He sank $1 million into the project, but his plans were derailed by the War of 1812. In 1813, the British took control of the territory, capturing Astor's town and rechristening it Fort George.

After the war, Astor renewed his relentless campaign for domination of the North American fur trade. During the war, Astor had lent generously to the U.S. government, and after the war he began to call in favors. In 1816, he convinced Congress to pass a regulation barring non-U.S. citizens from participating in fur trading in the United States, except as employees. This allowed him to push out of the Mississippi Valley his Canadian and British rivals. He continued to drive westward, taking control of St. Louis and moving toward the Rockies. He won an almost complete monopoly on American fur trading.

Then, after quashing his rivals, he seemed to grow tired of the game. In 1834, he sold all of his fur interests and focused his attention on his real estate holdings.

Astor had the foresight to recognize that land in the rapidly growing city of New York would soon be far more valuable than furs. As a result, he had been building a substantial real estate empire. Some he obtained through mortgages on which he foreclosed. Other land came to him by luck. When Astor's next-door neighbor, Aaron Burr, was forced to flee after killing Alexander Hamilton in a duel, Burr sold Astor a long-term lease for valuable land in what is now Greenwich Village. Astor also invested heavily in farmland on Manhattan Island, in an area that would become the future heart of New York City. He and his heirs followed the strategy of holding on to their land and leasing it to others to develop. As land values in the city continued to rise, so did the Astor fortune.

Despite his vast resources, Astor begrudged the spending of every penny. He had agreed to invest $1,000 in John Audubon's *Birds of America*, but every time the artist came to collect, Astor complained that his cash was very tight. On Audubon's sixth visit, Astor again said his cash was tied up in investments. He turned to his son to confirm that they had no money in the bank. His son, William, who had not been paying attention to the conversation, listed hundreds of thousands of dollars deposited in multiple banks. Astor finally gave Audubon his check.

Even as he approached death, so weak and infirm that breast milk was the only nourishment his sensitive stomach could tolerate, Astor remained an unfeeling landlord. One day one of his agents walked in as the frail Astor was receiving his daily exercise, which consisted of being tossed up and down in a blanket. As he was bouncing up and down, Astor grilled his agent about a certain unpaid rent. The agent protested that the woman who owed the money had suffered recent misfortunes and simply couldn't pay, but Astor insisted, "She must pay!" The agent sought out Astor's son, William, who gave him the money for the rent and told him to take it to his father. When the agent returned with money in hand, the elder Astor said smugly, "I knew you could get it if you only went about it in the right way."

To his last breath, the nation's richest man was passionate about his land. He had seen how rapidly inexpensive farmland had become prime city real estate. His final words were reportedly, "Could I begin life all over again, knowing what I do now, and had money to invest, I would buy every foot of Manhattan Island."

His son, William Backhouse Astor, tried to make up for his father's omissions, purchasing control of even more of the nation's most powerful city. By the time of his death in 1875, William, known as the "Landlord of New York," owned the land under more than 700 buildings and houses, many of them crammed with poor tenants. He is credited with creating many of the slums of nineteenth-century New York.

While the Astor men were conquering New York real estate, their wives were playing a dominant a role in New York high society. The queen of all was Caroline Astor, the wife of William Backhouse Jr., grandson of founder John Jacob. Caroline, a member of the respectable old Schermerhorn family, became the self-appointed arbiter of New York society. The 400 people who could fit into the ballroom that stretched the entire length of her mansion at 34th Street and Fifth Avenue defined the new American nobility. While a large fortune alone was not enough to gain admittance to this elite circle—as evidenced by the exclusion of the Goulds, Harrimans, and Morgans—it was nearly impossible to gain entrance to Mrs. Astor's January Ball without substantial wealth. Mrs. Astor presided over her balls like a queen, her short figure covered in satin, diamonds, and pearls. As a result of her efforts, "New York became the undisputed social Mecca of America and Mrs. Astor's Fifth Avenue mansion its holiest shrine." (The family had come a long way from the days when the rough John Jacob had once wiped his hands on his hostess's dress at a dinner party.)

Caroline insisted on being called *the* Mrs. Astor, informing her friends and the post office of the change. This infuriated the wife of her nephew, William Waldorf Astor, who, of course, considered herself *the* Mrs. Astor. It was clear there was not enough room in New York society for two Mrs. Astors, so William Waldorf—stating that America "is not a fit place for a gentleman"—moved to England. There he established himself among the British nobility, moving into a castle and becoming a viscount. His son's wife, Lady Astor, became the first woman member of Parliament, and other descendants gained control of Britain's two largest newspapers—the *Times* and the *Observer*.

As a parting shot to his aunt, William Waldorf replaced his mansion—next door to hers—with the first Waldorf Hotel. With all the traffic from her new neighbor, Mrs. Astor was forced to move. She traded up to a white marble double mansion at 65th Street and Fifth Avenue, replacing her 400-person ballroom with a 1,500-person ballroom flanked by a grand staircase. In her later years, the senile Mrs. Astor used to stand at the top of this staircase, dressed in her diamond tiara, pearl collar, and diamond stomacher, greeting the ghosts of long-dead guests. To the end, she was most in her element presiding over a grand ball.

The house she left behind when she moved, on the site of the present Empire State Building, was replaced by a second hotel, the Astoria. The Waldorf and Astoria hotels operated side by side for years until the two branches of the family were reconciled and the hotels were joined into the Waldorf-Astoria.

The Astors are believed to have made more money and kept it longer than did any other family in American history, thanks to the provisions made by the family's founder. Astor made sure his wealth stayed in family hands by setting aside half his fortune in a generation-skipping trust for his grandchildren. He also specified that his children make similar arrangements for their heirs, to prevent any profligate inheritors from squandering the fortune or giving it away to charity. Protected in this way, the Astor fortune in America and Britain topped $200 million by the third generation.

The British line of Astors continues to live comfortably, although not quite as extravagantly as in its heyday. Many of the Astors live in small townhouses and flats. Even the more luxurious country mansions have toned down their elegance. Hever Castle, home of one Astor branch, boasted more than thirty full-time servants in the 1920s, but by the 1980s, Lord Astor and his family were making do with only three servants. Some of the Astor heirs, whose fortunes have been depleted by high British taxes and diffused among many family members, have supplemented their inheritances with professions and enterprises. Several have returned to the old family business of operating farms, less for nostalgia, perhaps, than for the break on land taxes.

The American Astor dynasty came to an end with Vincent Astor, Caroline's grandson. He was the last of the Astors to turn up among the wealthiest Americans, appearing on the list compiled by B. C. Forbes in 1918. Even then, he was overshadowed by the new fortunes of the Rockefellers, Carnegies, and others.

Vincent's father, the fourth John Jacob Astor, had been a passenger on the ill-fated maiden voyage of the *Titanic*. He is remembered for his courage in valiantly ushering his pregnant wife into a lifeboat and then going down with the ship. Vincent, in college at Harvard at the time of his father's death, inherited $69 million, the bulk of his father's estate.

For a time, Vincent lived in the white marble mansion on Fifth Avenue, bravely carrying on his grandmother's tradition of the annual Astor ball. Then, tired of the pomp, he sold the mansion in 1925 for $3.5 million and moved into a town house. Vincent, who had no heirs when he died in 1959, left almost all his fortune to a charitable trust. He thus violated the ironclad rule of keeping the Astor money in the family and virtually ended the great wealth of the American branch of the Astor empire. The great Astor mansion on Fifth Avenue—with the grand ballroom that was once the center of America's Gilded Age—was torn down to make way for the Temple Emanu-El synagogue.

Rich, but Not Rich Enough

Donald Trump

(1947–   )

THE DONALD IS OUT-TRUMPED

Few names are associated with wealth and power more than modern real estate tycoon Donald Trump. He puts his name on his properties the way other people monogram shirts. When it comes to wealth, however, the master of "the Art of the Deal" finds himself out-trumped by less flamboyant rivals. Although he appeared on several lists of the wealthiest Americans in the 1980s, with estimates of $1.7 billion or higher, he ultimately fell off the *Forbes* 400 list, thanks in part to business reversals during the recession at the end of the 1980s. No matter. The real estate mogul is still at the table, launching a comeback with a whole set of new casinos and other business initiatives. In November 1995, he wrote an essay for the *New York Times Magazine* modestly titled "I'm Back," and subtitled "I'm soaring once again." Whatever he does, you'll know about it. "I like being public," he admits. "That way, everyone can see what I do."

4

Stephen Girard

(1750–1831)

The Cabin Boy Who Became
the Richest Man in America

Est. wealth: $7.5 million

Stephen Girard, a French immigrant and Philadelphia banker, is believed to have been the first person to be recognized as the "richest man in America" (before he was dethroned by John Jacob Astor). The sea brought Girard to the shores of America, and it was shipping that started him on the way to building his fortune of more than $7 million by the time of his death in 1831.

The eldest of five children of a sea captain in Bordeaux,

Girard was described as "the ugly duckling" of the family. At the age of eight, he became blind in one eye, and this evil eye later added to the sternness of his image. Son of a navy captain, Girard loved the sea. At fourteen, he ran away from a troubled home life, spending nine years sailing between Bordeaux and the West Indies. Starting as a cabin boy, he rose to take command of a trading vessel at twenty-three, becoming France's youngest captain.

He settled in Philadelphia by chance. While sailing from New York in May 1776, his ship became enshrouded in fog off Delaware. His rescuers told him the Revolutionary War had begun. He headed quickly for safe port in Philadelphia, where he sold his ship and cargo (only part of which belonged to him). With the proceeds, he opened up a small grocery store and wine business.

Girard took an oath of allegiance to the colonies, but his true allegiance was to trade. He made a small fortune by secretly trading with the British during the occupation of Philadelphia and through slave trading. He also financed privateers and continued a brisk trade with Santo Domingo despite shifting proscriptions of the war. When it became illegal to ship sugar and coffee, his cargos became "lumber." He also was known to mix low-grade flour into his high-grade flour, a change that couldn't be detected until bread was made. Girard soon built a fleet of eighteen ships, all named after French philosophers in honor of his native land.

He had married a servant girl in 1777, but after their first child died at birth, his wife went crazy. She lived out the rest of her life in an asylum. Girard, who never remarried or had children, lived alone in a dingy, four-story house on Water Street in Philadelphia. He was an eccentric who kept a cage of singing canaries on his desk and converted to vegetarianism late in life.

Girard used his shipping fortune to enter banking. He was the largest investor in the First Bank of the United States, and when the bank's charter expired he bought the building and cashier's house for $120,000. In 1812, he used these resources to open Girard Bank with capital of $1.2 million. And while the War of 1812 destroyed many merchants, Girard kept earning more money from shipping. He also helped the U.S. government finance the war—for a 10 percent commission.

Girard could easily have been the model for Dickens's Scrooge in *A Christmas Carol* (published in 1840). Girard declared that work "is the only pleasure I have on this globe." He started his day with a spoonful of Holland gin and a cup of strong black coffee. He was a cruel taskmaster with his employees. When he founded Girard Bank he cut the salaries of the employees who came from the First Bank of the United States. A watchman who had always received an overcoat at Christmas got nothing from Girard.

Like Scrooge, Girard also seemed to have a Christmas conversion. He died at the age of eighty-one on the day after Christmas in 1831. Imagine the surprise when the will of this skinflint was opened, and his relatives, apprentices, and even servants received bequests. The city, state, hospitals, orphan societies, and other charitable organizations also received gifts. But the largest bequest of $6 million went to the institution that would bear his name, Girard College, a school for male orphans in Philadelphia.

As Kenneth Fisher commented, "Had he lived another seventy-five years, the wealthy, influential Girard may have rivaled the powerful J. P. Morgan! Unlike Morgan, however, Girard's empire died when he did in 1831."

5

Andrew Carnegie

(1835–1919)

Man of Steel

Est. wealth: $475 million

(much of it given away before he died)

Andrew Carnegie, the twinkly-eyed Scottish founder of a steel fortune, is probably best known for giving most of his money away. His "gospel of wealth" made him one of the most prominent of the early philanthropists.

Carnegie was born in Scotland, the son of a poor weaver, at a time when the Industrial Revolution was putting weavers out of business. His mother kept them alive by sewing shoes, with young Andrew threading needles by her side. She wanted a better life for her sons, so the family moved to America when he was twelve. His father worked in a cotton factory where Andrew also worked for $1.20 per week.

Carnegie didn't let his lack of a formal education stand in the way of his learning. As a boy he was a messenger in a Pittsburgh telegraph office. When he was sent to deliver congratulatory messages to the theater, he would wait to arrive until just after the curtain went up so that he would be invited to stay and watch the performance of Shakespearean plays.

Carnegie was an avid reader, devouring books on politics, history, and science. As a teenager, he wrote letters to the editor of the *New York Tribune* and other papers, giving his opinions on issues such as slavery. He continued to write letters to newspapers throughout his life.

In his youth, Andrew was known for his honesty. As a messenger boy, he once returned $500 he had found, equal to ten years of his wages at the time.

Carnegie was promoted to telegraph operator and went to work for the Pennsylvania Railroad. He became one of the first telegraph operators who could recognize the letters by sound. Soon he was working as assistant and private telegraph operator for the superintendent of the railroad's Pittsburgh division. The position came with a $35 monthly salary. He later recalled: "I couldn't imagine what I could ever do with so much money!"

As always, he kept his eye out for opportunities, and it wasn't long before he found them. With his skill in telegraphy, Carnegie became the personal telegrapher and secretary to Thomas Scott, superintendent of the Pennsylvania's western division. With Scott's mentoring and support, Carnegie learned about management and entrepreneurship during his twelve years with the railroad, and he rose through the ranks to become a superintendent. Scott also introduced Carnegie to the world of investment, and by 1863, Carnegie's investments in railroad cars, oil, and other ventures were generating $45,000 in income per year. Carnegie helped with military transportation during the Civil War, taking troops to Washington and loading trains with wounded soldiers after the Battle of Bull Run.

After the war, the railway business boomed. It was the construction of many huge iron bridges that caught Carnegie's attention. In 1862, with Scott and a few other partners, he had established the Keystone Bridge Company to build iron bridges. In 1865, Carnegie left the railroad to run the bridge company. He used his railroad contacts to build Keystone into the largest and most successful bridge maker in the nation. Then, Carnegie moved into the iron business and subsequently to the iron rail business. Carnegie at first resisted moving from iron to steel but later became one of its most stalwart converts, constructing a large steel plant near Pittsburgh.

Carnegie raised the quality and drove down the cost of steel, with more efficient plants and processes. He introduced new accounting and inventory systems, producing the most accurate and detailed cost controls of any business of his day. He often said, "Watch the costs, and the profits will take care of themselves." Once while touring a new steel mill that could cut costs by 50 cents per ton, Carnegie noticed his assistant looked troubled. He asked what was wrong. The assistant—Charles M. Schwab (who would later rise to fame as a financier)—said he was disappointed because he had just thought of a way to save another half dollar a ton, but it would mean tearing down the new mill. Carnegie replied, "Go ahead and tear it down."

Carnegie maintained that his secret was surrounding himself with bright associates, wizards of science and finance. He hired people like Schwab and coke king Henry Frick. He once suggested that his epitaph should read "Here lies a man who was able to surround himself with men far cleverer than himself." He took good care of these associates, whom he considered more important than iron ore or plants. Some of the heads of his departments became millionaires themselves.

A devoted son, Carnegie didn't marry while his mother was alive. In 1887, shortly after her death, the fifty-two-year-old multimillionaire married his close friend Louise Wittfield. She was a capable hostess and didn't object to his giving away most of the family fortune. They spent half the year in a castle in Scotland and later bought a 40,000-acre tract and built Skibo Castle there, which remained their favorite residence.

Led by Carnegie, the United States raced passed Great Britain as leading supplier of the world's steel. At thirty-five, Carnegie had laid out a plan that included retirement once his fortune reached $50,000. Yet, he was over sixty-five before he sold his steel company to J. P. Morgan's United States Steel for more than $400 million in 1901. One of his first acts was to turn $5 million of his earnings back into a pension and benefit fund for his workers.

Then he began disposing of the fortune he had so carefully built, becoming one of the most famous philanthropists. He said, "There is no idol more debasing than the worship of money." His "Gospel of Wealth," published in the *North American Review* in 1889, became a blueprint for benevolence. He divided a man's life into two periods—a time of accumulating and a time of distributing wealth. Among Carnegie's benefactions were the establishment of 2,811 public libraries and the donation of 7,689 organs to churches. He also established Carnegie Hall in New York and the Carnegie Institution in Washington.

In ten years, Carnegie gave away more than $350 million. Then he tired of philanthropy. (As he complained in a newspaper article in 1913, "the way of the philanthropist is hard.") He established the Carnegie Foundation with an endowment of $125 million—the first modern philanthropic foundation. In later years, he became a proponent of world peace, building the Peace Palace at The Hague.

One of his most unusual gifts was in response to a request from Woodrow Wilson, then president of Princeton University. Wilson brought Carnegie to the New Jersey campus to discuss giving a gift to the institution. (Former partner and rival Henry Frick had already given an organ, which was Carnegie's trademark gift.) Carnegie was interested in supporting athletics, but he deplored the violence of football. He thought rowing was a more dignified sport, so he gave a gift to support it—but not a racing shell, as most donors would have done. Instead, he gave a lake—known as Lake Carnegie—carved out of a river running along the edges of the campus.

Carnegie was a devoted patriot. He wrote several books, including *The Triumph of Democracy*, praising his adopted nation and attacking the European monarchies. The book, published in 1886 with a disrespectful inverted crown on its cover, sold more than forty thousand copies. In 1908, he was offered a British title by King Edward, but he turned down the honor because he would have had to give up his U.S. citizenship.

Andrew Carnegie was not a gambling man. He eschewed speculation on Wall Street. He "never bought a share of stock on margin in his life, yet he did make one gamble of titanic proportions—and won. He wagered everything he possessed on the economic future of the United States." During economic depressions, he invested in his plants, confident of a recovery. During times of prosperity, these investments allowed him to expand to meet new demands. The nation grew and prospered. And so did Carnegie.

When he died at his summer home in Massachusetts in 1919, at the age of eighty-four, he was survived by his wife and a daughter. But the Carnegie legacy and the Carnegie fortune had already been diffused across the length and breadth of the nation he had adopted as his home.

6

Alexander Turney Stewart

(1803–1876)

The Merchant Prince

Est. wealth: $50–$80 million

Alexander Turney Stewart is credited with founding the first department store in the United States in 1848. His New York department stores were huge, lavish marble emporiums. They were monuments to the newfound buying power of Americans and the abundance of goods for those with the power to purchase them. A. T. Stewart had the power. By the time of his death in 1876, he had built a fortune of over $50 million.

Stewart was born near Belfast, Ireland, in 1803. His father died shortly after Stewart was born, and he was placed in the care of his grandfather. His grandfather wanted him to enter the ministry, and he sent Stewart to an academy in Belfast. But after his grandfather's death in 1820, the seventeen-year-old Stewart left the school to travel to New York City. Stewart, who had studied ancient Greek and Roman history at Trinity College in Dublin, taught at a private school. When he later returned home to Ireland to claim a $5,000 inheritance, he bought some Irish lace and linens, which he sold in New York. The teacher learned a lesson about the opportunities in trade that he would never forget.

In 1823, he opened a small dry goods store on lower Broadway. He and his wife lived above the store. There were hundreds of small stores, but Stewart stood out because of his distinctive approach to his customers and a shrewd sense for business.

He was among the first to discover the value of service to customers. At the time, most stores sought to extract the best bargain with no concern for building relationships or reputation. Stewart was known to throw in an extra ribbon or spool of thread into the packages of his customers as a bonus. His motto was: Never let a customer go. Customers knew that he would give them the best goods for the best price. And they beat a path to his door.

Although not known for philanthropy, he enhanced his reputation by sending a boatload of supplies to aid the Irish during the potato famine and by donating $50,000 worth of clothing and blankets to the victims of the Chicago fire. His reputation improved even more during the Civil War: While other merchants made fortunes on the conflict, Stewart supplied uniforms and blankets to Union troops at cost.

Stewart was also a shrewd dealer. He would arrange for an assistant to make extravagant claims about their products. Then Stewart would pretend to overhear and tell off the assistant. He would turn to the customer and explain the truth about the product. In the process of this carefully rehearsed show, he gained the confidence of his customers. He also gained a reputation as a cold operator when he bought, at auction, stocks of rivals who failed during the 1837 depression.

Stewart was a tough taskmaster. He paid low wages and stalked the floors of his stores, firing salespeople on the spot for transgressions. As fawning as he was to his customers, he considered his employees "simply machines." They were fined for lateness, long lunches, wrong change, and a host of other "offenses."

An innovator, he was the first to organize his stores into

departments and the first to use display windows to show his merchandise to pedestrians on the street. He owned factories around the world that supplied his retailing empire.

If A. T. Stewart was already the talk of the town by the mid-1840s, it was nothing compared to what happened next when he began constructing a huge building near New York's City Hall. It was so massive people called it "Stewart's Folly." But not after it opened. In 1848, he opened the doors of this giant marble dry goods palace, which featured huge pillars, sweeping ceilings, and glass chandeliers. People were in awe.

Then, he topped this achievement by building a larger store closer to the heart of town, at Ninth Street and Broadway Avenue. It was the largest retail store in the world. This eight-story, $2.75 million monument to retailing, called the "Cast Iron Palace" or "Business Palace," opened in 1861 and covered an entire city block. When an architect suggested hanging a large sign with Stewart's name on it, the founder objected. "People know whose store it is," Stewart said.

The store was the forerunner of the large department stores of Macy, Wanamaker, and others. It did more than $100,000 in business a day. By 1870, Stewart became the first retailer to sell over $10 million in goods per year. (Compared to less than $1 million in sales at Macy's and less than $3 million at Marshall Field). For many years, Stewart claimed the largest volume of retail sales in the world.

His next project, a personal one, was every bit as grand. Perhaps inspired by the classical studies of his youth, Stewart set about building a $1 million marble mansion at Fifth Avenue and 34th Street. The neo-Babylonian structure featured huge Corinthian columns and massive recessed windows. Its interior was lined with marble, boasting a sweeping staircase, classical white statues, and a large, valuable collection of artwork. Stewart and his wife moved into the home in 1869, when he was sixty-six.

When Stewart was nominated to be secretary of the treasury by his friend President Ulysses S. Grant, the merchant prince was elated. At last, he would gain the respect from the New York socialites that all his millions had not earned him. But rival congressmen, infuriated that Grant had not chosen political cronies to fill his cabinet, protested the appointment. They turned up a little-known statute barring anyone involved in trade or commerce from leading the treasury. Stewart's nomination was withdrawn.

Spurned in his political ambitions, Stewart turned his energy to expanding his empire. He created a "City Beautiful" on Long Island, which would become Garden City. It was intended as a paradise for working people. Meanwhile, his retail business and real estate holdings made him the richest man in New York.

When he died in 1876, at the age of seventy-three, a crowd of eight thousand turned out for his funeral. But his story didn't end there. Two years after he was buried, his remains were taken from their resting place by blackmailers and held for ransom. His widow paid $25,000 for their return. They were then ensconced in a beautiful tomb at the heart of the cathedral he had built in Garden City. After his death, A. T. Stewart and Company was transferred to his executor, Henry Hilton, for $1 million. It was renamed E. J. Denning and Company, but the new company was unsuccessful.

In contrast to the founders of the Astor and Vanderbilt empires, Stewart was a mild man who concentrated on small sales rather than million-dollar deals and political manipulations. But he was just as focused on business. As a biographer once wrote, "He thinks money, lives money, makes money; it is the end and aim of his existence." When he was asked about the secret of his success, he replied, "Work, Work, Work!"

7

Frederick Weyerhaeuser

(1834–1914)

Lumber Baron

Est. wealth: $200 million or more

Frederick Weyerhaeuser was the Paul Bunyan of the American timber industry—larger than life. The growth of the nation created a huge demand for wood—for housing and fuel—and Weyerhaeuser filled it. In the process, he harvested a personal fortune estimated at well over $200 million.

Born in Germany, Weyerhaeuser came to the United States when he was twenty. He worked on a construction gang for the Rock Island & Peoria Railroad in Illinois. Then "Dutch Fred," as he was known, took a job with a lumber company working at a sawmill. He was promoted to foreman.

In contrast to other businessmen in his time, he was known

for being kind and fair to his employees. But he did know how to take advantage of an opportunity. In the panic of 1857, he used his savings from his work in the lumber business to take over the Coal Valley lumberyard at a sheriff's auction. Three years later, he had earned $8,000 from the lumber operations. In partnership with his brother-in-law, Frederick C.A. Denckman, Weyerhaeuser gained control of a second mill.

In 1870, he helped organize a cooperative of seventeen lumber companies—the Mississippi River Logging Company. The company mined logs from the North, floated them down the Mississippi, and turned them into lumber to sell in the Midwest. Directed by his timber company based in Tacoma, Washington, Weyerhaeuser's loggers cut their way through Wisconsin, then moved to Minnesota and finally on to Idaho. It is said the extensive clearings they made in Minnesota opened the way for the wheat fields that became a central part of the commerce of the Twin Cities.

In Minnesota, Weyerhaeuser had another piece of good fortune. His next-door neighbor in St. Paul was James J. Hill. Hill, the railway man (who is also among the Wealthy 100), was struggling with a problem. In building the Northern Pacific railway, he had been given enormous "alternate" land grants in the Inland Empire—between the Rockies and Cascades. But Hill had no use for the land. When Weyerhaeuser looked out across these verdant forests, he had an idea.

Weyerhaeuser and his associates bought 900,000 acres at $6 per acre. Thus he locked up the last great stands of timber in the United States. It may be an exaggeration, but legend has it that by the turn of the century, the Weyerhaeuser family and associates controlled 62,500 square miles, an area larger than the entire state of Wisconsin. The family also had interests in more than twenty sawmills.

Weyerhaeuser and his German-born wife Elizabeth had four sons, all of whom played a role in developing his timber business. The eldest, John P. Weyerhaeuser, worked closely with his father starting in 1907 and became president of Weyerhaeuser Timber Company when his father died in 1914. John's son, John P., Jr., graduated from Yale and worked in various timber businesses before becoming president of Weyerhaeuser Timber Company in 1946. He led the company until 1956. His eldest son, George, was named vice president of the company in 1957, president in 1966, and later CEO.

Overcutting of the forests, along with a shift in building materials from wood to steel and cement, reduced the size of the family's timber holdings after Frederick Weyerhaeuser's death. But Weyerhaeuser's descendants continued to play a central role in the nation's timber business. In the 1930s, they still controlled 18 percent of the timber capacity in the United States. In 1959, with paper making, lumber, and other diverse activities, Weyerhaeuser Timber Company was renamed Weyerhaeuser Corporation. By the end of the 1970s, it owned eight pulp mills, five paper plants, eleven paperboard plants, forty-nine container and cardboard plants, and thirty-two lumber plants. The company controlled 5.7 million acres of forest land. It had more than 48,000 employees and net sales, in 1979, of $4.4 billion. But in the 1980s, after diversifying into a variety of businesses, the company lost its leadership in the forest products industry to rival Georgia-Pacific.

Although ecologists generally offer scant praise for lumber companies, Weyerhaeuser's high-yield, scientific forestry and concern for environmental impact won the company the distinction of being designated "Best of the S.O.B.'s" by *Audubon* magazine. Weyerhaeuser pioneered the concept of replanting, with the slogan "Timber is a crop."

From a single sawmill, Weyerhaeuser became the leading timberman in the world, purchasing an estimated 2 million acres by the time of his death. By 1990, the company owned 5.8 million acres of forest in the Northwest and held rights to 13 million acres in Canada. The land included Mt. St. Helens, and the company's corporate headquarters in Washington, between Seattle and Tacoma, now commands a spectacular view of Mt. Rainier.

8

Jay Gould
(1836–1892)
Mephistopheles of Wall Street
Est. wealth: $75–$150 million

Jay Gould, known as the "Mephistopheles of Wall Street," was one of the most notorious rascals of American business history. Even in a time when the most upright businessmen routinely engaged in stock watering, land grabs, and political manipulations, Gould stood out as one of the most ruthless. And, despite the best efforts of his many enemies, he got away with it. His estate at his death was valued at about $75 million, but his true wealth could have been as high as $150 million or more.

Gould, the son of a poor Connecticut farmer, started out at the bottom and clawed his way to the top. He worked for a local blacksmith and as a clerk before learning rudimentary skills in surveying. At eighteen, he began using his talents to draft county maps of New York. By twenty-one, he had managed to save $5,000, which he invested, in 1857, in a tannery in partnership with New York leather merchant C. M. Leupp. Gould, ruthless in his pursuit of wealth, quickly developed a plan to wrest full control of the business from his partner, and his enemies claimed Gould was responsible for driving Leupp to suicide later that year.

Gould was eerily pale and cold, with deep-set glaring eyes, and a full square-cut beard like a terrier's. He was described by author Arthur Howden Smith as "a pasty-faced little bearded man, who was probably hated by more Americans than Benedict Arnold—and whose surest title to immortality, perhaps, is that he was the only man who ever swindled Vanderbilt and got away with the loot unpunished."

Gould's most famous showdown with the Commodore was a fight for control of the Erie Railroad—a five-hundred-mile trunk line from New York to the Great Lakes. Vanderbilt wanted to absorb this competitor into his growing rail network. In 1867, Gould joined two associates, Jim Fisk and Daniel Drew, to battle the Commodore for the Erie.

The fight became an all-out war. To block Vanderbilt, Gould and partners illegally issued new stock for the railroad, literally cranking out some 100,000 stock certificates on a printing press in the basement of the Erie offices. Vanderbilt obtained an order to arrest them from a New York judge. Gould, Fisk, and Drew packed $6 million in Erie funds into suitcases and fled to New Jersey—out of reach of the state court. They surrounded themselves with more than a dozen policemen and three twelve-pound cannons in Taylor's Hotel, which they renamed "Fort Taylor."

Gould painted a picture for the public of the giant Vanderbilt beating up tiny rivals. When Gould ventured back into New York, Vanderbilt had him arrested in Albany for his swindles at the Erie. Gould posted bail. Meanwhile, he sent carpetbaggers with bags of $1,000 bills to bribe the legislature. Gould ultimately managed to have all his actions declared legal by the New York legislature, but only after spending an estimated $1 million in bribes in a bidding war with Vanderbilt. Weary of the battle, Vanderbilt conceded. The Commodore commented about a later minor skirmish with Gould and Fisk, saying in his sailor's dialect, "From now on, I'll leave them blowers alone." And he did.

Gould and Fisk continued to manipulate Erie stock by issuing new shares and using their own holdings to drive the price up and down at will. Their reign of terror was ended by angry Erie share-holders who took control away from Gould. Gould gave them land and securities that he said were worth $6 million in exchange for his 200,000 Erie shares and an agreement to leave. Gould took out an estimated $20 million from Erie as he drove the railroad into the ground. As the final insult, his "$6 million" in land and securities turned out to be worth only $200,000.

Gould and Fisk orchestrated another low point in American business history with an attempt to corner the gold market in 1869. They bought up the equivalent of twice the entire U.S. floating gold supply. (Although the supply on the market was only about $15 to $20 million, more gold could be purchased because some traders sold it short.) And they used backroom pressure on President Grant—through a friend, A. R. Corbin, brother-in-law to the president—to try to keep the U.S. Treasury's supply of some $75 million in gold off the market. As gold prices rose, the government caught wind of the scheme and released $5 million in gold from the treasury on September 24, 1869.

This sparked the gold panic known as Black Friday. The price of gold plunged $25 in fifteen minutes. Thousands of investors were ruined, and one newspaper compared the scene that followed to the battlefield of Gettysburg.

Although there were many casualties, Gould was not one of them. As usual, he watched the rising prices and unloaded his gold just before the crash—using insider information from sources within the government who tipped him off to the plans for the Treasury sale. Gould sold quickly and quietly, walking away with an estimated $11 million. Gould failed to pass on this information to his partner James Fisk, and Fisk was ruined

After having done enough damage in the East, Gould next turned his acquisitive mind to the West. He accumulated railroads—the Denver Pacific, Kansas Pacific, Missouri Pacific, and Union Pacific. By 1890, he owned half of the total trackage in the Southwest, a total of 15,800 miles. He also added the Western Union telegraph company, defeating a second Vanderbilt, William Henry, to gain control of the telegraph line.

After years of dirty deals that ruined many Wall Street investors, Gould had only a few friends in New York and was shunned by high society. But even here, the persistent Gould used his ample fortune to find ways around the problem. When he was excluded from obtaining a box at the old New York Opera, he didn't get mad. He got even. He set about raising money from other social climbers to build a bigger and better opera house—the New York Metropolitan Opera.

Gould died of tuberculosis at age fifty-six, in 1892, and his $75 million fortune was placed in trust for his six children. His eldest son, George, was given control over the family fortune. (George had run the family business for the last five years of the elder Gould's life.) But George was neither as ruthless nor as talented in business as his father. After losing money on railroad investments, he was forced to step down, and the estate was divided.

Gould's reputation haunted the family even many years after his death. When Gould's youngest daughter, Anna, died in 1961, she gave the family's Tarrytown, New York, estate, Lyndhurst, to the American people. It was her intention that it be established as a memorial to her mother and father. U.S. officials accepted the gift, but there was such an outcry about creating a shrine to one of the most ruthless of the robber barons that the tours of the mansion focused primarily on its architecture rather than the sordid life of its owner.

Jay Gould's youngest son, Howard, who died in 1959, proved to have a talent for investment, leaving an estate worth $62 million, most of which was not inherited from his father. Great-grandson Kingdon Henry Gould followed in his progenitor's footsteps, focusing on parking garages rather than railroads. Kingdon's share of Jay Gould's fortune—diluted by poor investments, taxes, and a large family—probably amounted to less than $1 million. Kingdon became a multimillionaire in the 1960s by building a parking lot empire in Washington, D.C., Baltimore, and Los Angeles. And the specter of Jay Gould followed him. In 1966, when the *Washington Post* wrote a series of critical articles on the new parking lot moguls in Washington, the paper noted that Gould was the great-grandson of "the Mephistopheles of Wall Street." In the end, although none of the Goulds was destitute, Jay Gould's reputation had more staying power than his fortune.

Prominent but Poor

Jim Fisk

(1834–1872)

JUST IN IT FOR THE EXCITEMENT

Jim Fisk, Gould's frequent partner in crime, was not as good as Gould at holding on to his prizes. After losing most of his fortune in the gold crisis, Fisk died in a blaze of bullets in the Broadway Central Hotel—shot down at the age of thirty-seven by a rival in pursuit of the beautiful Josie Mansfield. The public was surprised to learn that he left behind only "a paltry $1 million," mostly in real estate and stock, with many claims against his fortune. Some of his money had gone to his wife, but she lost her inheritance through bad investments soon after his death. Fisk's passing did have a favorable economic impact on Erie railroad stock. When news of his death reached investors, the stock rose more than four points on the expectation that its future was more secure now that he was gone.

Daniel Drew

(1797–1879)

THE DREW TREASURE: $148.22

Daniel Drew, once a powerful financier, helped to educate James Fisk and Jay Gould in the wily ways of Wall Street. He taught them too well. Although the three triumphed over Vanderbilt in manipulating Erie stocks, Drew ended up the big loser. Although he once had assets as high as $15 million, his protégés drove him to bankruptcy before his death. Drew held secret talks with Vanderbilt, and his angry former partners turned against him. Gould and Fisk manipulated stock prices in a way that led to a huge loss for Drew. When he died in 1879, Drew's estate was valued at just $148.22. His promised gift to the Drew Theological Seminary remained unfulfilled. Long after his death, people were convinced that he must have hidden some treasure somewhere. The only daughter of William Drew lived on a secluded farm near Port Elizabeth, New Jersey. When her grandson visited her property in 1972, he found it pitted with holes from treasure seekers, the evidence of years of fruitless search by seekers after the nonexistent prize.

9

Stephen Van Rensselaer

(1764–1839)

The Last Patroon

Est. wealth: $10 million

Stephen Van Rensselaer was the last of a landed aristocracy that had been given extensive empires under Dutch rule. He controlled a million acres of New York State and also wielded political power as a U.S. Congressman. In 1835, he was second only to John Jacob Astor as the richest man in America, but he lived long enough to see the feudal source of his power eroded by the forces of commerce and democracy.

The patroons—given huge land grants in the New World—had the same powers as lords of European feudal estates. Tenants needed permission from the lords to entertain a guest for more than twenty-four hours. They were forced to do all their business within the manor, and usually became so indebted to the lord that they could not leave. At the height of his influence, Stephen Van Rensselaer had between 60,000 and 100,000 tenants living on his estate.

Van Rensselaer is the only member of the *Wealthy 100* whose fortune came entirely from inherited wealth. He inherited the estate when he was just five years old, after his father's death in 1769. He was the eighth patroon in an unbroken line of family who had controlled the manor. After attending Harvard, Van Rensselaer took up residence in the manor house with his wife, Margaret Schuyler, a member of one of New York's leading families.

At the height of his power, he would drive to New York in a black carriage pulled by four horses, with a gilded Van Rensselaer coat of arms on the doors. Van Rensselaer's British valet would sit across from him in the carriage, and his personal army of mounted soldiers trotted behind. The citizens of Manhattan would line the streets, and some would even bow before this last vestige of royalty in the new democracy.

The Last Patroon served as a major-general in the New York State Militia, leading a troop of six thousand men during the War of 1812. The soldiers, stationed on the Niagara, made an attack on the Canadian shore, but the attack failed when many of them refused to cross the river. Van Rensselaer was defeated, and he resigned his commission.

Van Rensselaer, who had served in the state legislature and run twice unsuccessfully for governor, was elected to Congress in 1822. There, he cast the deciding vote in the 1825 U.S. presidential election (which came down to a vote in the House of Representatives). He was thought to be committed to candidate William H. Crawford, but after saying a prayer before his decision he surprised his colleagues by making John Quincy Adams president of the United States.

Van Rensselaer was also very active in advancing the economic progress of New York state. In 1824, he founded the Rensselaer Polytechnic Institute in Troy, New York, for instruction in the "application of science to the common purposes of life." It was one of the first schools to train civilians in mechanical arts such as chemistry, natural history, and agriculture. He also served on canal commissions that helped develop plans for a waterway linking the Hudson with the Great Lakes, and he personally financed a geological study following the Erie Canal across New York.

The last of the old-style aristocrats was decidedly liberal in his attitude toward democracy. He leased out more of his land to tenants, but still refused to sell any of it. He was known as a generous landlord. Instead of passing his estate on to his eldest son, as was the patroon custom, Van Rensselaer divided it among his ten children.

He was so lax in collecting rents that, at his death on January 29, 1839, his tenants owed him more than $400,000. When his heirs began trying to collect, the tenant farmers rose up in what became known as the Van Rensselaer Rebellion. Tenants refused to pay, launching a bloody rebellion against the patroon system that eventually had to be put down by the state militia. After more than a decade of subsequent conflict, New York's highest state court ruled against the Van Rensselaers in 1852. The son of the Last Patroon sold all the land to the tenants, and much of his widow's remaining estate was lost to an unscrupulous lawyer.

Less than fifty years after Van Rensselaer's death, his entire estate—nearly a million acres at its peak—was in the hands of strangers.

The great family manor house in Albany, which had overlooked the family holdings on the Hudson River, was later torn down and carted off to Williams College in Massachusetts. There it was reassembled as a fraternity house but eventually fell into disrepair. The last vestige of the beauty and glory of the original manor house is the manor hall with French wallpaper preserved in the American Wing of the Metropolitan Museum of Art in New York City.

10

Marshall Field

(1834–1906)

Field of Dreams

Est. wealth: $140 million

Marshall Field started out on the ground floor of Chicago. Although he is best known for his retailing business, which continues to this day, he owed most of his fortune to the rapid appreciation of Chicago real estate.

It was easy to see how Field made money in real estate in those days. Chicago grew quickly as the hub of railways and the home of mills, packing houses, and manufacturing companies. In 1830, a quarter-acre of downtown land could be purchased for as little as $20. By 1894, the same piece of land was worth $1.25 million. Field, who had purchased downtown land at bargain-basement prices, soon found himself sitting on a fortune.

49

The son of a Massachusetts farmer, Marshall Field came to Chicago at the age of twenty-one to work in a wholesale dry goods house. He earned just $400 per year, saving half his earnings by sleeping at night in the store. In 1865, Field joined with other future multimillionaires Levi Z. Leiter and Potter Palmer to found the Field, Leiter & Palmer dry goods store. The owners, wearing frock coats, were known for greeting their patrons at the door, and Field's standards of customer service made him a standout among retailers. His skill in selecting managers and handling employees also contributed to his success. Eventually, Field bought out his partners and founded Marshall Field & Co.

Field lost the store in the Chicago Fire of 1871, and the store burned down again in 1877. But he rebuilt, and the store kept growing. By the time of his death, Field's company did an estimated $68 million per year. Shortly after his death, Marshall Field & Co. opened the largest store in the world in downtown Chicago, with 450 departments spanning 73 acres on 13 floors.

The reach of Field's empire extended far beyond Chicago. He built huge factories and clothing mills across Europe, Asia, and South America to supply his stores. He even had wool mills in Australia. He used his retailing and real estate earnings to invest in 150 companies, including industrial, transportation, utility, and mining corporations.

Field introduced several innovations in retailing, including marking fixed prices on products. Field also is credited with starting the policy of allowing customers to exchange goods if they were dissatisfied. The customer was king, and Field particularly catered to female customers with his slogan: "Give the Lady What She Wants."

His personal life was less fortunate than his business career. His wife, daughter, and son chose to live abroad while Field stayed in Chicago. His son, Marshall Field II, whose poor health prevented him from joining the family business, shot himself a year before his father's death. The family said the shooting was an accident, but it was rumored to be a suicide. Field was shaken by his son's death and the newspaper photographers and reporters who hounded him for days after the incident.

As a family friend commented before Field's death, "You have no home, no family . . . nothing but money."

Field's $140 million fortune was bequeathed primarily to two grandsons, Marshall Field III and Henry Field. Field's 22,000 word will was one of the longest ever probated in the Chicago court.

Most of the money was set aside in trust until the year 1954, when the youngsters would be in their fifties. Field also gave ten acres of land to the University of Chicago and donated $9 million to establish the Field Museum of Natural History in Chicago.

His grandson, Marshall Field III, founded the left-wing New York newspaper, *PM*, and later launched the *Chicago Sun* to challenge the conservative *Tribune* (owned by descendants of Cyrus McCormick). The younger Field took a beating in wars between the two papers, but managed to keep the paper alive by merging it with the afternoon *Times* to create the *Sun-Times*. In 1942, the *Tribune* blocked Field's paper from joining the Associated Press until 1945, when the U.S. Supreme Court ordered the AP to accept the *Sun-Times* as a member. By 1946, Field had built up the paper's daily circulation to 400,000. That same year, he launched *Parade* magazine, building a circulation of 3.5 million. Field owned radio stations in Chicago and Cincinnati. By the 1960s, the younger Field had amassed a fortune estimated at $168 million. His eldest son, Marshall Field IV, succeeded him as head of the publishing business.

11

Henry Ford

(1863–1947)

*After Two Failures, Rode
the Model T to Fame and Fortune*

Est. wealth: More than $1 billion

Henry Ford transformed the automobile from a toy of the rich to transportation for every man. He was a tinkerer who worked on strange contraptions in the garage behind his home. He was an entrepreneur who, at the age of thirty-nine, had little more to show for his troubles than two failed car companies and a few racing trophies. Then, between 1908 and 1927, his assembly lines turned out more than 15 million Model Ts. Ford reshaped the countryside and transformed the American way of life. In the process, he counted his cars in the millions and his wealth as $1 billion or more. Ford is one of the best examples of his own words: "I refuse to recognize that there are impossibilities."

As a child growing up on a farm outside Dearborn, Michigan, he had a natural interest in mechanical objects. He would take apart clocks—even if they weren't broken. A friend once said that "every clock in the Ford home shudders when it sees Henry coming." But he became an expert in fixing clocks and developed an interest in mechanical tinkering that became his lifelong obsession and the source of his fortune.

He never liked farm life. At sixteen, he left for a job as a machinist in Detroit, cleaning clocks at night. His salary was $3 per week. As the young Ford was fixing mainsprings, his own gears were turning. He began formulating a plan for mass-producing watches. He built dies and even secured a partner. He could make two thousand watches per day, but he had no way to sell them. It would be several decades before his interest in mass production would find an appropriate focus.

Ford's father wanted him to be a farmer, but Ford left the farm for Detroit—leaving behind the land that was his only inheritance. Ford worked as an engineer at the Edison plant in Michigan. But his dream was in a garage behind his house, where he worked through the night building his automobile. His neighbors called him "crazy Henry." His first little gasoline-powered "quadricycle" rolled out of the shop in 1896. His designs were not the first. Perhaps not even the best. But he had built his first car.

Still, this quirky inventor was a long way from success. He founded one company to build cars. It failed. He founded another. It dissolved. In 1902, at age thirty-nine, Henry Ford had two failed car companies behind him. And the odds were against him. Between 1900 and 1908, five hundred car companies were formed, but only a handful survived.

Anyone with less courage and tenacity might have given up and gone back to engineering. Not Henry Ford. Maybe it was the confidence and reputation he had gained through building race cars. (His 999, driven by Barney Oldfield, had set a new American record by crossing a five-mile course in five minutes, twenty-eight seconds in October 1902.) Maybe it was the realization that he finally had the experience to make it work. He formed the Ford Motor Company in 1903 with $150,000 in capital, only $28,000 of it in cash. None of it was from Ford, who contributed his talent and expertise in making cars. Ford's backer was Alexander W. Malcomson, a leading Detroit coal dealer, and their initial small successes attracted other investors. Ford's first cars were largely constructed by outside suppliers, particularly the Dodge Brothers, who would later challenge Ford as rivals in the auto industry.

This time, the company clicked into gear. Ford's dream of creating "a motorcar for the great multitude" was on the verge of being realized. He moved from the Model A to the Model T—the

"Tin Lizzie" as it was affectionately known—which was introduced in 1908. Ford and his engineers worked long into the night designing the new car, while Ford sat on his mother's old rocking chair, believing it would bring him good luck.

While most cars at the time cost more than $1,000, within eight years of its launch, the Model T was selling for as little as $345. The automobile, once the exclusive luxury of rich city dwellers, suddenly became a fixture in rural America. This Model T was called "the greatest single vehicle in the history of transportation."

To produce this car for the common man, Ford completely rethought the manufacturing process. He built one of the most efficient production lines in history. He used standardized parts instead of handcrafted ones. (The Model T initially came in red, green, black, blue, and two shades of gray, but in 1914 Ford's streamlining eliminated all colors except black.) He didn't set out to become the father of mass production but rather kept experimenting with new ideas that evolved into his assembly line. Gustavus Swift had introduced the idea of an assembly line in meat packing (actually "disassembly" lines), and others such as Samuel Colt and Henry Leland had developed interchangeable parts. Ford put these ideas together on a scale that had never before been attempted. In 1913 and 1914, he introduced a single continuously moving assembly line, cutting the average assembly time for a chassis from 728 minutes to 93 minutes.

To keep these efficient factories rolling, he needed a dedicated workforce. He shocked the world by introducing his famous $5 a day salary in 1914. At the time, Detroit auto plants were paying $1.80 per day for unskilled labor. He became an overnight celebrity and was hailed as an enlightened business leader. But his generosity to employees was paternalistic, and he later fiercely fought the unionization of his plants.

In 1907, Ford built a $285,000 red-brick home on Detroit's fashionable Edison Avenue. After his successes, he constructed a $2 million mansion in Dearborn. To keep out beggars and would-be inventors who were constantly showing up at his door, Ford positioned the gatehouse of the mansion a mile from his front door.

It was reported that Ford and his son, Edsel, had a fortune worth $1.2 billion between them in the 1920s. The New York *Evening World* speculated on what Ford could do with such a fortune. Among the possibilities: buy absolute control of U.S. Steel, General Motors, and the New York Central railroad; buy the entire gold reserve of the federal banks; or purchase all the wheat, oats, potatoes, and tobacco in the United States in 1925.

But he wasn't much for pomp and circumstance. He once turned down a dinner invitation from President Franklin Roosevelt to meet with the king and queen of England in 1939 because Mrs. Ford was having a meeting of her garden club that day.

Ford wasn't even all that interested in money. Ford and his son on three occasions were reportedly offered $1 billion or more by investors to sell the company. Ford's response: "I'd have the money but no job." Money was not the object. When he was asked about the size of his fortune, he replied, "I don't know or care!" He used to stuff checks in his pockets. One day, a check for $85,000 fell out of his pocket, and another for $125,000 was found in a suit at the dry cleaners.

Ford loved simple pleasures—leaning against birch trees and touring the countryside with his pals Thomas Edison, Harvey S. Firestone, and naturalist John Burroughs. There is a story that one day the three were cruising along in Ford's Model T when a lamp blew out. Ford stopped at a gas station to buy a new one. The conversation went something like this:

"You know," Ford said to the shopkeeper, "the man who made this lamp is out there in the car."

"Not Thomas Edison," the shopkeeper exclaimed.

"The same," said Ford.

Noticing Firestone tires on the shelves behind the counter, Ford added, "And by the way, Harvey Firestone is out there, too." The shopkeeper was in awe.

As he prepared to leave, Ford added: "And my name," he said smiling, "is Henry Ford!"

"Hey, wait a minute," said the shopkeeper, looking out at the bushy-bearded Burroughs, "if you tell me the other man out there is Santa Claus, I'll call the sheriff."

The automaker was an anti-intellectual and didn't care for small talk. He once said: "I don't like to read books. They muss up my mind." After his defeat in a run for the U.S. Senate in Michigan, which he blamed on Jewish voters, Ford began to publish the *Deaborn Independent* in 1918. With relentless anti-Semitic diatribes, Ford and his editors built the small weekly to a national circulation of 472,000 by 1923. With articles such as, "The International Jew: The World's Problem," the paper continued its anti-Semitic propaganda until Ford attacked Jewish lawyer Aaron Sapiro in 1925. Sapiro filed a $1 million defamation suit, which was settled out of court. A humbled Ford issued a formal retraction of his anti-Semitic statements and a personal apology to Sapiro. The paper was shut down in 1927.

Ford also was one of the nation's most visible pacifists. When World War I broke out in Europe, he had the notion to travel to Europe to try to stop the war. He chartered an ocean liner and took about 150 Americans there to plea for peace. The "Peace Ship" earned him the ridicule of the press.

Once Ford's peace efforts failed, and it was clear the war could not be prevented, Ford put the full force of his factories behind the war effort. He produced trucks, tanks, and other vehicles. Again, in World War II, when Ford was in his eighties, he constructed the world's largest aircraft-assembly plant to build B-24 Liberator bombers.

Ford had a single-minded focus. As he celebrated his fiftieth wedding anniversary, a reporter asked him the secret of a successful marriage. "The same as a successful car," he replied. "Stick to one model." This single focus was both his greatest strength and greatest weakness in business.

Ford had bought out his partners so that he could have a free hand. But his unwavering vision and dictatorial control eventually began to work against the company. As other car companies diversified, Ford clung to the formula that had made him successful. He saw his market share begin to slip from its record 55 percent in 1923. The company's losses mounted through the Depression, and Ford Motor Company dropped into last place among the big three.

His only son, Edsel, who had joined his father in running the business, died in 1943 at the age of forty-nine. After his son's death, Henry, then eighty, resumed the presidency of his company, which was now struggling.

Edsel's son, Henry, was discharged from the navy and returned to Michigan to help put the family business back in order. But Ford had planned to hand control of the company to Harry Bennett, the company's security chief whose men had thwarted attempts by the United Auto Workers to organize the Ford plants. The twenty-six-year-old Henry II carried a pistol to and from the office. Faced with persistent urging from his grandson's wife, Clara, and mother, Eleanor, and witnessing young Henry's success in winning support with the company, Ford began to reconsider his opposition. Finally, in 1945, Eleanor threatened to sell her 42 percent stake in the company if her son was not put in charge. The elder Ford, afraid that his company would pass out of family hands, capitulated and offered his twenty-eight-year-old namesake the presidency. The young Henry brought in talented managers, including "whiz kids" Robert S. MacNamara and Arjay Miller, who later went on to become Ford presidents. Within four years, Henry had begun to turn the floundering company around.

Most of Henry Ford's fortune, largely stock in the company, went to the Ford Foundation to avoid estate taxes. But to give the family continued control over the company, the stock was split into voting and nonvoting shares, with the family retaining the voting shares. It was ironic that a man who had opposed philanthropy in life (although he did give away $37 million during his lifetime), established one of the richest private foundations in the world. When Ford's wife, Clara, died in 1950, the foundation inherited an even larger stake in the company.

The Ford Foundation was ultimately responsible for selling off shares in the company. In 1956, the foundation convinced Ford family members to allow it to sell off a block of 7 million shares. The family made sure it would retain a majority of the votes on the board, but after the sale the Ford Motor Company was owned by more than 350,000 voting investors. After Eleanor's death in 1976, even more of the family shares were sold to the public. Still, *Fortune* reported in 1989 that Ford descendants owned $2 billion in stock, controlling 40 percent of shareholder votes.

Henry Ford II ruled the company with an iron fist for thirty-five years until his retirement in 1979. He had the final word in matters, sometimes saying "my name is on the building" ending all discussion. He never hesitated to fire executives, including Lee Iacocca, who was dismissed as president in 1978 and who later took charge of Chrysler. Henry Ford II was the last member of the family to head the dynasty. The company Henry Ford had so jealously guarded and kept in family hands was now widely owned and operated by professional managers.

Rich, but Not Rich Enough

Thomas Edison

(1847–1931)

THE $15 BILLION MAN

In 1928, Congress awarded a gold medal to Thomas A. Edison for his service to humanity. In the proclamation, the legislators figured that the inventor of the light bulb, phonograph, motion picture, and so many other items had made contributions worth $15.599 billion to humanity. (It is not certain how this very precise accounting was done.) Edison was very adept at turning his inventions to profit and died quite well off with a fortune estimated at about $12 million.

Prominent but Poor

Charles Goodyear

(1800–1860)

RUBBER CHECKS

Charles Goodyear's development of the vulcanized rubber used in tire manufacturing made his name a household word, but he lived to see his wonderful invention snatched from his hands. A host of manufacturing giants seized his idea. Goodyear engaged in protracted litigation, but only succeeded in driving himself to bankruptcy. As Gustavus Myers remarks, Goodyear died "loaded down with worries and debts, a broken-down man, at the age of 60." And the United States Commissioner of Patents reported in 1858: "No inventor probably has ever been so harassed, so trampled upon, so plundered by that sordid and licentious class of infringers known in the parlance of the world, with no exaggeration of phrase, as 'pirates.'" (The other tire making giant, Harvey S. Firestone, fared much better. By the time he died in 1938, he and his family owned shares in Firestone's company worth $17 million. It was still not enough to put him among the top 100.)

12

Andrew W. Mellon
(1855–1937)

13

Richard B. Mellon

(1858–1933)

Est. wealth: Over $350 million each

Banking Brothers

Andrew and Richard Mellon, partners to the end, had a working relationship that is rare among the founders of multimillion-dollar fortunes and rarer still among siblings.

The two brothers who would dominate U.S. banking and industry worked in adjacent offices at the bank, separated only by a saloon style swinging door. They spoke and acted as one, prefacing their statements by saying, "My brother and I . . ." They each had unlimited access to one another's funds. When one brother bought stock, he would frequently buy an equal portion for the other. When one decided to contribute to philanthropy, they both did. Until Andrew left to become secretary of the treasury, they sat at identical mahogany desks, ate lunch together, and spent week-ends in each other's homes.

Perhaps what made the relationship work is that they had complementary personalities. Andrew, the older brother, was slen-der, shy, and soft-spoken, with piercing blue-gray eyes. Richard was bearlike, gregarious, and full of spirit. Andrew worked on the books, while Richard—or Dick, as he was known to almost every-one—met with customers. Andrew was sophisticated and cos-mopolitan, while Dick was decidedly not. (He had half of a buffalo head hanging in his home, much to the chagrin of his wife.) Yet, as a team, they were one of the most powerful forces in finance and industry in the early 1900s.

Their father, Judge Thomas Mellon, had expected it to work out this way. The Judge's family had emigrated from Ireland to Pittsburgh in 1818 when he was five. Inspired by Franklin's auto-biography, Judge Mellon became a successful lawyer and entre-preneur. He was elected judge of the common pleas court of Allegheny County. After a career on the bench, he established a bank, T. Mellon & Sons, which he hoped would help provide for some of his eight children. For Richard and Andrew, it did.

In Pittsburgh, the brothers were at the center of many grow-ing industries—including coal, steel, oil, and railroads—and they invested shrewdly in a variety of firms. Through the Mellon bank, the two brothers built the Aluminum Company of America, the Koppers coke company, the Carborundum abrasives company, and many other enterprises. They also bought a controlling interest in a large Texas oil strike that became Gulf Oil. They had a keen eye for recognizing small businesses and new inventions that would soon become big enterprises, so they often beat other investors into emerging industries.

A young inventor, Charles Hall, had been rejected by a num-ber of investors before he brought his idea to the Mellons. It was a process for making aluminum, for which Hall received a patent in 1889. The Mellons recognized the importance of this new light-weight metal and created the Pittsburgh Reduction Company, which later became the Aluminum Company of America. From alu-minum, the Mellons moved to control the raw materials like baux-ite, and downstream products such as radiators and wire. They built a steel company, which they later sold to U.S. Steel. They also helped another inventor develop a coke-making process, which Mellon acquired for $300,000 and built into a $15 million business, thanks to the increased demand for steel during World War I.

The irony is that the retiring Andrew Mellon, described as "an anonymous figure even to his contemporaries," was appointed secretary of the treasury by President Warren G. Harding in 1921—at the age of sixty-five. He also was later appointed ambassador to Great Britain.

Had it not been for Andrew's appointment, the extent of the Mellon fortune might never have been known. In the age before the SEC and disclosure laws, the Mellons were completely overlooked when B. C. Forbes identified his list of the thirty wealthiest Americans in 1918. The Mellon investments were so complex that when Andrew was appointed secretary of the treasury, he had to resign from the boards of fifty-one corporations to avoid a conflict of interest.

Andrew Mellon, who served under both Harding and Calvin Coolidge, has the noble distinction of being the last secretary to succeed in reducing the national debt. He also has the distinction of helping to keep taxes down for wealthy Americans like himself.

Besides smoking Havanas, Andrew had one other true extravagance—he drove a custom-built automobile, constructed entirely from parts made by his businesses. While it may not have resembled a luxury car, it cost $40,000.

After finishing his service as ambassador to Great Britain, Andrew returned to Pittsburgh in 1933, at the age of seventy-eight, to resume his work at Mellon National Bank. But a short time later, Andrew was devastated by the death of his brother Richard. Andrew devoted his last years to philanthropy, donating his 126 paintings—including Rembrandts, Vermeers, and Titians—worth more than $35 million, to found the National Gallery of Art in Washington.

While Andrew's focus was in Washington, Richard's was firmly fixed on Pittsburgh, where he ran the family banking business until his death in 1933. In contrast to his more sophisticated, art-collecting brother, Richard had rather unorthodox tastes. For example, in his elegant mansion in Pittsburgh, Richard kept a coat rack made entirely of buffalo horns that he had collected during business trips to Montana.

Richard was fiercely dedicated to his native city and used his fortune to help improve it. He supervised the creation of major new buildings in the downtown area for Gulf, Koppers, Mellon National, and Union Trust.

In 1937, Andrew and Richard each had over $200 million, but they had already given much of it away to their children (a total of $310 million by 1937). By the time Andrew died, he had only $37 million in his personal estate.

Richard's son, Richard King Mellon, carried on the family business. He started out at Mellon Bank as a messenger in 1920, and when his father died in 1933, the thirty-four-year-old Richard King was left to run the family business by himself, while his uncle Andrew was preoccupied with a messy tax case in Washington. Richard King—whose father once took him on a tour of the former homes of Pittsburgh millionaires who had abandoned the town—became one of the driving forces of the city's renewal. He is credited with transforming Pittsburgh from a gritty and sooty steel town to a clean and modern city. He spearheaded urban renewal projects in Pittsburgh in the 1940s and 1950s that demolished more than ninety old buildings and created the thirty-six-acre Point State Park. Richard King died in 1970 at the age of seventy-one. He had passed along most of his estate to his four adopted children and his grandchildren. The remaining fortune was divided between his widow, Constance, and the Richard King Mellon Foundation.

In contrast to Richard King, Andrew's son Paul had little interest in the family business. While attending college at Cambridge, he worked in the bank during the summers but found it held little interest for him. After two unsuccessful entrepreneurial ventures—a restaurant and a business that made plastic bathtubs—he devoted his time to art and literature. His French Impressionist paintings are considered the most important collection held in private hands today. Following his father's example, Paul gave away more than $250 million in paintings. In 1978, he and his sister Ailsa donated nearly $100 million worth of art to the East Wing of the National Gallery. In 1995, the eighty-eight-year-old Paul still had a personal fortune estimated at more than $1 billion. The Mellon family also continues to play a prominent role in running major corporations such as Alcoa, Gulf Oil, and the Mellon Bank.

A survey of wealthy Americans by *Fortune* magazine in 1957 put four Mellon heirs near the top of the list, just below J. Paul Getty. A similar survey in 1968 put three Mellons (including Richard King and Paul) in the $500 million to $1 billion category. In 1995, *Forbes* estimated the total Mellon fortune at $5.4 billion.

14

Sam Moore Walton

(1918–1992)

The Wizard of Wal-Mart

Est. wealth: $22 billion

Wall Street woke up one morning in 1984 to find it had been invaded by a troupe of hula dancers and ukulele players. In their midst, stood a small, grandfatherly gentleman who looked like he could be a tourist from some backwater town in Arkansas, which is where he actually came from. But there he was, in this bastion of high-powered finance, wearing a Hawaiian shirt, grass skirt, and a string of colorful leis over his suit.

Sam Walton had made a bet with his employees that if they produced a pretax profit of more than 8 percent, he would hula down Wall Street. Once again, the phenomenal company had exceeded expectations. Walton proceeded to do what he described later as "a pretty fair hula." As usual, he was dancing all the way to the bank.

Sam Walton was the founder of one of the most successful businesses in American history, and he has become a business folk legend. He was known for his folksy, honest values as much as his shrewd business sense. In 1985, the year after his dance down Wall Street, Walton led the *Forbes* 400 list as the richest man in America. The year before his death in 1992, the Walton fortune had topped $22 billion, although he had divided it among his wife and four children. Walton would protest, "It's just paper—all I own is a pickup truck and a little Wal-Mart stock."

By 1995, the business that had begun with one store in Arkansas was a sprawling empire of more than two thousand Wal-Mart and Sam's Club stores in every part of the United States. Wal-Mart had become the nation's largest retailer.

Walton was a natural salesman. He was born in Oklahoma and grew up in Columbia, Missouri. During the Depression, his father barely kept them alive selling whatever he could get his hands on. The young Walton worked his way through college at the University of Missouri by running a paper route. His fraternity brothers at Zeta Phi nicknamed him "Hustler Walton" in a profile in a 1940 fraternity newspaper.

Upon graduation, Walton interviewed with two retail companies—Sears Roebuck and J.C. Penney. Each offered Walton a job. On June 3, 1940, he began working as a management trainee in J.C. Penney's Des Moines, Iowa, store. His salary was $75 a month. He worked there for some eighteen months, learning the retail business. One of the highlights of these early beginnings was the day J.C. Penney himself visited the store and personally showed the young Walton how to tie and package merchandise, how to wrap it with very little twine and very little paper, yet still make it look nice. It was an example of personal involvement that Walton would emulate in store after store.

Walton was drafted into the army in 1942 and served stateside in the military police. After he was discharged at age twenty-seven, Walton followed up on his dream of opening his own retail store. His variety store in Newport, Arkansas, part of a national chain of Ben Franklin stores, was so much of a shoestring operation that when the landlord refused to renew his lease in 1950, Walton had to move across the state to Bentonville. By 1962, he had built a chain of sixteen Ben Franklin stores.

After watching the rise of large discount stores in New England, Walton became convinced that small variety stores such as Ben Franklin would soon be driven out. In 1962, after pleading unsuccessfully with the national management of Ben Franklin to open a large discount store, Walton opened his own discount store—the first Wal-Mart Discount City in Rogers, Arkansas.

Walton's secret of success was an innovative warehousing system that allowed him to focus on the small towns that many of the larger retailers had ignored. For most retailers, it was not cost-effective to transport goods out to rural areas. But Walton began developing central warehouses with stores arranged around them like the spokes of a wheel—all the stores within one day by truck from the warehouse. He received volume discounts for the huge purchases sent to his warehouse, shaving 2 to 5 percent off his costs, which allowed him to serve rural America as efficiently as other large retailers had served city residents. With little competition, Wal-Mart quickly dominated retailing in these backwoods markets.

During the next eight years, he opened thirty stores, clustered around a series of central warehouses. In 1970 he took the company public and in 1983 he opened his first Sam's Wholesale Club which offered even steeper discounts to members who bought bulk goods.

Success didn't change Sam Walton. When it was announced that he was America's richest man, the media thundered into town. He joked later that they were probably expecting to find him "diving into a pool full of money" or lighting "big fat cigars with $100 bills while the hootchy-kootchy girls danced by the lake."

What they found was good ol' boy Sam Walton, who drove around Bentonville in a beat-up pickup truck with cages for his bird dogs in the back. He sported a Wal-Mart baseball cap and had his hair cut at the local Bentonville barbershop. He still would start off his Saturday morning meetings with his associates by giving the Arkansas Razorbacks' cheer—the pig calls rising into the still morning air.

Walton had a rare combination of small-town values and a worldwide vision. He was genuine enough to capture the hearts of his associates and customers in his rural stores and broad enough to stretch out from the small town of Bentonville, Arkansas, and take on the world. He knew how to run a retail business and how to offer value to customers. He danced around the retail giants like Macy's and Sears in the large cities and sprawling malls to build his stronghold in rural America.

If you asked him what three things mattered most in retailing, he'd probably say, "The customer, the customer, the customer." Walton saw himself as the customer's agent, negotiating on their behalf with manufacturers such as Procter & Gamble, Colgate Palmolive, Johnson and Johnson, Coca-Cola, Pepsi, and Gillette to get the best possible deal—meaning the lowest price. He continued to streamline the store delivery process with innovative approaches to warehousing, and computer and satellite links with headquarters and manufacturers. A cross-docking system in his warehouses allowed goods to be moved quickly from manufacturers' trucks at one side of the warehouse to Wal-Mart trucks on the other—greatly reducing the stock sitting in inventory.

Walton was a direct and powerful presence in his stores. He flew millions of miles in his small planes to keep in touch with his retailing empire. "Once I took to the air, I caught store fever," he said. Having his own plane allowed him the luxury of moving about the country at will, to talk to anyone he deemed interesting and informative. And fly and talk he did. He once spotted a Wal-Mart truck and had the pilot set him down so he could hitch a ride on the eighteen-wheeler.

His first plane was a secondhand, old two-seater Air Coupe, which he bought for $1,850. Over the years, he and the company have owned nearly twenty aircraft. Not one of them was new. Walton prided himself on the fact that Wal-Mart never owned a jet until after the company sales approached $40 billion.

To the end, he looked more like a Wal-Mart customer than the owner of the operation. When he received the Presidential Medal of Freedom from President Bush, shortly before his death in 1992, Walton filled the audience with Wal-Mart associates. He saw it not so much as a personal triumph but rather as the collective success of the company he had founded.

Walton's company was extolled in the pages of the *Harvard Business Review* and studied by MBA students. Wal-Mart, which used to be the tiny upstart, became the feared giant, eliciting protests from small rivals when it moved into a new region. Sam Walton didn't start out with a grand vision of conquering the retail world. As he would modestly explain the roots of his success: "Friend, we just got after it and stayed after it."

Following Walton's death from bone cancer in 1992 at the age of seventy-four, control of the company and its chairmanship passed on to his eldest son S. Robson Walton, but the entire family remained involved either in the business or the family's investments. If the fortune had remained in the hands of one person, it would have easily overshadowed those of Warren Buffett and Bill Gates. Even with one-fifth of the fortune each, there were only ten people ahead of the Walton heirs on the *Forbes* list in 1995.

James G. Fair
(1831–1894)

Est. wealth: $45 million

James Cair Flood
(1826–1888)

Est. wealth: $30 million

William S. O'Brien

(1825–1878)

Est. wealth: $12 million

John W. Mackay

(1831–1902)

Est. wealth: $30–$60 million

The Silver Kings

The four "Silver Kings"—two miners and two stockbrokers—launched one of the most famous hostile takeovers of one of Nevada's leading silver mines. They then went on to buy their way and mine their way into the most lucrative mineral strike in American history—the Consolidated Virginia mine, which produced more than $100 million in silver and gold. All four men became multimillionaires and were collectively known as the Silver Kings.

James Fair, the mastermind of the operation, was one of the ablest miners in the West. He had run successful mining operations in California and then moved to Nevada, where he became a mining superintendent. It was there that he met his future partner John Mackay.

When Mackay drifted into Nevada in 1860 from the gold fields in California, he didn't have a cent to his name. Born to a family of poor Irish immigrants, he had headed to the California gold fields in 1851, where he spent ten years in mining without anything to show for it. After working in Virginia City, Nevada, he soon earned enough as a timberman, placing timber to support mine shafts, to buy an interest in several mines. His mines were so unsuccessful that when Mark Twain, then a reporter at the local paper, suggested to Mackay that they switch jobs, Mackay declined saying, "I've never swindled anybody and I don't intend to start now."

Mackay's luck began to improve when James Fair came to him with a business proposition. Fair had his eye on the Hale and Norcross mine, one of the richest mines in Nevada, currently controlled by banker William Sharon who had overextended himself in exploring new parts of the mine. When Sharon was forced to cut his dividends to shareholders because of his expenses, many of these unhappy shareholders were anxious to sell. Fair and Mackay, who believed they could extract great wealth from the low-grade ore in the Hale and Norcross using modern equipment and processes, saw the opportunity to take control of the mine.

In 1865, Fair and Mackay headed to the San Francisco Mining Exchange. There they sought out two young brokers who were just getting started in the business, James Flood and William O'Brien. Flood and O'Brien had been partners in a saloon near the exchange, called the Auction Lunch. While the jovial O'Brien swept customers in off the street, Flood stayed behind the bar talking with the brokers at the new exchange. He soon was acting on tips on the mining stocks. The two sold the saloon and established a brokerage to which the two prospectors from Nevada came.

Fair, Mackay, Flood, and O'Brien staked almost all their combined wealth on the enterprise. They quietly bought up stocks in the Hale and Norcross mine, tunneling underneath Sharon's empire. By the time Sharon realized what was happening, it was too late. The four future Silver Kings had seized control of his mine. Flood and O'Brien continued to expand their Nevada holdings, while Fair and Mackay tunneled deeper into the earth. Within three years, in their Consolidated Virginia mine, they discovered what became known as the Big Bonanza, the largest mineral strike in the history of the nation. Between 1873 and 1882, Consolidated Virginia yielded more than $105 million in silver and gold. The four men used their earnings to establish the Bank of Nevada. All four men were multimillionaires.

James Fair, who managed to triple his Comstock fortune through buying California real estate and other business deals, won a seat in the U.S. Senate in 1881. Fair's six years in Washington were unremarkable, except that he made headlines when his wife of twenty-two years, Theresa, filed for divorce charging "habitual adultery." Fair found himself on the covers of newspapers across the nation, and Theresa was granted the largest settlement at that time, a total of $5 million dollars.

After his divorce, Fair was given custody of his two sons, who ran wild while he attended to business deals. His son Jimmy committed suicide, and his second son Charles Lewis was killed in a car accident with his wife near Paris in 1902. His two daughters, who remained with Theresa, married into the most respected families on the East Coast. The youngest married William K. Vanderbilt, Jr., and the eldest married Herman Oelrichs. Fair was not invited to the weddings. The elder Silver King, a millionaire many times over, was often found in a drunken stupor in a seedy hotel room near the Golden Gate Bridge. He died at the age of sixty-three in 1894.

Flood, the financial genius of the Silver Kings, retired to San Francisco where he built two huge mansions, one on Nob Hill (which became the home of the Pacific Union Club) and the other at Menlo Park. He was besieged by claimants to his fortune and by press attacks, which continued long after his death.

Flood, who as a teenager had worked as an apprentice carriage-maker in New York, now bought himself the finest carriages in San Francisco. The polished wheels and silver harnesses glistened as he drove through the streets, with coachmen in plum-colored livery.

One newspaper compared the scene of Flood going through the town to that of "Queen Victoria arriving to open Parliament."

Of the four men, O'Brien, known as the "jolly millionaire," probably enjoyed his fortune the most. He never married, and he lived in the house he bought for his widowed sister and her three children. He shunned the fancy balls and dinners, preferring instead to sit in the backroom of a San Francisco saloon gambling with his old friends, the way he did in the old days. The only difference was that now he kept a large stack of silver dollars at his elbow, and any player who was down on his luck could help himself. Although O'Brien didn't have great mining skill or financial talent, he helped smooth the sometimes stormy relations among the other partners and eased public ill will against the four overnight multimillionaires. At his death, he left his $12 million fortune to his two sisters. "He has more friends in all walks of life, and fewer enemies, than ... most rich men," wrote a local newspaper.

Mackay, the youngest of the Comstock partners, had a boxing ring built in the basement of his bank in San Francisco. He loved a good fight. In 1883, Mackay sold his Nevada mining shares and turned to a new fight, this time taking on financier Jay Gould in the trans-Atlantic telegraph business. Mackay started a rate war with Gould that drove prices from 75 cents per word down to 12 cents. Both sides lost millions. Finally Gould conceded. He complained, "There is no beating John Mackay. If he needs another million or two, he goes to his silver mine and digs it up." (Although this helped Gould salve his wounds, Mackay actually had sold his Comstock holdings by this time.) After his success in dominating the Atlantic cable business, Mackay turned to the Pacific where he built the first trans-Pacific cable to Manila in 1901.

Mackay's wife, Marie, probably enjoyed his riches more than he did. She bought a house in Paris where she lived with their two sons, while Mackay spent his life in bachelor quarters in Virginia City and San Francisco hotels. There was no indication of estrangement; Mackay and his wife just moved in different worlds. Mackay visited his family in Europe a few weeks out of the year, which was all he could take of high society. Even during those visits, he substituted a slug of bourbon for wine at dinner and made sure the French chef was coached in preparing corned beef and cabbage.

Around the time Mackay sold his mining interests, a reporter from a London newspaper calculated that his income exceeded $10,000 per day. (Mackay protested it was a mere $2,900 per day.) Yet when he was polled by a New York journal about whether wealth brings happiness, he replied with an emphatic "No."

16

William Weightman

(1813–1904)

Rx for Riches

Est. wealth: $80 million

William Weightman founded one of the first U.S. pharmaceutical firms and made his fortune in producing sugarcoated quinine pills. His investments in Philadelphia real estate also made him one of the largest and wealthiest city landowners.

Born in England, Weightman had come to the United States to work for his uncle at the age of sixteen. The uncle, John Farr, was the founder of a Philadelphia chemical manufacturing company. As a boy, Weightman worked in the laboratory. He soon

75

developed a reputation as a brilliant chemist as well as a shrewd businessman, and his uncle made him a partner in the firm in 1836, at the age of twenty-three.

The young Weightman led in the development of new chemicals and the manufacturing processes to produce them. He made the company one of the leading manufacturers of quinine sulfate, used to treat malaria. But by the mid-1800s, the supply of quinine was threatened. Quinine was originally made from the bark of the cinchona trees from the Andes Mountains in South America, but in the middle of the nineteenth century, the supply of trees began to die out. The price of quinine soared. Weightman then pioneered the development and manufacture of cheaper alkaloid substitutes for natural quinine—cinchona, cinchonidine, and cinchonine. This assured a steady supply of the drug, and the new synthetics had some advantages over the original medicine.

Weightman's firm became one of the international leaders in chemical manufacturing and pharmaceuticals. In addition to developing quinine, the company also introduced citric acid and developed a system for manufacturing it. After Weightman's death, the chemical company he founded joined with another major Philadelphia chemical firm and then was absorbed into Merck & Company in 1927.

Weightman invested in theaters, hotels, office buildings, businesses, and residential blocks in the heart of Philadelphia. His chemical business and his real estate investments made him the richest man in Pennsylvania.

Weightman was active in local business and civic affairs, serving on the boards of several banks and the Philadelphia College of Pharmacy. He scorned high society, preferring instead to lavish his attention on his garden of rare flowers at his mansion in Germantown.

In addition to his Philadelphia estate, Weightman built the Weightman Cottage at Franklin and Washington Streets in Cape May, New Jersey. His son, William Weightman, Jr., desiring a better view, later broke the building into two cottages, which he moved to Ocean and Beach Drive. Legend has it that the farmers who undertook the move with mules and wagons found the building too large and cut it in two. It remained two buildings, known as the Lafayette Hotel cottages.

Aside from a few small bequests, Weightman left nearly his entire $80 million fortune to his daughter, Ann. In 1907, the *New*

York Times included Ann Weightman Walker, then sixty-five, in its survey of wealthiest Americans. The *Times* estimated her fortune at more than $120 million, the bulk of which she inherited from her father. Weightman placed no restrictions on his daughter's use of the money. Weightman's other heirs were shocked when he ignored the seven children of his two deceased sons, John Farr Weightman and William Weightman, Jr., as well as three other grandchildren.

The widow of William Weightman, Jr., contested the will on behalf of her children, and the suit dragged on for months in the Philadelphia courts. Ann Walker eventually won the right to keep her fortune. Walker, who had been married to a lawyer, lived in regal fashion in New York, with country homes in Atlantic City and the Philadelphia suburbs.

17

Moses Taylor
(1806–1882)
City Banker
Est. wealth: $40–$50 million

Moses Taylor was one of the most powerful and prominent bankers in New York. As president of the National City Bank of New York, he provided support to coal and iron works, railroads, telegraphs, and gas companies.

Moses Taylor's father had been a confidential agent of John Jacob Astor. Taylor was educated in New York private schools before joining a New York importer as a clerk at the age of fifteen. In 1834, at twenty-eight, Taylor set up his own business with $15,000 of his own savings and another $35,000 that he borrowed from his father. Moses Taylor and Company began specializing in importing Cuban sugar. Taylor later expanded into importing coffee and fruit. A year after he set up the business, his store was destroyed by the great fire of 1835. Two years later, the Panic of 1837 shook many New York businesses, but Taylor's continued to grow.

While most investors suffered huge losses during the panic, Taylor used the opportunity to purchase stocks at low prices. He bought a controlling interest in the Delaware, Lackawanna & Western Railroad for just $5 a share. Seven years later, the stocks had soared to $240 per share.

Taylor's success in trading, investing, and banking came from following a policy of holding on to large cash reserves, which later became the hallmark of his City Bank. This policy allowed him to take advantage of downturns and to acquire assets cheaply at a time when other investors were scrambling for cash. Taylor also was known for his full understanding of all the complex details of the businesses in which he participated.

His success in trading led him into the shipping business where he became a director of the Pacific Mail Steamship Line and the United States Mail Steamship Line. Just four years after starting his business, he had built a personal fortune of more than $200,000.

In 1837, Taylor was elected to the board of directors of City Bank. The bank was designed to serve the merchant community. Taylor also realized that banking was not just a necessary adjunct to the trading business, but it could also be a profitable enterprise in its own right. During his two decades as director, he helped shape the bank into one of New York's most powerful institutions. He shifted its focus from providing short-term commercial loans to merchants, to financing long-term projects. In 1856, he was named president of the bank, which was renamed National City Bank after the Civil War. By the time of his death in 1882, the bank had assets of more than $16 million.

Through the bank and his own personal investments, Taylor became one of the foremost independent financial investors of the era. He bought New York real estate, and he invested in several New York gas companies that were later brought together into the Consolidated Gas Company of New York. He also became involved in the coal industry in Scranton, Pennsylvania, particularly in the Lackawanna Iron and Coal Company. From coal, his interest turned to the railroads that carried the coal.

In the decade after the Civil War, Taylor was a leader in railroad investment. His investment in the Delaware, Lackawanna &

Western Railroad led to an interest in a midwestern railroad empire. Taylor invested in the Michigan Central and a network of railroads stretching southward from Kansas City. He ultimately lost the network during a battle between Jay Gould and Commodore Vanderbilt. Taylor sold most of his stock to Vanderbilt, and the two became close allies throughout the last years of Taylor's life. Taylor also built a network of southern railroads in Georgia, South Carolina, and Texas.

Taylor financed telegraph pioneer Cyrus Field, who laid the first trans-Atlantic telegraph cable from Valentia, Ireland, to Trinity Bay, Newfoundland. The project was near collapse on several occasions. Field began laying the cable in 1859, but the process proved so difficult that the company did not start successful operations until 1866. Taylor, who was the treasurer of the company, continued to have faith in the project. He supported Field and the business until its ultimate success.

Taylor left his estate—estimated at between $40 and $50 million—to his wife Catherine and their five children. Although Taylor's two sons took little interest in the family business, his son-in-law played an active role in Taylor's businesses during his life and after Moses's death. His daughter Albertine married Percy R. Pyne, who had started as a junior partner in Moses Taylor's trading firm. Pyne later was named vice president of the National City Bank. When Taylor died, Pyne succeeded him as president of the bank, until 1891 when Taylor's protégé James Stillman took charge of the bank.

The bank that Taylor had built played a powerful role in American business under Stillman's leadership. With the infusion of Rockefeller oil money, it became the first billion-dollar bank in the nation. Taylor's grandson, Moses Taylor II (1871–1928), also took an active role in many of his grandfather's enterprises. He served as president and then chairman of Lackawanna Steel, until it was sold to Bethlehem Steel in 1922. He also became a director of the National City Bank and the Consolidated Gas Company of New York.

18

Russell Sage

(1816–1906)

Market Manipulator

Est. wealth: $100 million

Russell Sage was a shrewd market manipulator who made his fortune in railroad and telegraph stocks. He brought the system of puts and calls to Wall Street—using all his political and financial wiles to amass a fortune of more than $100 million.

Sage, in his cheap, black baggy suits and frayed banker's vests, watched every dollar of his empire. Sage used to pilfer notebooks and other amenities after the board meetings of Western Union, on which he served. One day, when he was about to depart with an inexpensive fan, an assistant, at the request of fellow board member J. P. Morgan, challenged him at the door. The assistant pointed out that the fan was property of Western Union. Sage turned on him angrily. "I'll have you know that I *am* Western Union!" he said. And he stormed out clutching the stolen fan.

Biographer Paul Sarnoff, in *Russell Sage: The Money King*, describes a scene that conveys the vigor and ruthless opportunism of Russell Sage. Sage always rode the trolley to his free lunch at the Western Union board meeting because he claimed he could not afford a hack. One day the eighty-six-year-old multimillionaire leaped for a trolley car running board. He bounced off and fell in a heap on the ground. A crowd rushed over. After a few moments, Sage leaped up and shook his fist at the trolley, cursing it for not stopping. Sage then proceeded to call his doctor and to file a lawsuit against the trolley company. Sage was always on the lookout for new opportunities, no matter how small. "If you take care of the pennies," he would say, "the dollars will take care of themselves."

Sage had few pennies to take care of as a young man. He was born in a covered wagon heading west. His family, fleeing the famine in New England in 1816, was starting on a fifty-five-day journey to Cincinnati, the first leg of a trip to Michigan. Sage was born before they left New York. The family stopped and settled in the Mohawk Valley in New York. At twelve, young Sage clerked in his brother's grocery store, earning just $4 per month. He saved and earned enough through trading so that he soon opened his own store. As a young man, he vowed that he would never live in poverty. He earned money from horse brokering, retailing, and shipping—as well as making loans to friends—so that by twenty-one, he had already become a wealthy and prominent citizen of Troy, New York, where he was elected an alderman and later named treasurer of Rennselaer County.

Sage's idols were John Jacob Astor and Governor De Witt Clinton, and he gained power both in business and in politics. It was a mix that served him well. In 1852, when he was only thirty-six, Sage was elected to the U.S. Congress. There, he found out that the New York Central needed the Troy & Schenectady line to expand its operations. As a director of the line, he convinced the city of Troy to sell the twenty-one-mile railroad to a small company for $200,000, less than a third of its worth. The company that bought the stock was a dummy company set up by Sage. Then Sage turned around and resold the line to the New York Central for $900,000 and a seat on its board of directors. Sage found the combination of business and politics very lucrative.

After serving two terms in Congress, Sage returned to New York where he continued trading. He worked out of a dingy, third-floor office, sitting in a swivel chair once owned by George Washington. He created the system of puts and calls—options to buy or sell stocks within a specified time period—which allowed investors to bet on the rise and fall of stocks. Of course, not being a gambling man, Sage often manipulated the prices of the stocks to make sure the odds were stacked in his favor. He was a contrarian investor, advising "Buy straw hats in the winter when nobody wants them, and sell them in the summer when everybody needs them."

Sage, who made loans at high interest to everyone from Congressmen to small investors, was arrested in 1869 as part of a usury ring for his loansharking. During downtimes, he offered strapped investors loans from his fortune, at a very high premium. Sage protested that he was only trying to serve his fellow man. Then he used his connections to avoid a jail sentence.

Given their common interest in railroads and money, it is no surprise that Sage became good friends with Jay Gould. The two men teamed up to take control of the Pacific Mail Steamship line, netting them about $5 million. After the crash of 1873, they bought the depressed stocks of Union Pacific. With Sage's support, Gould then went on to build an extensive Western railroad empire. Gould and Sage also teamed up to take control of the Atlantic and Pacific Telegraph Company, which became Western Union. This is not to say that Sage trusted Gould. Sage once tapped the telegraph wire between the younger man's home and Wall Street to keep an eye on his partner.

Sage had no children and little time for the dalliances of the rich. A former cook once claimed he fathered her son, and a female painter sued him claiming that he had an affair with her when he was posing for a portrait. But these may have been opportunists seeking a piece of his fortune. Sage was never found guilty, and there was little to indicate that he had time in his life for such diversions from his true passion, making money.

Sage's first wife died in 1867. Two years later he married Margaret Olivia Slocum of Troy. After Sage's death in 1906, Margaret became famous for giving away the fortune that Sage had so meticulously assembled. She made gifts to universities, churches, and charitable organizations and left more than $40 million to charity when she died in 1918.

Her largest gift was a $10 million donation to establish the Russell Sage Foundation. The Foundation, the first general-purpose philanthropic foundation in the United States, was chartered to use "any means" to improve "social and living conditions in the United States of America." It became one of the foremost contributors to the professionalization of the field of social work, supporting research, education, housing projects, and a variety of other initiatives. Ironically, among the many early social studies the funds of the usurious Russell Sage helped support was a research project on consumer credit.

Sage's widow, who had suffered under his austerity throughout his life, now was free. She commented at the first meeting of the Sage Foundation board of trustees, "I am nearly eighty years old, and I feel as if I were just beginning to live."

Margaret Sage, however, often attached her husband's name to the gifts. In addition to the foundation, there is the Russell Sage College in Troy, New York, and the Russell Sage Institute of Pathology at the City Hospital. Thus the name of the man who was known in life for his stinginess and opposition to philanthropy became associated in death with generosity and charity.

19

John I. Blair

(1802–1899)

40,000 Miles Per Year

Est. wealth: $60–$90 million

John Blair was born on a small farm on the banks of the Delaware River near Belvidere, New Jersey. There is a story that Blair's family was so poor that when he was ten, he told his mother, "I have seven brothers and three sisters. That's enough in the family to be educated. I'm going to get rich." So he did. He built the largest railroad network of any individual, and through government grants associated with the railroad projects, assembled land holdings of more than 2 million acres, becoming one of the richest men in America.

Blair didn't waste any time building his fortune. He started working in a country store when he was eleven. By the time he was eighteen, he had his own store. By the time he was twenty-seven, he owned a chain of five general stores and four flour mills. He owned several teams of horses to haul produce to New York City and bring back goods for his stores.

Blair then entered the coal and iron mining business. In 1846, he established the Lackawanna Coal & Iron Company. But the coal and iron had to be taken out of the hills to be sold, so he organized the Delaware, Lakawanna & Western Railroad. Blair served as director of the railroad until his death.

Blair's interest in politics led him to the Republican convention in Chicago in 1860, where a young Illinois lawyer, Abraham Lincoln, was nominated as the candidate for president. Blair's visit to Chicago made him aware of the vast opportunity for railroads in the West. With Oak Ames and William Durant, Blair received the charter to build the Union Pacific Railroad, one of the important last legs of the transcontinental railroad line.

Blair and other investors laid the first 100 miles of the Union Pacific west from Omaha to Promontory Point, Utah, where it met with the Central Pacific from California. The Union Pacific received generous government land grants along the route, accounting for more than 18,000 square miles of territory— roughly the area of Vermont and New Hampshire combined.

Blair began building a network of railroads through Iowa, Wisconsin, Kansas, Nebraska, Dakota, Missouri, and Texas. Known as the "Railroad King of the West," Blair owned more miles of railroad than any other individual in the world and at one time served as president of sixteen different railroads. He also put together sites for more than eighty towns along his routes.

At home in New Jersey, however, Blair didn't flaunt his riches. Throughout his life, he lived in the same home in Blairstown, New Jersey. It was a small village, far from the megamansions and bustle of New York where many other railroad barons made their homes. He served on the board of trustees of Princeton University, where Blair Hall bears his name. Active in politics, he won the Republican nomination for New Jersey governor in 1868. But even after personally spending over $90,000 on the campaign, Blair lost to his Democratic opponent.

Blair's energy was as boundless as the railroads he controlled. Even at the age of ninety-two, he was known to arrive at the office at 5:30 A.M. In his younger years, he traveled an average of 40,000 miles per year, personally surveying his railroad empire. When he reached eighty-five, he decided it was time to cut back on his business travel. So he reduced his tour to a mere 20,000 miles per year.

By the time of his death, at age ninety-seven in 1899, Blair had given away more than $5 million to charity, including gifts to the Blair Presbyterian Academy, Lafayette and Grinnell colleges, and to the construction of more than one hundred churches in the towns he built in the West. With land holdings that would cover an area half the size of his native state of New Jersey, his estate was estimated at between $60 million and $90 million.

20

Cyrus H. K. Curtis

(1850–1933)

Post Master

Est. wealth: $174 million

Founder of *Ladies' Home Journal*, Philadelphia publisher Cyrus Curtis bought the *Saturday Evening Post* for $1,000 in 1897. It had only two thousand subscribers, and its pages were filled with sentimental fiction and mediocre poetry. Through fierce determination, he lifted up the *Post* to make it one of the most loved and successful American magazines, a publication Will Rogers once called "America's nickelodeon."

Curtis was born in Portland, Maine, in 1850. He was forced to leave high school after his family lost their home and all their possessions in the great Portland fire in 1866. Curtis worked as an errand boy. When he was nineteen, he became a salesman for a dry goods store in Boston. He then sold advertising for newspapers including the *Boston Times* and *Independent.*

In 1872, after observing the newspaper business, he established his own paper, the *People's Ledger.* In contrast to the serialization of most weeklies at the time, Curtis featured an entire story in a single issue. To save printing costs, he moved the paper to Philadelphia in 1876. After selling his first paper, he established the *Tribune and Farmer* in 1879, a four-page weekly.

At this paper his wife began writing a column for women, focusing on issues such as cooking, needlework, flowers, fashion, and parenting. The column was so successful that it became the basis for a monthly supplement in 1883, the *Ladies' Journal and Practical Housekeeper.* In its first year, the *Ladies' Home Journal* attracted twenty-five thousand subscribers. Curtis sold the paper to devote his attention to this new magazine.

With the *Journal,* Curtis established the model for success in mass market magazines. He advertised heavily, spending more than half a million dollars during the first five years, with the help of generous allowances from the advertising agency N. W. Ayer and Son. He attracted popular authors to the magazine, including Louisa M. Alcott, Mark Twain, and Bret Harte. Within a year, Curtis drove circulation up to 100,000.

Curtis also hired a very talented editor, Edward W. Bok, who led the magazine for thirty years. Under Bok's leadership, the magazine took on controversial issues such as women's suffrage, sex, and venereal disease.

Curtis placed great trust and control in the hands of his editors. When shocked advertisers pressured Curtis to rein in his editor, Curtis told them, "Go talk to Mr. Bok about it. He is the editor." But with that trust came great responsibility. Bok once described his boss's motto as: "Make good or hang yourself." By 1893 the magazine's circulation had topped 1 million.

With his interest in advertising, Curtis also was a pioneer in market research. He hired Charles Parlin, a high school principal who developed systematic research on the magazine's demographics. This research was then used to help advertisers create marketing plans.

In 1897, Curtis took on his greatest challenge. The *Saturday Evening Post* seemed like a lost cause, overpriced even at $1,000. Curtis was the only one who believed in it. He set out to use advertising to promote it, as he had done with the *Ladies' Home Journal,* with ads in newspapers in forty-four cities and in weekly magazines. During his first three years of ownership of the magazine, he ran up a debt of more than $900,000. Many of the original 2,000 subscribers, upset by the change in format, deserted the publication. Yet by 1900, Curtis was boasting a circulation of more than 250,000. Of course, he was giving most of them away or offering them as special ten-cent subscriptions to *Ladies' Home Journal* subscribers. It was only the stubborn determination of Curtis that kept the publication running.

As with the *Journal,* Curtis again had a stroke of genius when he hired an editor for the new publication. George Horace Lorimer became editor-in-chief in 1899 and retained the position until 1936. The magazine was offered at five cents a copy, half the price of rivals such as *Harper's Weekly.* Designed to reflect middle-class America, it avoided both high-brow intellectualism and low-brow sensationalism.

By 1937 the *Post* had become the largest-selling weekly magazine in the world, with a circulation of more than 3 million. When Curtis died in 1933, the circulation of the *Ladies' Home Journal* had reached 2.5 million. With these two flagship publications, the Curtis Publishing Company took in $2 of every $5 spent on national magazine advertising.

When Curtis died in 1933, just before his eighty-third birthday, he left a fortune estimated at $174 million from his publishing enterprises. He donated $2 million to the Franklin Institute, $1.25 million to Drexel University, and $1 million to the University of Pennsylvania. *Life* magazine overtook the *Saturday Evening Post* in circulation in 1942, and new magazines eroded the position of the *Journal.* With $20 million in losses in 1968, Curtis Publishing sold the *Ladies' Home Journal* and shut down the *Post* a year later.

21

Edward Henry Harriman

(1848–1909)

The Wizard of Railroad Finance
Est. wealth: $100 million

Edward Henry Harriman started his career on Wall Street, but it was his success in turning around struggling railroads that made him his fortune of more than $100 million. His skill at building and using railroads as assets made him one of the most powerful railroad men in American history.

At first glance, Harriman might not have appeared to be one

of the dominant forces in American business. He was a small, soft-spoken man who wore baggy trousers and a soft hat pulled over his receding hair line. His stern eyes peered from thick, wire-framed glasses perched above a walrus mustache. Yet beneath this unassuming exterior, Harriman was "a human dynamo," a man with persuasive vision who "would rather battle than eat."

Harriman was not easily intimidated, even by the imposing J. P. Morgan. As a small shareholder in the Erie Railroad, the young Harriman challenged J. P. Morgan's plan for reorganizing the railroad. Morgan assumed that anyone who dared to challenge the plan must have substantial backing. He asked Harriman, "Whom do you represent?" Harriman quietly replied, "I represent myself."

Harriman was born in 1848, the son of a poor rector of St. John's Church in West Hoboken, New Jersey, but he came from a respected family. He left school at fourteen to become an errand boy for D. C. Hayes, a Wall Street broker. In 1870, at the age of twenty-two, the young Harriman borrowed $3,000 from his uncle Oliver Harriman, who also was a Wall Street broker, and bought his own seat on the New York Stock Exchange. Two years later, he started E. H. Harriman & Company with two partners. As he later would say, he "started out with a pencil and this" tapping the pencil to the side of his head.

After finding success on Wall Street, Harriman turned his sharp insights to railroads. He first became involved in railroads in 1879 after he married Mary Averell, daughter of the president of the Ogdensbury and Lake Champlain Railroad. Working with his new father-in-law, the twenty-eight-year-old Harriman gained control of the Lake Ontario Southern Railroad in 1881, which he reorganized and sold at a large profit two years later. He then reorganized the Illinois Central and helped with the reorganization of the Erie.

Harriman became a legend on Wall Street by taking poorly performing railroads and turning them around. Harriman took on his greatest challenge in 1895, the Union Pacific Railroad, which had become "a streak of rust" after it was bankrupted by unscrupulous investors and placed into federal receivership. Harriman revived the line with an infusion of $8 million, and it became one of the most efficient and profitable railroads in the country. Harriman continued to make improvements, boosting annual profits from $14 million in 1899, to $20 million one year later. He added the Oregon Railway, Kansas City Southern, and Chicago & Alton. Harriman spent so much money upgrading rail lines that others had written off that he was called "mad Harriman."

Unlike railroad investors such as Jay Gould and Jim Fisk, who drove many of the railroads they owned into the ground, Harriman saw his holdings as more than paper investments. He built the value of these assets by effective management and careful improvements. Then he used that equity to purchase more railroads.

When the last of the western "Big Four" partners died, Harriman took control of the Southern Pacific, making him the most powerful railroad owner in the West. Harriman fought a famous showdown with another railroad mogul, James J. Hill, for control of the Northern Pacific and Burlington. This battle of giants—with the Rockefellers and others lining up behind Harriman, and J. P. Morgan supporting Hill—shook Wall Street. Share prices for Northern Pacific stock skyrocketed from $100 per share to more than $1,000 in 1901, ruining investors and sparking a financial panic.

The two sides called a truce, establishing the Northern Securities Company, joining the interests of Hill and Harriman. In 1904, the U.S. Supreme Court dissolved Northern Securities, and Harriman was forced to sell out for more than $50 million. He used the funds to continue to build his railroad empire, which ultimately included ten major railroads and five steamship firms, along with interest in coal, real estate, oil, and several street railways.

Even the United States was not broad enough to contain Harriman's transportation ambitions. He envisioned a worldwide transportation system, which he set about building. In the early 1900s the Pacific coast was dotted with Harriman's steamboats. He organized and funded an expedition to Alaska with his family and a shipload of scientists. He also made plans for a line of steamers carrying passengers to Asia that would connect with the new Manchurian Railroad in China or the Trans-Siberian railroad in Russia. He traveled to China in 1905, but unstable political conditions put a damper on his plans for a global transportation system.

Harriman was a quick thinker, brilliant strategist, and tough fighter. As author George Redmond comments in *Financial Giants*, "Once he determined upon an object to be had, he would pursue it with ceaseless energy and let nothing stand in his way. If it could be had peaceably, well and good. But if necessary, he would summon all the forces at his command to the conquest."

When he was asked by banker James Stillman what interested him most in life, Harriman replied, "I guess it is to be told that some big thing can't possibly be done, then to jump in with both feet and goddam well do it."

When Harriman died in 1909, he was survived by his widow, three daughters, and three sons. His son William Averell Harriman took over running the Union Pacific. During the New Deal, he served as an administrator of the National Recovery Administration. He went on to become governor of New York and one of the most prominent American diplomats. William Averell also built the nation's first winter resort in Sun Valley, Idaho, in the 1930s.

22

Henry Huttleston Rogers
(1840–1909)
From Whale Oil to Standard Oil
Est. wealth: $100 million

Even as a child, Henry Huttleston Rogers was alert for business opportunities. Rogers, whose family had come to Massachusetts on the *Mayflower*, grew up in the small town of Fairhaven, near the heart of the American whaling industry. When he was just fourteen, he worked as a newsboy and closely followed the reports on whaling in the papers he sold. One day he saw a story about a whaler with a heavy cargo of sperm oil that was lost at sea. Rogers knew the news would lead to a jump in the price of oil.

Rogers took all his papers to one of the leading merchants in town and offered him the whole stack to keep his rivals from finding out about the lost ship. The merchant paid $200. Rogers learned there were great opportunities in oil speculation. Rogers used this same business sense when he turned to a different type of oil—crude oil—by becoming one of John D. Rockefeller's partners in Standard Oil. He eventually built a fortune of over $100 million.

When the crude oil industry was just forming around the rich oil fields of western Pennsylvania, Rogers and a partner left Massachusetts to enter the business. They each put up their entire $600 savings to build a small, successful refinery. In Pennsylvania Rogers met oil pioneer Charles Pratt, who asked Rogers to help him run his Brooklyn refinery. When Rockefeller absorbed Pratt's business into Standard Oil, Rogers, who had a genius for organizing and leading businesses, was made a senior executive in the huge financial trust.

Early on, Rogers showed his understanding of oil and his natural abilities for invention. While working for Pratt, he developed and patented machinery for separating the valuable solvent naphtha from crude oil. At Standard Oil, Rogers originated the concept of using pipelines to transport oil, and he organized the National Transit Company to carry out the idea.

Rogers also showed a talent for leadership. After John D. Rockefeller dropped out of the day-to-day management of the oil business, Henry Rogers became virtual manager of the enterprise. With William Rockefeller, Rogers extended the holdings of Standard Oil far beyond the oil industry. Rogers branched out into gas, copper, steel, banking, railroads, and insurance. There were very few businesses in which Rogers didn't have some role. He even founded the Atlas Tack Company, the largest tack manufacturer in America.

During the 1890s, working on the Anaconda copper mine in Montana, Rogers established the $75 million Amalgamated Copper trust. He then used some of the most ruthless business tactics, including watering stock and seizing rival properties, to extend his copper empire.

During the Panic of 1907, Rogers was so wealthy from Standard Oil that he built the $40 million Virginia Railway from West Virginia's coalfields to Norfolk, all on his own personal capital and credit.

A tall, handsome man, Rogers was as witty, charming, and generous in private life as he was merciless in business. He was good friends with Mark Twain and helped support the author after Twain suffered financial setbacks because of the failure of his publisher.

Rogers was a devoted citizen of his small hometown of Fairhaven, where he often spent weekends and summers. He built a town hall, paved streets, and constructed school buildings, a library, and a church.

Rogers worked up to the time of his death in 1907 at the age of sixty-nine. He had married Abbie Palmer Gifford from his hometown during a visit home in 1862, and they had four children before her death in 1894. After her death, Rogers married Emelle Augusta Randall, who survived him along with a son and three daughters. His eldest son, Henry H. Rogers II, who had helped run several of his father's businesses, took charge of the extensive family holdings after his father's death.

23

John Pierpont Morgan
(1837–1913)
The Most Powerful Banker in American History
Est. wealth: $118 million

John Pierpont Morgan used to joke that he could trace his ancestry back to Henry Morgan, the seventeenth-century pirate of the Caribbean. He named his yacht *The Corsair,* and it was rumored on Wall Street that he flew the Jolly Roger above the Stars and Stripes. Arrogant and determined, Morgan built the most powerful financial firm in American history, and he created some of the most important American industrial firms—including U.S. Steel and General Electric. Morgan was so powerful that when the nation itself came close to collapse, it turned to Morgan for assistance.

Despite the huge sums of money that passed through his hands, Morgan left a fortune less than a tenth the size of Rockefeller's—estimated at just over $100 million, much of it in works of art. But Morgan had power that far exceeded Rockefeller's. Around the turn of the century, *Life* magazine published a cartoon in which someone asked, "Who made the world?" The response:

"God made the world in 4004 B.C., but it was reorganized in 1901 by James J. Hill, J. Pierpont Morgan, and John D. Rockefeller."

Morgan was a direct and forceful dealmaker. Clutching a cigar in the corner of his mouth, he was known to conclude multimillion dollar deals in a matter of minutes. Morgan's financial power and personal bearing were impressive, even to his staunchest enemies. As Theodore Roosevelt once said, "We were fundamentally opposed, but I was struck by his very great power and his truthfulness. Any kind of meanness or smallness were alike wholly alien to his nature." Morgan was gruff and brusque. When a fellow Wall Streeter asked Morgan about the cost of building his extravagant yachts, Morgan reportedly replied, "If you have to ask, you can't afford it."

Morgan entered the financial world from a position of strength. His father, Junius Spencer Morgan, was a leading financial force in London. J. P. Morgan was an average student, graduating from high school near the middle of his class. His senior essay, not surprisingly, was on Napoleon Bonaparte, and he showed an early talent for business. When the principal sent him to the store to buy erasers, Morgan returned with far more change than expected. "I bought them at the wholesale rate," he explained.

Morgan was sent to college in Germany, where he studied mathematics. He then joined his father's firm in London in 1856. The young man's mathematical abilities soon made him a master of foreign trade and other intricacies of the business. His abrupt and fearless style, while not endearing personally, allowed him to take initiative and responsibility early in his career. In 1857, his father sent the twenty-year-old J.P. to New York to serve as clerk at the company that was the U.S. representative of the London house.

Morgan showed early audacity and initiative. During a trip to New Orleans to study the cotton and shipping business, he came across a captain who needed to sell a cargo of coffee. After talking to merchants in the area, Morgan bought the entire cargo, using a draft from the New York company. When his superiors in New York found out about it, they were livid, but they quieted down when he told them he had already sold the cargo at a tidy profit. Four years later, at the urging of his father, Morgan established J. P. Morgan & Company, which his father appointed as his new U.S. agent.

The House of Morgan in New York became the heart of

America's financial center. The J. P. Morgan & Co. offices at the intersection of Broad and Wall streets in New York became known simply as "the corner." From this epicenter, reverberations were felt across the United States and around the world.

Morgan was in the center of most of the major business deals of the age. He was a key figure in a brutal battle with Jay Gould and James Fisk over control of the Albany and Susquehanna Railroad. Morgan also handled one of the largest railroad stock sales in the nation's history. William Henry Vanderbilt, under increasing public pressure to reduce his 87 percent share in New York Central railroad, wanted to sell 250,000 shares of stock in the railroad. Vanderbilt feared that the $25 million stock offering of such a major railroad could create a panic in the United States. With his father's help, Morgan quietly sold the stock in Europe, becoming a member of the board of directors of the railroad in the process.

Morgan used his power to save the United States from the gold crisis in 1895, and also to personally profit from it. In the wake of a financial crisis, the government supply of gold had slipped to just $41 million and was falling by about $2 million a day. Morgan was asked to step in. After Morgan had secured $50 million in gold from investors in Europe for a private gold bond sale, President Cleveland said he changed his mind, preparing to make a public sale instead. As they discussed the issue in Washington, a report came in that the reserves had sunk so low that the government's supply of gold could be exhausted with the presentation of one outstanding draft. With this news, Cleveland approved the private sale of gold bonds by Morgan and August Belmont, the American agent for the Rothschilds.

The gold crisis was averted, and government reserves soon topped $100 million. But Morgan and Cleveland were sharply criticized for the deal. Rival politicians such as William Jennings Bryan claimed Cleveland had mortgaged the country's future to line Morgan's pockets. When Morgan was asked to reveal the extent of his profits to a Congressional committee, he refused.

Morgan helped create, in addition to his own firm, some of the most important and successful American companies. An early supporter of Thomas Edison's Edison Electric Light Company, Morgan stepped in in 1890 when the company had accumulated $3.5 million in debt. Morgan helped Edison merge with another major electric company to create General Electric in

1891. In 1901, Morgan added Andrew Carnegie's steel company to a number of other steel makers to create the United States Steel Company. The first billion-dollar U.S. company, U.S. Steel controlled 60 percent of the steel industry. The $400 million deal made Carnegie, in Morgan's words, "the richest man in the world."

Morgan also orchestrated the creation of International Harvester in 1902, from McCormick, Deering, and other manufacturers. The new firm controlled 80 percent of the harvester trade. Morgan played a central role in other great consolidations, including American Telephone & Telegraph, Western Union, and Westinghouse.

Morgan and his collaborators were involved in so many different businesses that a Congressional committee, which issued its report shortly after Morgan's death in 1913, estimated that Morgan and partners, along with the leaders of a few major banks, held 341 directorships in 112 major companies. This small group of men controlled assets of more than $22 billion.

When Morgan died in 1913 at the age of seventy-five, he left his collection of paintings, valued at more than $50 million, to the Metropolitan Museum of Art, where he had served as president before his death. After Morgan's death, his son, the younger J. P. Morgan, had to sell some of the paintings, reportedly to meet expenses on his father's estate.

J.P., Jr., succeeded his father as head of J. P. Morgan and Company. He continued to extend the bank's reputation and presence in international finance. He became the sole purchasing agent for the French and British governments in America. In 1915, he organized a syndicate of 2,200 banks to underwrite a war loan of $500 million to support Great Britain and France during World War I. And because of his support of the Allies, the younger Morgan was shot by a German sympathizer but was not seriously injured.

As the United States became a financial power, Morgan's role shifted from providing European capital to America to providing American capital to the world. But the stock market crash in October 1929 again threw the nation's finances into turmoil. Morgan tried to organize a group of bankers to rally the market as his father had done in 1907, but he failed to stop the panic. His eldest son, Junius S. Morgan II, born in 1892, joined J. P. Morgan & Company in 1915 and served as a director of the firm until his death in 1960.

J. P. Morgan's goal was not to amass the largest fortune but rather to build an enduring organization. In this he succeeded. The powerful Wall Street firm that bears his name to this day is, perhaps, his greatest achievement. As he once described the business he had founded, "We have built for all time and all generations; we will survive for hundreds of years after you are dead and buried, and our business will go on without interruption under the direction of men as yet unborn who will be trained to conduct it—we are an institution."

The institution he created remains one of the most powerful U.S. banking firms, with a portfolio of $89 billion by 1990 and earning more than $1.3 billion in 1995. It continues to raise money for governments and large corporations.

24

Col. Oliver H. Payne

(1839–1917)

Colonel Cash

Est. wealth: $178 million

Oliver Hazard Payne made his first conquests on Civil War bat-
tlefields, where he rose to the rank of colonel. Then he took that
same fighting spirit into his business and political deals, becoming
one of the leaders of Rockefeller's Standard Oil empire.

Payne's father was a successful merchant and railroad man
who later became a representative and U.S. Senator from Ohio.
When the Civil War broke out, the younger Payne interrupted his
studies at Yale in 1861 to enter the Union Army as a lieutenant in
an Illinois regiment. He fought at New Madrid, Corinth, and
Booneville, Mississippi. He soon was promoted to colonel. He was
seriously wounded but returned to fight the battle of Pickett's Mill.

In that battle, he received a commendation for "faithful and meritorious services." After the grueling march on Atlanta under Sherman, he resigned from the service and turned his attention to business.

When he returned to Cleveland, Payne became a pioneer in the petroleum business. His company, Clarke, Payne & Company was one of the rivals of John D. Rockefeller. After jousting for years with Rockefeller, Payne joined forces with him in Standard Oil. Payne served as treasurer of the company.

Payne's rising financial power created a scandal for his father in Washington. When the elder Payne was elected to the U.S. Senate in 1884, there were charges that the younger Payne had secured his father's seat in the Senate through $100,000 in bribes to members of the Ohio legislature. (At the time the legislature appointed senators.) It was said that Payne sat at a desk at the Columbus Hotel with a stack of bills at his side, doling out payments.

There was a Senate investigation with more than fifty witnesses called to the stand. But the case was dropped, perhaps more for lack of political will than for lack of evidence. It was also charged that the elder Payne was a puppet of Standard Oil.

Colonel Payne moved to New York in 1884 and gradually dropped out of the oil business. With the "Standard Oil Gang," he made investments in banking and industrial companies, including the American Tobacco Company and the Tennessee Coal and Iron Company, until it was absorbed into U.S. Steel.

His greatest extravagance was yachting, and he built the largest, fastest, and most luxurious steam yacht in the country, *Aphrodite*. He sailed to Europe and later around the world.

A confirmed bachelor, Payne contributed $500,000 to found Cornell Medical College and gave the school a total of $8 million in gifts. When he died in 1917, he left $1 million apiece to the New York Public Library, Yale University, and Lakeside Hospital. The bulk of his fortune, valued at $178 million, was left to his favorite nephews, Harry Payne Bingham and (William) Payne Whitney. The latter more than doubled his $75 million share of the estate.

25

Henry C. Frick
(1849–1919)
"I'll See You In Hell"
Est. wealth: $225 million

Henry Clay Frick was the iron fist behind the smiling face of
Andrew Carnegie. While the positive and progressive Carnegie was
preaching his "gospel of wealth," Frick was unequivocally practic-
ing what biographer Samuel Schreiner called a "gospel of greed."
Frick didn't have time for Carnegie's benevolent public face. He
was strictly, bluntly about business. He knew how to make money,
and he made plenty of it, for both himself and Carnegie. And
nobody stood in his way.

Frick didn't see the world through Carnegie's rose-colored
glasses. Years after the former partners angrily parted ways, Frick
nursed the old grudge and looked on critically as Carnegie began

making a public display of giving away his fortune. Frick considered it hypocrisy. The two men lived for years just blocks from each other, in mansions on New York's Fifth Avenue. Carnegie, wanting the whole world to love him, anxiously sought to improve his relationship with his old partner. As his health began failing in 1919, Carnegie sent word to Frick that he would like to arrange a friendly meeting. Frick's reply: "Tell Mr. Carnegie I'll see him in hell, where we both are going." A short time later, Carnegie died, and within the year, the much younger Frick—perhaps anxious to keep his appointment with his former partner—was also dead.

When Frick once was asked to explain the secret to his success, he replied in typical no-nonsense fashion: "There is no secret about success. Success simply calls for hard work, devotion to your business at all times, day and night."

Frick was born on a little dirt farm in Westmoreland County, Pennsylvania. Even early on he had an eye for art, but he could indulge only in tacking cheap magazine illustrations to his walls. As a bookkeeper living in a sooty miner's house in Pennsylvania, Frick discovered the value of coke, a high-temperature fuel that became key to the steelmaking process. As the steel industry heated up, the demand for coke increased. The area Frick lived in was rich in bituminous coal, which was ideal for making coke. With a $10,000 loan from Thomas Mellon (Andrew Mellon's father), Frick built a huge coke-making enterprise.

By 1882, H. C. Frick Coke Company controlled 80 percent of coke production before Frick sold a half interest to Andrew Carnegie. His company soon produced more than 1 million tons of coke per year, employed 11,000 men, and owned 1,200 coke cars. And Frick was known as "the Coke King of Pennsylvania."

Shortly after Frick had earned his first million in the coke business, he went to New York with his friend Andrew Mellon. Frick had just turned thirty. They stopped to admire the Vanderbilt twin mansions, the symbols of power on New York's Fifth Avenue. The two young men tried to guess how much it would cost to keep them up. Frick would soon find out. Twenty-five years later, he was living in one of these very mansions.

Frick, a quiet and enigmatic man who stayed out of the limelight, was like Carnegie's dark double. This nefarious image was darkened substantially during the bloody Homestead Strike in 1892. When Carnegie cut wages, discontented laborers in the Homestead plant rose up. In the past, Carnegie had given in to workers' pressures. But Frick stood firm, and emerged as "the first large-scale union buster," who effectively crushed the steel industry's union movement for more than four decades.

A week after the Homestead strike, an angry Polish-Russian immigrant decided to assassinate Frick. He crept into Frick's Pittsburgh office and shot him twice, once in the ear and a second time in the neck. He then pulled a knife and stabbed Frick repeatedly. Rescuers rushed to Frick's aid. Cool and collected, despite near-fatal wounds, Frick shouted to rescuers to check the man's mouth. He had a capsule containing enough explosive to blow up the office.

After the incident, Frick bound up his wounds and continued working until the end of the day. He refused anesthesia when doctors removed the bullet from his neck. The incident not only earned Frick the grudging admiration of even his most ardent critics, but it set back the unionization movement considerably. His only statement to the press: "I do not think I shall die, but whether I do or not, the Carnegie Company will pursue the same policy and win."

Although Carnegie respected Frick's management abilities, there was no love lost between the two men. To Carnegie's chagrin, Frick continued to profit from the coke enterprise even as he was selling his product to the Carnegie plants. Carnegie tried to buy out Frick's share of the steel enterprise. An enraged Frick chased the small Carnegie down the hall, and Carnegie wisely dropped the subject.

But J. P. Morgan offered them a way out of their relationship when he absorbed Carnegie Steel into U.S. Steel. Carnegie earned $400 million from the deal, and Frick took $60 million. With his own fortune from coke, Frick now had more than $77 million, becoming one of the "Pittsburgh Millionaires."

Frick indulged in his own philanthropies, although not on the scale of Carnegie. He donated an organ and chemistry laboratory to Princeton University and set up the Henry C. Frick Educational Commission. His most famous act of benefaction was rescuing the Dime Savings Bank on Christmas Eve in 1915. The bank, which built its reputation by opening accounts with as little as a dime from thousands of school children, shut its doors, swallowing the children's Christmas funds. Frick stepped in to save Christmas, wiring the bank $170,000 to pay all school accounts in full.

On Saturday afternoons, Frick was known to sit in the parlor of his Fifth Avenue mansion while an organist played majestically on his three-hundred-year-old, $100,000 French pipe organ. Surrounded by Rembrandts and Van Dycks, Frick would sit on a large Renaissance throne and page through the *Saturday Evening Post*. As one journalist noted, "Surely Frick must have felt, as he sat there, that only time separated him from Lorenzo and the other Medicis."

He later gave the home, along with its organ and art collection, to the public, with a $15 million endowment for its maintenance. After the death of his widow in 1931, the mansion at Fifth Avenue and 70th Street was opened to the public. Thousands of people have viewed the Frick Collection and enjoyed concerts at the mansion.

Frick's fortune, estimated by B. C. Forbes and a group of respected American bankers at $225 million one year before his death in 1919, was left to his family. Frick's son, Childs, died in 1965 after a life of scientific achievement. Grandson Henry Clay Frick II pursued a medical career in New York. Perhaps the most visible of Frick's children was his daughter, Helen Clay Frick. She was active in philanthropy—continuing to develop her father's renowned art collection in New York—and in defending her father's reputation before her death at the age of ninety-six in 1984. In 1965, she sought an injunction against a Random House book called *Pennsylvania: Birthplace of a Nation* that made a few brief but unflattering references to her father. After two years in litigation, her case was rejected.

26   32

Collis Potter Huntington
(1821–1900)

Est. wealth: $50–$70 million

Mark Hopkins
(1813–1878)

Est. wealth: $20 million

Leland Stanford
(1824–1893)

Est. wealth: $19 million

Charles Crocker
(1822–1888)

Est. wealth: $20–$40 million

The Big Four

The "Big Four" built the Central Pacific Railroad—tunneling through mountains and across deserts to drive the golden spike into the last leg of the U.S. transcontinental railway system. These four men, three merchants and a former prospector, came to dominate business and politics in the western United States. By 1870, they controlled one of the largest railroad empires in the country, and they were all multimillionaires.

Collis Potter Huntington was the son of a Connecticut tinker who was so poor that local officials took away Collis and his other children and sent them to live with local farmers. The fourteen-year-old Collis spent a year as an apprentice on a neighbor's farm. After the year, he worked at a general store and as a peddler selling watches from a horse and buggy before opening a store with his brother in Oneonta, New York. In 1848 at twenty-seven, Huntington left New York to open a new store in the rich gold-mining region of California.

Always alert for opportunities, when Collis was delayed for three months crossing the isthmus of Panama, he increased his capital from $1,200 to $5,000 through shrewd trading. He used the money to set up a hardware store in Sacramento. He later joined with a partner, Mark Hopkins, who would become the second member of the Big Four, to open a new store. The Huntington & Hopkins Hardware Store became one of the most prosperous retail-wholesale firms in California. Through their involvement in city politics—as members of the Know-Nothing party—Huntington and Hopkins met fellow merchants and future partners Leland Stanford and Charles Crocker.

Stanford was the son of an innkeeper in New York. He originally trained to practice law in Wisconsin, but after his law books were destroyed in a fire, he followed the Gold Rush to California in 1852. There, he and four brothers set up a general store selling supplies to miners. A lucky stake in a mining operation netted him $400,000. He also was active in California politics, helping to organize the Republican party in the state.

Charles Crocker, the last of the four, came to California from Indiana with his younger brother during the 1849 Gold Rush. After working in placer mines, Crocker opened a store in Sacramento, where he became a prominent citizen and was elected to the state legislature in 1860.

The four men would often meet to discuss politics and business in a vacant room above the Huntington & Hopkins store. It was there in 1860 that Huntington introduced his future partners to an eccentric engineer named Theodore "Crazy Ted" Judah. Judah had come up with a route to run a railroad through the perilous Sierra Nevada mountains. He spent over a year seeking financial backing for a survey of the route, but no bank would put up the money for the project. The four Sacramento merchants decided to back the project with $35,000 and to begin surveying and building tracks into the silver-mining country.

The partners had virtually no experience with railroads. They had access to only about $195,000 in capital. But with lobbying by Huntington in Washington (greasing the wheels with bribes), Congress passed the Pacific Railway Act in 1862 granting Central Pacific the right to build the railroad from Sacramento to meet the Union Pacific railroad. Huntington telegraphed Stanford: "We have drawn the elephant, now let us see if we can harness it."

"Harnessing the elephant" turned out to be a significant challenge. The proposed rail line stretched across 689 miles of deserts and mountains. Construction began in 1863, and even with crews working through the winters, it took more than five years to complete. The builders of the Central Pacific, moving east from Sacramento, raced against the Union Pacific, moving west from Omaha. Since they were paid by the government in cash and land grants for every mile completed, the crews worked year-round and even sometimes through the night.

The four partners of the Central Pacific worked smoothly together. Huntington handled Washington relations, while Stanford, who had been elected governor of California in 1861, took care of local government. The burly Crocker oversaw construction work, while the scholarly Hopkins managed the books and the office.

As the Central Pacific worked its way toward the advancing Union Pacific tracks in the East, it faced a shortage of workers. Crocker had a Chinese servant, Ah Ling, and he hit upon the idea of hiring Chinese workers for the railroad. Soon the Central Pacific had assembled an army of 10,000 Chinese workers who would do the grueling work of building the railroad. They slaved through sun and snow, chiseling out the Summit Tunnel in the Sierra Nevada, *by hand*, for wages of only $1 per day. In 1869, the Central Pacific met the tracks of the Union Pacific in Promontory, Utah, where the famous golden spike was hammered home.

The government had paid for almost the whole project, thanks to Huntington's lobbying in Washington and Stanford's efforts in California. The partners received $16,000 for every mile of track across the flat lands and $48,000 for every mile across the mountains. (When the federal government announced the premium for mountainous tracks, Stanford quickly arranged for the state geologist to redraw the maps of the Sierra Nevada, adding an extra twenty-four miles to the width of the mountain range.) In addition, Stanford had arranged for California to pay them $10,000 for every mile of track laid in the state. In all, the partners were given $25 million in government bonds and 4.5 million acres of land.

Although the railroad was almost entirely financed by the government, the profits were kept by the partners. (Their company books, which would have told exactly how much they had made, were "accidentally" lost in a fire when they were requested by Congress.)

In 1865, even before the Central Pacific was completed, the four men established the Southern Pacific Railroad Company, a forty-seven-mile railroad from Sacramento to San Francisco. The new company built a line from San Francisco to Los Angeles, which was completed in 1876. By 1884, the Southern Pacific stretched from the West Coast to New Orleans. The partners had also built Reno, Nevada, Fresno, California, and other towns along the route. Next to the federal government, Southern Pacific became the largest landlord in California, Nevada, and Utah, controlling more than 3.8 million acres. In 1979, the magazine *New West* commented: "The hidden empire of Southern Pacific is so vast that it controls virtually every important area of policy and growth in California."

As the partners, led by Huntington and Stanford, became the dominant force in the Western business, they also were the subject of intense criticism and even open protests. Workers, backed by sugar millionaire Claus Spreckels, drew up plans for a "People's Railroad" to compete with Southern Pacific in the San Joaquin Valley. William Randolph Hearst frequently railed against Huntington and Southern Pacific in his newspapers, and author Frank Norris, in *The Octopus*, offers a scathing portrait of the Mussel Slough massacre, a violent confrontation that erupted between the railroad and farmers who had set up homesteads on land that the railroad considered its own.

Huntington ended up the wealthiest of the four, with a fortune estimated at between $60 and $70 million before his death in

1900 at the age of seventy-nine. With all the time he spent lobbying in Washington, Huntington had made sizeable East Coast investments, including gaining control of the Chesapeake and Ohio Railroad. He extended that line to Huntington, West Virginia, and he also built the town of Newport News, Virginia, as a deep sea terminal for the line. Then Huntington built the Chesapeake & Ohio Railroad. He also served as president of the Mexican International Railway and the Pacific Mail Steamship Company.

Twice married, Huntington had two adopted children, but his business interests were passed on to his brother's son, Henry E. Huntington, then fifty, who received one third of his uncle's shares in Southern Pacific.

Leland Stanford, during his two-year term as California governor, was credited with keeping the state loyal to the Union during the Civil War and advancing the interests of the Central Pacific, including helping pass seven acts of "benevolence" toward the Central Pacific. He pushed through a bond issue to help finance the railroad and obtained land grants in California for the railroad that was destined to join the East and West.

In 1885, Stanford was elected U.S. senator, joining a group of wealthy men known as the "Millionaire's Club" in the Senate. He continued his fight against the government regulation of business. Unconcerned about conflicts of interest, Stanford served as president of the Central Pacific from its inception until his death in 1893.

Stanford is probably best known for founding one of the nation's most prominent universities. Stanford's only son and namesake died of typhoid fever in 1884 at the age of fifteen. In his honor, Stanford and his wife, Jane Lathrop Stanford, founded Stanford University in 1885, with a gift of $20 million and land for the campus on his ranch at Palo Alto.

Charles Crocker, who built a personal fortune of between $20 and $40 million, was seriously injured in a carriage accident in 1886. He never fully recovered and died two years later. He left his fortune to his three sons and a daughter. Crocker had established a bank in San Francisco with his son and a partner in 1886 that became the Crocker National Bank in 1906. Crocker's son, William H., served as its president until 1936. After the San Francisco earthquake in 1906, William played an important role in arranging for loans from New York banks to rebuild the city. Control of the bank passed to William's son, William W., in 1936. The younger Crocker served as president until 1956, when the bank merged with the Anglo-California National Bank to become the Crocker-Anglo National Bank.

Mark Hopkins was the most invisible and mysterious member of the quartet. While his partners entered politics and built huge mansions, Hopkins lived simply and worked behind the scenes. Huntington once said of Hopkins that he "was the truest and best man that ever lived. He had a keen analytical mind, and was thoroughly accurate."

Hopkins' simple life is attested to by the amounts the four partners withdrew from Central Pacific for personal accounts and expenses. In one five-month period, Stanford drew $276,000, Huntington took $57,000, and Crocker withdrew $31,000. But Hopkins drew only $800.

Hopkins preferred spending his time in a little cabin he had constructed in the Sierras. The cabin was on the outskirts of a resort known as Hopkins's Spring that he and Stanford established near Donner Pass. Hopkins lived a modest, perhaps severe, existence. He ate little, and neither smoked nor drank.

Hopkins was such a mystery in his personal life that even his biography is controversial. There were apparently two Mark Hopkinses in Sacramento at the same time, one from New York and one from North Carolina. To make matters worse, the poorer, New York Mark Hopkins also worked at Central Pacific. When he died, his wife went to work for the richer, North Carolina Mark Hopkins as his housekeeper. After his death, she claimed to be his widow and inherited most of his $20 million estate, much to the chagrin of his North Carolina descendants.

Judah, the engineer and visionary of the Central Pacific railroad, benefited least from the project. When he complained about the questionable tactics of his partners, they began easing him out. By 1864, the partners had taken over his shares, and he died virtually penniless a few years later.

Peter A. Widener

(1834–1915)

A Streetcar Named Success

Est. wealth: $100 million

Peter Arrell Widener built the largest transit empire in the nation and became the richest man in Philadelphia.

The son of a Philadelphia brick-maker, Widener dropped out of high school to work as a butcher's boy at his brother's meat shop. Widener was soon in business for himself and became an important figure in the city's Republican party. During the Civil War, Widener used his political connections to secure a government contract to supply mutton to Union troops within a ten-mile radius of Philadelphia, earning him $50,000. Widener used his earnings to expand his chain of meat stores, and he also began purchasing street railways in Philadelphia.

Widener had a brief but fruitful career in city government. He served on the board of education and was appointed city treasurer in 1873. City jobs at the time carried large salaries, so he became quite wealthy through his government work. He ran unsuccessfully for mayor in 1877 and failed in his attempt to be nominated for state treasurer.

In 1875, Widener and partner William Elkins formed the Continental Street Railway Company. Using political contacts and deep pockets, Widener and partners took over rival company Union Passenger Company in 1880, giving them control of almost all the north-south and east-west lines in the city. By 1882, their lines carried nearly 33 million passengers per year. In 1883, Widener and his partners founded the Philadelphia Traction Company. They began an aggressive program of converting the horse-drawn cars into cable cars. It cost more than $10 million and took five years to install one ten-mile stretch of double tracks. In the 1890s, the partners began installing an electric trolley system. Because of strong public opposition to the overhead wires, the transit company had to agree to repave city streets to obtain government approval to install the electric systems. These joint activities required millions of dollars in investments, but by 1895 the company had expanded its business to carry more than 100 million passengers.

In the mid-1890s, with a virtual monopoly over city transit, Widener's group began taking over rapid transit lines running out of the city. They leased thirteen rapid transit franchises. Even though the partners had a virtual monopoly, fixed-fare rates eventually undermined the system. As costs rose and rates remained the same, profits fell. Eventually, the city government took greater control of the lines.

Widener also worked with Thomas Fortune Ryan and William Collins Whitney in New York, helping to finance and to plan the strategy for their dominance of New York transit. Widener and his partner William Elkins also moved on to invest in rail systems in Chicago, Pittsburgh, and Baltimore. Soon they owned more miles of streetcar tracks than any other syndicate, with a total capitalization estimated at $1.5 billion.

At the time Widener started in the transit business, rail cars were drawn by horses. Widener was among the pioneers in implementing cable cars, then electric cars. He created the most modern and efficient transportation system in the nation.

Widener also invested in other areas. He helped organize the U.S. Steel Corporation and the American Tobacco Company. He invested in Standard Oil, as well as railroads and mortgage companies.

Widener built a beautiful home called Lynnewood Hall in the Elkins Park section of Philadelphia. He filled it with art by Raphael and Rembrandt, along with one of the finest collections of Chinese porcelain in the United States. Widener, who had an impressive library, was well read and a skillful conversationalist.

Widener and his wife, Hannah, had three sons, but only one survived his father. George D. Widener took over his father's transit interests shortly before his father's death. George married Eleanor Elkins, daughter of his father's partner, in 1883, and they had two sons and a daughter. George and his son Harry died in the sinking of the *Titanic* in 1912 on their way home from London. Harry, who was twenty-seven when he died, was an avid book collector and had bought a 1598 copy of Sir Francis Bacon's *Essaies* shortly before his death. He reportedly quipped before setting sail for America that "I'll take a little Bacon with me in my pocket, and if I am shipwrecked, it will go home with me." After his death, his mother, who had survived the sinking of the *Titanic* in a lifeboat, donated her son's book collection to Harvard College to establish the Harry Elkins Widener Memorial Library.

When the elder Widener died in 1915 at the age of eighty-one, he was the richest man in Philadelphia. He left a fortune estimated as high as $100 million to his surviving younger son, Joseph, and George's son and daughter. Widener had also contributed an estimated $11 million to charity, including establishing a training school for handicapped children. His Broad Street home was donated as a branch of the Philadelphia Free Library, and his art collection was given to the city.

Widener's son, Joseph, was a financier and sportsman who owned the Belmont Park and Hialeah racetracks along with a substantial art collection that was donated to the National Gallery. At his death in 1943, his fortune of $20 to $30 million, along with his share of his father's trust, was passed on to his son and daughter. His son Peter, grandson and namesake of the founder of the fortune, was haunted by his wealth. In 1940, eight years before his death at age fifty-three, he published an autobiography, which he wrote, in his words, "to set myself up as a horrible example of what an empty existence it is to be the son of great wealth ... ".

Number 28 is James Cair Flood, who was one of the Silver Kings (see page 70).

29

Nicholas Longworth
(1782–1863)
The Man Who Owned Cincinnati
Est. wealth: $15 million

Nicholas Longworth, called "the Western millionaire," was the largest landowner in Cincinnati, one of the largest cities in the United States at the time. His secret to wealth was purchasing worthless farmland and holding on to it until it became valuable city property in the bustling metropolis. By the time of his death, this strategy had created a fortune estimated at $15 million.

Longworth became interested in real estate speculation by accident. Longworth was born in Newark, New Jersey, where he was trained as a shoemaker. He moved to Cincinnati at the age of twenty-one. He arrived on a flatboat in 1803 with little more than the clothes on his back. Cincinnati was no more than a frontier outpost, with a population of only eight hundred people. Longworth studied law under Judge Jacob Burnet, becoming a frontier lawyer in just six months.

One of his first cases was a man accused of horse stealing. There were few crimes more despicable at the time than stealing horses, and the punishment was death. Longworth somehow managed to win the case, but his client had no money to pay the fee. He gave Longworth two secondhand copper stills. But the tavernkeeper who operated the stills was just expanding his business and was reluctant to part with them. Instead he offered Longworth thirty-three acres of land on Western Row (which became Cincinnati Avenue). By 1851, this land was worth almost $2 million.

This was how Longworth got into the business of real estate. As he continued to practice law, he constantly added to his land holdings in what would become the heart of Cincinnati's business district.

At that time, Cincinnati was little more than a village, but Longworth was confident in its future. He bought for "trifling sums whatever was rejected by everyone else . . . acquiring some of the most valuable portions of the present city and its immediate suburbs," reported a *Harper's Weekly* cover story in 1863. Settlers swarmed into Cincinnati. By 1830, the population topped 24,000, and by 1860, it had grown to 171,293 residents. Longworth's land was now in the center of this growing city. In 1819, he was making so much money from real estate that he gave up the law to manage his property. By 1850, he owned so much land that he reportedly paid the second highest tax bill in the United States, $17,000. Only William B. Astor in New York paid a higher bill, just over $23,000.

Longworth also founded a huge vineyard where he produced more than 500,000 bottles of wine per year. His grapes were renowned among wine producers across the United States.

His garden that surrounded his mansion on Pike Street in Cincinnati was open to the public. *Harper's* reports, "If his gardeners were not on hand, Mr. Longworth himself was chaperone for those who came to visit his garden. And he was a ready writer, full of wit, humor and sarcasm." There is a story that Abraham Lincoln even came to see these famous gardens and mistook Longworth for the gardener.

It was no wonder. The gardeners often dressed better than the eccentric Longworth. He wore an old, discolored hat and his clothes fit loosely. His shoes were unshined and oversized, with leather hanging from them. He dressed so poorly that one hot day when he was walking through town, he stopped on a stoop to wipe the sweat from his forehead. As he held his hat in his hand, a passing gentleman, taking him for a beggar, dropped a quarter into the millionaire's hat. Longworth, displaying his characteristic sense of humor, put the coin in his pocket, saying, "Thank you, Sir. I never earned a quarter so easily in my life."

Longworth was a study in contrasts. In business, he was ruthless—foreclosing mortgages and using his legal knowledge to best his opponents. He was parsimonious and dressed so simply that he looked "more a beggar than a millionaire." But in his personal life, he was sometimes generous to a fault. There is a story of how a beggar came to his office and pointed to his gaping shoes on his feet. Longworth kicked off one of his own shoes and asked the beggar to try it on. It fit, so Longworth gave him the other. It was hardly expected behavior from a multimillionaire. But after the beggar left, Longworth—true to form—instructed a boy to buy him another pair at the shoe store, but not to pay more than a $1.50 for them!

Longworth was known for supporting charities that others would turn away. Once a friend sent a committee of Mormons to Longworth with a note saying that "since these people were not Christians, and seemed to be abandoned by everybody that professed to be, they probably came within his rule." Longworth helped them without hesitation.

With his $15 million estate, *Harper's* estimated that upon his death his taxes were higher than those of any other man in the nation—more than $17,000. When he died in 1863, at the age of eighty-one, he left his fortune to his son and three daughters.

Longworth's great-grandson and namesake served as speaker of the U.S. House of Representatives from 1925 to 1931. He married Alice Roosevelt, daughter of President Theodore Roosevelt. His descendants contributed Eden Park to the city and helped to found Cincinnati's art museum. Longworth's Pike Avenue mansion later became the Taft Museum, and the gardens he tended so lovingly were preserved as one of the city's attractions.

30

Philip Danforth Armour

(1832–1901)

Pork-Barrel Profits

Est. wealth: $50 million

At nineteen, Philip Armour set out with three friends from his hometown of Stockbridge, New York, determined to reach the gold fields of California—on foot. One of the young men died on the way. Two turned back. Six months later, Armour alone arrived on the West Coast. He found no gold but survived by sheer determination. He dug ditches for $5 per day. In five years, he had saved $8,000.

On the way home from California, Armour stopped in Milwaukee, and it was there that he returned to settle. Using his savings, he set up a produce business. Toward the end of the Civil War, he built a huge fortune speculating on contracts for pork. Just before the surrender of the Confederacy, Armour secured contracts for pork at $40 per barrel. When the war ended, pork prices dropped to just $18 per barrel. He made a $22 profit per barrel, earning $1 or $2 million.

Armour then moved into the meatpacking business. In 1867, at the age of thirty-five, he and two brothers moved south from Milwaukee to Chicago. Chicago, at the center of the railroads and with a ready supply of grain for feed, was an ideal location for meatpacking. Armour and his brothers established Armour & Co., which became the largest meatpacking company in the nation.

Armour was among the first to see the power of the new refrigerated rail cars for taking the meatpacking business nationwide. Until that time, beef and pork for East Coast markets had to be transported alive in stock cars, a very inefficient process. The railroads were reluctant to adopt the refrigerated cars because it would reduce their business of transporting live cattle. Armour built his own fleet of cars, and his company soon transformed meatpacking from a seasonal business to a year-round enterprise.

In addition to packing meat, Armour expanded to meat byproducts, fertilizer, soap, margarine, tanning and leather, and other products. As the saying went, when a pig entered the yard, nothing got away but the squeal.

Outside of Chicago, Armour built his "Packing Town," a small city with its own bank, post office, and newspaper. He employed more than 15,000 people, and by 1894, *McClure's Magazine* estimated that his payroll topped $6 million per year. He had more than 1,400 railway cars, seven hundred horses to haul his wagons, the largest grain elevators in the world, and a glue factory that produced 7 million tons of glue per year. The stockyards were infamous for their noise and stench, and their poor working conditions were sketched in gory detail in Upton Sinclair's *The Jungle*, creating a national scandal.

Armour, a quiet but energetic man, had a single-minded focus on business. He would leave for the plant at five or six in the morning and work until 6 P.M. On most nights, he was in bed by nine o'clock. He once commented, "I do not love the money. What I do love is the getting of it."

Armour relished his wealth, which had grown to an estimated $50 million by 1893. Every morning, he would have a stack of one hundred crisp $1 bills placed on his desk. Throughout the day, he would give them away, one at a time.

In 1892, Armour heard a sermon by Dr. F. W. Gunsaulus on the topic of "What I Would Do If I Had $1,000,000." Armour, who *did* have several million, set up the Armour Institute of Technology to train skilled workers based on the minister's ideas, and he put Dr. Gunsaulus in charge of it. The Institute ultimately formed the core for the modern Illinois Institute of Technology.

Armour also was dedicated to the city of Chicago. During the panic of 1893, many frightened depositors wanted to withdraw their funds from the Illinois Trust and Savings Bank, which was rumored to be on the brink of collapse. Armour and several other wealthy Chicago citizens reassured the crowd that they had faith in the bank. Armour demonstrated his faith by offering to cash any personal checks from his own accounts. As many as a thousand investors turned up at Armour's office, and he made good on his pledge by cashing their checks, saving the bank.

When Armour died in 1901, he left his $50 million estate and control of the firm to his son J. Ogden. At the time, the business had more than $100 million in annual revenues. J. Ogden continued to expand his father's holdings, increasing revenues by five times over the following sixteen years. He was believed to be the richest man in the world. After World War I, however, J. Ogden's fortunes declined after he made a number of poor investments, including speculating in German marks. At one point, he lost $1 million per day for 130 days. Even the great Armour fortune was ultimately depleted. He gave up financial control of his father's company in 1923. At the time of his death in 1927, J. Ogden's estate was valued at only $20,000. As he once said, "The world is a worse place for a young man with a lot of money than for one without any."

31

Bill Gates
(1955–   )
Est. wealth: $15 billion

Paul Allen

(1953–   )

Est. wealth: $6.1 billion

Micro-Moguls

At the age of nineteen, William Henry Gates III, a Harvard dropout, established a company that would change the future of computing and business. By thirty-one he was a billionaire. At the age of forty, he was in a neck-and-neck race with investor Warren Buffett for the title of richest man in the world.

127

During a media extravaganza to launch Windows 95, comedian Jay Leno said of Bill Gates, "This man is so successful, his chauffeur is Ross Perot." In October 1995, Gates's personal fortune was estimated by *Forbes* at $15 billion. He is the youngest, most aggressive, most visible billionaire in American history. His partner, Paul Allen, who dropped out of actively running Microsoft when he contracted Hodgkin's disease, continues to be a player in high-technology companies using the fortune he built through Microsoft.

Gates, the son of a successful Seattle attorney and a university regent, grew up in an upper-middle-class neighborhood in a house overlooking Lake Washington. He was, as one of his teachers commented, "a nerd before the term was invented." When the World's Fair came to town in 1962, the seven-year-old Gates went from exhibit to exhibit—space, technology, computers, machines in the offices and homes of tomorrow. By the age of nine, he had consumed the entire *World Book Encyclopedia* from A to Z. (Today, Gates owns the most popular multimedia encyclopedia, Microsoft *Encarta*.)

His parents sent him to the private, all-male Lakeside School. His classmates used to describe the freckle-faced Gates as brash, goofy, funny, and arrogant. At Lakeside, Gates met Allen, and they became close friends and partners. Allen, the son of two Seattle librarians, grew up being dragged to museums and surrounded by books. (His mother brought twelve thousand books with her to the house her son later built for her on his Washington estate.) Allen's broad vision and active mind had always sought new challenges. "Even as a kid, every year I was interested in something different, whether it was chemistry or cars or physics or electronics or space travel or music," he told a *Fortune* interviewer in 1994.

Gates and Allen shared a fascination with technology along with an enthusiasm for adventure, risk taking, and entrepreneurship. While they were at Lakeside, the school installed its first terminal linked to a computer at a local company, purchased with the proceeds of a rummage sale held by parents. Gates and Allen soon became hackers, breaking into security systems at the leading firms around the country.

A local company had bought a computer from Digital with the stipulation that it would not have to pay for the machine as long as there were bugs in it. Gates and Allen, riding their bicycles to work, were hired by the company to find bugs in the system. They were so successful, Digital had to renegotiate the contract. The teenaged partners then pedaled their bikes to work at TRW, troubleshooting its new computer system that ran a dam and generating station on the Columbia River.

When Gates was a senior in high school, he and Allen created a company to read computer cards from machines that monitored traffic flow for local municipalities. Traf-O-Data, the company that ultimately became Microsoft, earned $20,000 in revenues in its first year.

After a summer working at Honeywell, Allen dropped out of college to join Honeywell's Boston office. Gates, who had scored a perfect 800 on the math portion of the SAT, followed Allen to the East Coast, enrolling in Harvard. When the first build-it-yourself minicomputers were developed, the two techies bought one and then offered to write a BASIC interpreter for the machine. When they successfully delivered the program to the manufacturer, Gates and Allen began selling the software to other companies in the growing personal computer market. Gates dropped out of Harvard to set up his business in Albuquerque, New Mexico. By 1980, with $8 million in revenues and eighty employees, Gates and Allen moved the company back home to Seattle.

Gates is fiercely competitive, sometimes abusive, and is known to throw things when he is angry. He is hard driving, commanding the respect of employees, partners, and rivals. Scrawny with an adolescent look, he moved into a room full of older businessmen and commanded their attention with his understanding of technology and his grasp of its implications for their businesses. He never pulled punches. It was this direct and forceful approach that gained him the respect of some of the largest corporations in the world—including GE, Texas Instruments, NCR, Radio Shack, and National Semiconductor.

While Gates can be caustic, Allen is known to be affable and courteous. (When Ticketmaster CEO Fred Rosen confessed to Allen that he didn't know how to operate a personal computer, Allen offered to fly to Los Angeles and teach him.) Allen has an uncompromising vision, while Gates can cut to the chase and get things done.

In 1980 Gates received a call from IBM. The company asked him to write an operating system for their new personal computer. Microsoft had never written an operating system, so they bought a system from Seattle Computer Products for $50,000 and modified it for the IBM computer. The system, ultimately called MS-DOS, rode the rising popularity of the IBM personal computer to become the dominant operating system for personal computers, with more than 90 percent of the market.

Eight years into the Microsoft miracle, Allen returned from a European business trip in 1983 with a high fever. After tests showed he had Hodgkin's disease, a cancer of the lymphatic system, he began to reassess his nonstop, hard-driving lifestyle. He left the day-to-day operations of Microsoft to Gates, although he remains on the board of directors and is one of its largest shareholders.

After Allen recovered from Hodgkin's disease, he began to enjoy his new freedom and wealth. He toured Europe, did scuba diving, and picked up the electric guitar. He constructed a country estate near Seattle, including two swimming pools and an indoor basketball court, with a Maserati and four Ferraris parked in the garage. He also bought a private jet and a 150-foot yacht.

Allen indulged his love for musician Jimi Hendrix by building a museum in Seattle to house Hendrix memorabilia, including the guitar he played at Woodstock. Allen indulged his passion for basketball by acquiring the Portland Trail Blazers basketball team.

By the 1990s, he was looking for new business challenges and began investing in multimedia start-ups. He founded multimedia software company Asymetrix and invested in America Online, Ticketmaster, and Egghead Software. He set up a $100 million think tank called Interval Research, which he hopes will play the kind of role in shaping the information superhighway that rival Xerox's Palo Alto Research Center did in developing Silicon Valley.

Gates continued to build Microsoft, with revenues topping $100 million by 1984. Gates moved from his success with DOS to the Windows graphical interface. He also launched what became leading applications programs in word processing, spreadsheets, electronic mail, and presentations.

Taking a page out of John D. Rockefeller's book, Gates initiated a practice of charging manufacturers for software per machine. Even if manufacturers installed another operating system, they would have to pay the same royalty to Microsoft (in exchange for a volume discount).

By 1995, Microsoft had more than eighteen thousand employees gathering around beer kegs on his sprawling Seattle campus. Thousands had become millionaires through their Microsoft stock. At the center of the campus was "Lake Bill," and the image of Bill Gates became synonymous with his company. The boyish face of the forty-year-old Gates beamed from the covers of *Time* and from his best-selling book, *The Road Ahead.* When he launched Windows 95, hard-core computer customers lined up at midnight like rock fans. Gates even turned up in the funny pages as the target of *Bloom County* humor, Bill the Nerd paired with Bill the Cat.

In the 1990s, Gates began enjoying the fruits of his labors, beginning construction on a $40 million home outside of Seattle, with video walls that can feature an ever-changing array of paintings and his own private trout stream. In 1994, the thirty-nine-year-old Gates married Microsoft executive Melinda French in Hawaii.

Microsoft, the tiny upstart, became the most powerful company in the computer business. *Business Week* headlines asked "Is Microsoft Too Powerful?" and in November 1995, a cover story on Microsoft in the *New York Times Magazine* featured an image of a gorilla and the question "How do you restrain an 800-pound gorilla?" In 1996, Microsoft faced new challenges from Internet rivals, such as Netscape and Sun, and investigations by the U.S. Department of Justice.

Gates's position as richest American also faced a new challenge from his close friend, Warren Buffett, who surged past Gates in February 1996 with a fortune of $16 billion. (*The Wealthy 100* list is a snapshot based on fall 1995 data.) Gates and Buffett first met at a Fourth of July picnic at Gates's parents' home through *Washington Post* publisher Katharine Graham, and the two immediately became good friends. They attended University of Nebraska football games and took a family vacation together in China.

As Gates wrote in a review of a biography of Buffett in *Fortune,* "I can't be neutral or dispassionate about Warren Buffett, because we're close friends. . . . I think his jokes are all funny. I think his dietary practices—lots of burgers and Cokes—are excellent. In short, I'm a fan." Gates and Buffett agree that it isn't good for their heirs to be saddled with too much of their fortunes, so they are essentially, Gates says, "working for charity."

Prominent but Poor

Albert Einstein

(1879–1955)

IF YOU'RE SO SMART, WHY AREN'T YOU RICH?

Bill Gates may be pretty brainy, but he's no Einstein. When it comes to wealth, however, Einstein was no Bill Gates. His estate at the time of his death in 1955 (the year Gates was born) was just $65,000. Perhaps the most valuable part of his bequest, his manuscripts, was left to Hebrew University. But wealth, as Einstein might say, is all relative.

Number 32 is Mark Hopkins, one of the "Big Four" who built the Central Pacific Railroad (see page 110).

Edward Clark

(1811–1882)

Est. wealth: $25–$40 million

Isaac Merritt Singer

(1811–1875)

Est. wealth: $13–$15 million

Sewed Up an Industry

Isaac Singer, a failed actor and tinkerer, seemed destined to be destitute rather than become one of the richest men in America. But Singer's design for a sewing machine, coupled with the business and marketing genius of his partner, Edward Clark, made their machine synonymous with sewing and made them both multi-millionaires.

Singer, born in Oswego, New York, in 1811, ran away from home at the age of twelve. He wanted to be an actor but never had much success on the stage. He drifted from state to state, keeping alive through his mechanical genius, which allowed him to earn a living in manufacturing and other businesses. While he was digging ditches in Lockport, Illinois, Singer invented a new rock drilling machine. Singer received a patent, but quickly spent the money he made from the invention. Then, while working for a printer in Pittsburgh, he came up with a new machine for carving type. He went to New York to build a business around the new invention, but a boiler explosion at his factory destroyed the plant. At thirty-nine, he was penniless again.

Singer was working in a Boston machine shop in 1851 when a customer brought in a sewing machine for repairs. Singer looked at the relatively new invention and proposed to his boss that the machine would work better if the needle moved vertically rather than horizontally and if the shuttle didn't move in a circle. Within eleven days, Singer had designed a superior sewing machine. With the help of the owner of the machine shop and another partner, Singer established I.M. Singer & Company to manufacture his machine. Unlike the leading sewing machine of that time—developed by Elias Howe—Singer's new machine had the capacity to do continuous stitching. It soon became the first practical domestic sewing machine.

Howe, however, sued Singer for royalties, and Singer fought Howe's claims for years. Finally in 1854, the courts ordered Singer to pay $15,000 in settlement. These patent troubles brought Singer into the office of Edward Clark, a lawyer at a major New York City firm. Singer, aware that his young company could use a skilled patent lawyer, asked Clark to join the company. Clark, then forty, left a promising career as junior partner in the law firm to become a half partner in Singer's fledgling business.

After a bitter three-year "sewing machine war" with Howe, Clark negotiated a settlement by organizing a patent pool. Manufacturers paid the pool $15 per machine, and it was divided among the inventors.

The two men were like vinegar and water. Clark was a straightlaced, dignified, button-down attorney. He was a dedicated family man and Sunday school teacher. Singer was a bohemian former actor who blasphemed like a sailor and left mistresses, wives, and children behind him. Clark was horrified by his partner's personal life. At one point, Clark's wife advised her husband to "Sell out and leave the nasty brute." But Clark stayed with the business, in spite of his antipathy toward Singer.

As much as they were polar opposites in their personal lives, Clark and Singer were a powerful combination in business. According to one observer, "Singer's inventiveness, mechanical know-how and boundless drive and energy were ideally complemented by Clark's cool acumen." Singer continued to develop the machine, receiving twenty patents between 1851 and 1863. Clark, meanwhile, made the machines a household necessity through aggressive advertising and innovative financing.

Clark introduced the first installment plans for the $100 machines, requiring only $5 down to buy a machine. He offered a $50 credit to anyone who exchanged a competing brand for a Singer. His advertising played on husbands' guilt about not providing their wives with the latest laborsaving device, and he set up women in store windows to demonstrate how easy the machine was to use. Without any advantage in patents, the company became the dominant force in the sewing machine industry. Then Clark led the worldwide expansion of the company. He set up operations in England, France, Germany, and Brazil. The arrival of Singer sewing machines was touted in Singer ads as "the herald of civilization." Singer sewing machines turned up in Manila and were carried into the jungles of Madagascar. When the Civil War interrupted the company's sales in the United States, foreign sales kept going strong. By 1965, the company had factories in twenty-nine countries with $642 million in sales.

Singer and Clark fought so much that neither would allow the other to become president of the company. As the story goes, a clerk interrupted one of their battles, and the result was that they named the startled young man president of the company.

Singer built one of the gaudiest coaches in New York, which the *New York Herald* described as "a regular steamboat on wheels." It was a massive canary-yellow carriage weighing 3,600 pounds and was drawn through the streets of New York by nine matched horses. The carriage, which carried more than thirty passengers, sported a small orchestra on top that played as Singer rattled through the streets. The contraption also had a separate nursery compartment, with beds, for his many children.

Early in his life, Singer had married Catherine Maria Haley, but he walked out on her and his two children in New York to resume his drifting life. After founding his sewing machine company, Singer lived on New York's Fifth Avenue with a mistress,

Mary Ann Sponsler, with whom he had eight children. When Clark found out that Singer had left behind his first wife, he insisted that his partner get a formal divorce and marry his mistress. Singer went through with the divorce in 1860, but he didn't marry his mistress. She caught Singer driving through New York with another woman, and she screamed at the top of her lungs from her carriage in the middle of the street. Singer assaulted her and was arrested.

In 1863, Singer withdrew from active control of the business and moved to Europe with yet another lover. He finally settled in England, where he married the twenty-one-year-old Isabella, and had two more children. When he died in 1875, at the age of sixty-three, his estate of between $13 million and $15 million, half of which was Singer stock, was divided among his twenty-three children. His son, Paris, who was eight when his father died, had a ten-year affair with dancer Isadora Duncan. Paris, who had fathered five children and separated from his wife before meeting Isadora in Paris in 1909, once rented the New York Metropolitan Opera House for her so she could perform for friends. After breaking up with Duncan in 1917, Paris moved to Florida where he established the exclusive Everglades Club in Palm Beach.

Clark's heirs, like the founder of the fortune, kept a lower profile. After stepping down from management of the company, Clark invested in real estate, including building the Dakota apartment building in Manhattan. His primary focus was in the town of Cooperstown, New York. When he died there at the age of seventy, he left his estate of between $25 million and $40 million to his only surviving son, Alfred, then thirty-eight. In 1939, his descendants established the National Baseball Hall of Fame in Cooperstown (based on the claim that Abner Doubleday had created the sport there), attracting more than 300,000 visitors every year. The Clark family had a total fortune estimated by *Forbes* at $550 million in 1995, including several charitable trusts that benefit Cooperstown.

Number 34 is Leland Stanford, one of the "Big Four" who built the Central Pacific Railroad (see page 111).

35

William Rockefeller

(1841–1922)

Brothers in Trust

Est. wealth: $150–$200 million

William Rockefeller, younger brother of John D. Rockefeller, started out in his own business before his brother made him a partner in Standard Oil. Although overshadowed by the reputation and billionaire status of his older brother, William was one of the driving forces of Standard Oil's success and expansion.

At sixteen, William started work as a bookkeeper for a local miller in his home town of Cleveland. By the time he was twenty-one, he had established a successful commission merchant business. Then John D. Rockefeller hired his brother, two years his junior, to manage the export business of his growing oil company.

The younger Rockefeller set up William Rockefeller & Company, a subsidiary of his brother's company, to handle the export business, and he moved to New York City to manage the operations. William later served as Standard Oil's president until the company was dissolved by federal regulators in 1911.

The two Rockefeller brothers were very different. While John D. had a genius for building profits, William was a master at handling people. John was dour and serious; William was jovial. John was cautious; William was adventurous.

William's skill at handling people was instrumental in bringing all the diverse and rancorous rival refining companies to the same table to form the Standard Oil monopoly. William also was a master salesman who played a central role in selling Standard's products around the world.

William also was a risk taker. His sense of adventure made him one of the driving forces of Standard Oil's expansion into many other investments. A key member of the "Standard Oil gang," William stretched Standard's tentacles into copper, railroads, gas companies, and many other businesses.

After Standard Oil was dissolved by U.S. trustbusters, William retired from active leadership of the company. He continued to pursue his investments in railroads and other companies. William and John built side-by-side estates in Tarrytown, New York. It was there that William died of pneumonia in 1922, at the age of eighty-one, fifteen years before his older brother (who lived to be ninety-eight).

William left a fortune of between $150 million and $200 million in trusts for his four surviving children. It was estimated that the structure of his estate produced more than fifty millionaires in successive generations. Although John D. Rockefeller was one of the most visible and generous philanthropists of his time, William didn't engage in philanthropy, at least not publicly. Two of his sons married daughters of banker James Stillman, one of William Rockefeller's partners in the "Standard Oil gang."

36

Hetty Green

(1834–1916)
The Witch of Wall Street
Est. wealth: $100 million

Henrietta Howland Robinson Green was a shrewd investor, one of the only women to master the man's world of Wall Street finance. She built a fortune that rivaled J. P. Morgan's. In an ugly, unwashed black dress, she also gained a reputation for unparalleled stinginess, earning the title of "the witch of Wall Street." Through "forgery, perjury, penury, genius, ruthlessness, and physical stamina" she became "the richest and most detested woman in America."

Green was born to a Quaker family in Massachusetts. Her father, a partner in a whaling house and a merchant in China trade, often took his only daughter with him to work. Young Hetty grew up surrounded by the foul-smelling barrels of whale oil and the equally foul world of investment. While other young girls were reading *Godey's Lady's Book*, Green was devouring the financial pages of the New York and Boston newspapers.

When her father died in 1865, Hetty, then thirty-one, inherited $6 million. When her aunt died shortly after her father's death, Green was due to inherit a life interest in over $1 million. She wasn't satisfied and went to court to claim her aunt's entire $2 million estate. She produced a highly suspect will that stipulated that no change could be made in her aunt's will without her being consulted. And it made Green the chief beneficiary of her aunt's estate. The case dragged on for five years, with handwriting experts testifying that the signature on the document was a forgery. Green lost her claim and fled to England to avoid forgery charges.

In 1867, Hetty married millionaire silk trader Edward Henry Green. A new kind of legal contract—the prenuptial agreement—kept their financial affairs completely separate. It wasn't to protect Mr. Green but rather to protect Hetty's fortune. In England the couple had two children. After eight years abroad, she then returned to New York and became active on the stock exchange.

On Wall Street, Green bought low and sold high, sweeping up stocks during financial panics. She also lent money to other traders during the Panic of 1906, earning interest off their misfortune. Green also drove several bull markets in railroad stocks and invested in government bonds and municipal bonds, as well as more than $5 million in Chicago real estate.

Hetty Green was legendary for her cheapness. She wore her plain, outdated black dress and shabby cape for so long, they turned green. From the capacious pockets of her dress, she would extract grimy ham sandwiches and graham crackers. She lived in boarding houses to avoid paying New York property taxes. She used to eat her cereal cold to save the cost of heating it up.

When her son Edward injured his knee in a sledding accident, Green dressed him in rags and tried to pass themselves off as a charity case at a free clinic. But the doctor recognized her and demanded payment. Green angrily took her son home and unsuccessfully treated him herself. Gangrene set in, and his leg had to be amputated.

Her husband, a more daring speculator than Green, went bankrupt in 1885, and she refused to underwrite his debts. They later separated. Green then lived with her daughter in a small Hoboken apartment and in New York City. Her relationship with her children was often strained. (When her daughter was once asked where her brother had lived during a certain period, she replied drily: "With my mother—if you can call that living.")

Green spent much of her time in court, fighting off claims to her fortune or other business attacks. One time when she was forced to represent herself in Chicago, she turned to theater to help her case. The multimillionairess turned up in the courtroom in her shabbiest dress. She pleaded poverty and persecution. And the sympathetic jury awarded in her favor.

Green detested lawyers. When she was asked why she had taken out a license to carry a revolver, she replied with wry humor, "Mostly to protect myself against lawyers. I'm not much afraid of burglars or highwaymen."

When Green's health began failing, her son Edward began managing her financial affairs. Green had groomed him as her successor, even paying for his college at Fordham, although she made him promise he wouldn't get married for twenty years after graduation so he could devote himself fully to the business. Edward proved skilled at managing the business, yet his mother paid him only $3 per day for "training."

After Green died in 1916 at the age of eighty-one, Edward married and followed his mother's example of drafting a prenuptial agreement. His $40 million estate was left to his reclusive sister, Mrs. Matthew Astor Wilks. When she died without heirs in 1951, most of her $100 million estate was consumed by taxes, with the remaining $25 million distributed to sixty-three charities.

37

James Jerome Hill

(1838–1916)

The Empire Builder of the Northwest

Est. wealth: $100 million

James J. Hill, born just three decades after Meriwether Lewis and William Clark blazed the first trails across the American Northwest, built a system of railroads from the Great Lakes to the Pacific Ocean. He established cities and farms and towns, becoming the driving force of settlement in the region.

Hill, the son of Irish immigrants, was born in Ontario. His father died when Hill was fifteen, and Hill came south to look for work. He took a job at a steamboat company in St. Paul, Minnesota, carrying wood and freight on his back for $2 per day.

St. Paul was then the farthest reaches of civilization, with great prairies stretching out to the west. Hill then became an agent for the Northwestern Packet Company. He later launched the Red River Transportation Company, plying steamboats between Moorhead and Winnipeg. As he neared forty, Hill was a very successful merchant. A short, stocky, bearded man, who was sightless in his right eye, he looked more like a prospector than a businessman. He was respected as a businessman in the St. Paul community but not considered a visionary.

Then Hill began his most ambitious project. The St. Paul and Pacific Railway—unfinished, in a state of disrepair, near bankrupt—had been written off as hopeless. There were already two transcontinental railroads, the Canadian Pacific Railway in Canada and the Northern Pacific in the United States. Some believed that there was no room for a third. These earlier railroads had been built with the help of huge outlays of government support. Now, Hill and a group of foolhardy investors were planning to create a rail line—without government support—stretching into a virtually uninhabited stretch of prairie.

Hill saw future settlements in the open territory. He pushed forward, through Minnesota, Dakota, and Montana to the North Pacific, ultimately creating a network of six thousand miles of tracks. The Great Northern Railway, completed in 1893, spanned from Lake Superior to Puget Sound, Washington. It was the first transcontinental railroad constructed without government aid.

To make the railroad a success, Hill also had to develop the towns around it. He offered breeding stock to farmers to help build the livestock business in the region. He sent demonstration trains out to show settlers better farming methods and negotiated grain rates and erected large elevators in Buffalo. The prairies soon were dotted with cities. Hundreds of thousands of farms were planted, and Hill's trains carried the harvests to market. One of these farms was owned by Hill himself, who raised horses, cattle, and thirty-five thousand acres of grain. When his rail lines reached the coast, Hill founded the first steamship line between the United States and Japan. He was soon doing $50 million in business per year with the Orient.

Hill, who initially scorned the speculation in railroads of Jay Gould and other investors, eventually teamed up with J. P. Morgan to expand his rail system with the acquisition of his competitor, the Northern Pacific and the Chicago, Burlington and Quincy line. These purchases drew the wrath of Edward H. Harriman, who quietly began buying up Northern Pacific stock. The stock prices shot from under $100 per share to more than $1,000. Faced with ruin, Hill and Harriman called a truce and agreed to share control of the Northern Pacific and Great Northern through the Northern Securities Company.

But trustbusters declared the alliance illegal, and the U.S. Supreme Court ordered it dissolved in 1904. After the ruling, Hill resigned as president in 1907 and became chairman. His son Louis took over as president. By the time Hill stepped down as chairman, at the age of sixty-nine, his Great Northern, which was once the mockery of St. Paul, earned gross profits of more than $66 million per year and carried an annual cargo of 15 million tons.

Hill put his fortune to work in a variety of philanthropic activities, including founding a theological seminary in St. Paul. He was a polished speaker and writer, often on issues of conservation and natural resources, and his speeches and writing were compiled into *Highways of Progress*, published in 1910.

Hill, who fathered ten children, died in 1916 at the age of seventy-seven. His son Louis served as chairman of the board of Great Northern until 1929, and another son, James, served as vice president of the railroad.

Even after the antitrust ruling, the Northern Pacific and Great Northern shared offices in St. Paul but were required to keep a wall down the center of the building to comply with the court order. In 1970, Chief Justice Earl Warren approved a merger between the Great Northern, Northern Pacific, and the Chicago, Burlington and Quincy. A decade later, the Burlington-Northern was merged with the St. Louis–San Francisco Railway, creating the longest railroad in American history, stretching twenty-six thousand miles.

38

Elias Hasket Derby

(1739–1799)

Trailblazer of American Global Commerce

Est. wealth: $800,000–$1 million

The Revolutionary War produced the fortune of Elias Hasket Derby, a merchant who gained his wealth in privateering and global trade, during and after the war. Unlike many successful Salem merchants, Derby inherited a successful business from his father. He built it into one of the most lucrative in the city. "King" Derby, as he was known, may have been America's first millionaire.

Before the war, Derby's father created a thriving merchant business in Salem, Massachusetts, importing sugar from the West Indies. Derby inherited the family business on the verge of the Revolutionary War. He first outfitted several of his ships for privateering, capturing British cargo during the war. Then, he took advantage of the birth of the new republic to establish trade in the farthest reaches of the globe. Through his daring and shrewd business sense, he blazed the trails of American commerce in all parts of the world.

By the end of the war, Derby could easily have retired with his earnings of more than $50,000 from privateering and trade. Instead, he immediately began building a global trading empire. In 1784, his ship *Light Horse* arrived in St. Petersburg, Russia, with a cargo of West Indian sugar, the first U.S. vessel to sail into the Baltic. In 1785, his *Grand Turk* reached the Cape of Good Hope and then headed to the Isle of France in the Indian Ocean. The Isle of France (now called Mauritius) became a very profitable trading center for Derby. The *Grand Turk* then sailed on to Canton, China, becoming the first New England ship to reach the Orient.

Encouraged by these successes, Derby sent ships to Manila, Batavia, Rangoon, Calcutta, and Bombay. His ships brought back exotic goods from all parts of the world to the shops of the growing American republic. Between 1788 and 1799, he sent out 37 ships on 125 different voyages.

Derby also profited from the turmoil of the Napoleonic Wars, when "neutral" ships such as Derby's were at a premium in Europe. Trading in a war zone, however, continued to be as dangerous as it was profitable. Derby's 355-ton ship, the *Mount Vernon*, outfitted with twenty guns, had several close calls with the patrolling French fleets in the Mediterranean. Each time, Derby's ship managed to outsail or outshoot its rivals.

Surprisingly, Derby was not a sailor. In fact, he never went to sea. A knowledgeable shipbuilder, he personally supervised the construction of many of his ships, and he took great care in choosing his captains. Like Andrew Carnegie in a later age, Derby subscribed to the principle of surrounding himself with good men. He chose his captains, who sailed for a year or more at a time, for their sailing skill and their ability as traders. He also rewarded them well, creating many of the largest family fortunes in New England. Derby's captains were so skilled that they lost only one ship (other than those captured) in Derby's entire career.

Derby was active in philanthropy and public affairs. He contributed guns and ammunition to the Continental Army during the Revolution and helped develop the country's original tariff acts. He built a large farm outside of Salem, where he experimented with new crops brought back by his sailing ships. He also erected the largest mansion in Salem at the urging of his wife, Elizabeth Crownshield, the daughter of a prominent Salem trader.

The eldest of their seven children, Elias Hasket Derby, Jr., unlike his father, was an active sailor. He made profitable trips to the Isle of France, Naples, and India, where he lived for three years. The younger Derby was largely responsible for the success of Derby's international trading, adding more than $200,000 to the family coffers. In 1800, while sailing on the *Mount Vernon* during the Napoleonic Wars, Derby was entertained by Lord Nelson and Lady Hamilton. Before he returned from that voyage, his father died in Salem in 1799, at the age of sixty, leaving what was believed to be the largest fortune created in America during the eighteenth century.

In recognition of the important contributions Elias Hasket Jr. made to the family fortune, his father left him half his estate. This sparked a feud with a brother-in-law, which resulted in a scandalous fistfight on the Derby wharf. Shortly after inheriting the business, the younger Derby retired to his father's princely Salem mansion. The cost of maintaining his extravagant lifestyle along with several business reversals forced him to return to trading after ten years. In an attempt to regain his fortune, he led an unsuccessful voyage to Rio de Janeiro and London in 1809.

In 1811, he successfully imported a shipload of 1,100 merino sheep from Lisbon, Portugal. He used the new herd to set up the first broadcloth loom in Massachusetts. Elias Jr. had four daughters and five sons. His eldest son, Elias Haskett III, worked in the law offices of Daniel Webster and became a prominent railroad lawyer. He built a large fortune through his legal work and his investments in railroads.

39

Warren Buffett

(1930–   )

The Sage of Omaha

Est. wealth: $12 billion

It is Monday, May 1, 1995. In Omaha, Nebraska, it's a gray day. A light rain is falling. But for four thousand people assembled at the Holiday Inn Convention Center, the sun was shining. The crowd is so big that several hundred people had to be seated in an overflow room. But they don't mind because, along with most other attendees, they are all lucky enough to be shareholders in Berkshire Hathaway, the New York Stock Exchange holding company run by billionaire Warren Buffett—"The Sage of Omaha." All had come to sit at his feet and listen. Most—including a surprising number of nonshareholders—were there to learn.

Berkshire's stockholders have reason to be happy. An investment of $10,000 in 1956 would be worth $80 million in 1995. While he made millions for his shareholders, Buffett built a fortune of more than $12 billion for himself, making him the second-richest man in America.

Not bad for a small man with thick glasses who owns little more than pieces of paper called stock, and who lets the owners

and managers of those companies in which he owns stock run things. Buffett compares himself to the late, great baseball manager Casey Stengel, who once described his job as "getting paid for home runs the other fellows hit."

A great deal of modesty from a man who has probably hit

more home runs on Wall Street than just about any other money manager. But modesty remains his mantra. While his friend Bill Gates is spending millions on a megamansion, Buffett still lives in the home he bought in 1958 for $32,000. His staff in 1994 was under a dozen, and the company offices—it's been suggested—could fit into half a tennis court. While other less wealthy men are collecting Ferraris, Buffett drives a vintage Lincoln. "Wall Street," he notes, "is the only place that people ride to in a Rolls Royce to get advice from those who take the subway."

Where did Buffett get his talent for making money? You could say it's in the genes. The Omaha native, born in 1930, was the son of a stockbroker who later became a Republican congressman. His mother was a reporter. The junior Buffett showed an early interest in numbers. As early as eight years of age, he started reading stock market books in his father's library.

Buffet started in the business at the bottom. Back in the early 1940s, stock prices were marked by hand in brokers' offices. Beginning at eleven years of age, Warren spent summers writing, erasing, and changing stock prices in the local Harris Upham office where his dad worked.

He was always entrepreneurial. As a youngster, he would buy six-packs of Coca-Cola for 25 cents and sell each bottle for a nickel—a 20 percent profit. (Soon, he would be trading the entire company.) After his father was elected to Congress and the family moved to the nation's capital, the thirteen-year-old worked two paper routes.

While most of his friends spent the money they earned, Buffet invested his capital, acquiring reconditioned pinball machines for $25, placing them in neighborhood barber shops, and eventually taking home about $50 a week. With a friend, he took his earnings and bought a 1934 Rolls Royce for $350 and rented it out for $35 a day. By the time he was sixteen years old, he had already accumulated some $6,000. That was in 1946.

Nearly twenty years later, in 1965, Buffett launched what is today known as Berkshire Hathaway, a holding company with a diverse portfolio of investments, including large positions in such well-known global companies as Coca-Cola, Gillette, and American Express, along with outright ownership of such smaller businesses as See's Candies and the Nebraska Furniture Mart. These smaller, often more local, companies sell everything from shoes to jewelry to candy to furniture to encyclopedias. Not only is Buffett an amazing stock picker and investor, he's also a master sales-

man. The day before Berksh.   annual meeting takes
place, he opens Borsheim's Jew   attendees can buy a
bauble or two, while at the meetin.   s of See's Candies
are on sale.

So what are the investment strategi.   rica's second
richest man? In a word: simplicity.

It's not clear whether he, or his like-minded .   ent guru,
Peter Lynch, said it, but both men espouse the strateg. of buying
companies any idiot can run because "sooner or later one will."

You don't need to be a computer genius—and Warren Buffett would be the first to admit he isn't—to appreciate the simple
concept of having a big position in a company like Coca-Cola, the
world's most recognized trademark. You don't need to be a
"techie" to appreciate the value of a company like Gillette. Almost
every day on this planet, in almost every country, almost every
man and many women engage in some form of shaving. Buffett
has a big position in Gillette. "It's far better to own a significant
portion of the Hope diamond," he observes, "than 100 percent of
a rhinestone." He sees his Cokes and Gillettes as rare gems.

While he wins more than he loses, Buffett is modest enough
to admit when he makes a mistake. A recent Berkshire Hathaway
annual report has a section called "Mistake Du Jour." For example, he sold 10 million shares of Cap Cities in 1993 for $63, only
to watch the shares dramatically rise thereafter. "I make more mistakes when I have a lot of cash around," he admits. "You're
tempted to do things with it."

He also sold out too soon on his investment in Disney. "In
the 1960s, the entire Walt Disney Company was selling for only
$80 million. At that time, they put $17 million into their new
pirate ride. So the company was selling at only five times [its]
rides. We took a stake for $5 million and sold it a year later for $6
million. Had we kept it, that $5 million would have been worth
over a billion dollars in the mid-1990s."

As big as Berkshire gets, it never loses Buffett's personal
touch. He likes smaller, privately-held companies whose owners
have built successful businesses and wish to stay on to manage
those concerns. While he does meticulously analyze the financial
health of these companies, he also believes it's imperative to like
the people involved. "We do things we enjoy with people we like,"
he writes in a recent annual report.

He says he never thinks about what the stock market is going
to do. "I think about what the company is going to do. If I buy the

right kind of business, with the right kind of people, then I'll be right over time. It's more important to be in the right business. I want to own good businesses, run by good managers." Buffett, with a keen wit, enjoys presiding over the annual shareholders meetings, where he has a chance to pass on his investment wisdom. When asked why so many directors of Berkshire Hathaway are named Buffett (one of them is Susan, his wife; another is Howard, his son), he replied, "It's good for family harmony."

And how much of his great wealth does he plan to pass on to his children? "Leave your children enough money so they can do anything but not do nothing."

Buffett makes it all sound so simple. And, in a certain sense, it is. As he writes, "It's probably true that hard work never killed anyone, but I figure, why take the chance."

By February 1996, Buffett's soaring Berkshire Hathaway stocks—which had risen 46 percent in 1995—had pushed his wealth to $16.6 billion, ahead of Bill Gates, making him the wealthiest man in the world.

40

Claus Spreckels

(1828–1908)

Sweet Success

Est. wealth: $50 million

Claus Spreckels was a fierce and dominant force in the West Coast sugar business, fighting off rivals and gaining control over plantations and productions to become "Sugar King of the West."

When the eighteen-year-old Spreckels emigrated to America from Hanover, Germany, in 1846, he started working in the grocery business in South Carolina. It was there he met his wife, Anna Christiana Mangel, in 1852. He eventually bought the grocery store but sold it in 1855 to open a grocery and retail store in New York City with his brother. In 1856, the two Spreckels brothers followed the Gold Rush to California, where they opened another grocery and retail store in San Francisco.

By 1863, after a stint in the brewing business, Spreckels entered the sugar business where he was to make his fame and fortune. Tapping the supply of sugar cane from the Hawaiian Islands, he established the Bay Sugar Refining Company. By turning west for their resources, he created a sugar business that was independent of the powerful established Eastern sugar companies.

Two years later, Spreckels sold the business and spent the next two years in Europe studying all phases of sugar production. He returned to California in 1867 and built the largest sugar refinery on the Pacific Coast. Within five years, the plant was processing more than 50 million pounds of sugar per year.

Spreckels was a pioneer in the industry. He patented a new process for making hard, or "loaf," sugar in 1874. He also was an early experimenter in the sugar beet industry, establishing sugar beet ranches in California.

In 1876, Spreckels faced a crisis when U.S. regulators, under pressure from American sugar growers in Hawaii, planned to allow Hawaiian sugar to be imported duty-free. The move would have expanded sugar manufacturing in Hawaii, undermining Spreckels's West Coast business. Before the reciprocity treaty with Hawaii was ratified, Spreckels bought up most of the year's sugar crop in Hawaii. He also established his own forty-thousand-acre sugar plantation, the largest plantation in Hawaii. With control of much of Hawaii's sugar cane production, Spreckels then bought a fleet of ships between Honolulu and San Francisco, cornering sugar transportation between the Islands and the West Coast.

With his control over the supply of raw material secured, Spreckels then turned his attention to dominating the West Coast refining business. By 1884, he had used his control over sugar cane farming and transportation to drive most of the smaller refiners out of business, and he acquired a one-third interest in his largest rival, American Sugar Refining Company. Spreckels had gained a virtual monopoly over sugar production and could dictate prices to the Hawaiian growers.

His enterprise also was large enough to attract the interest of the established East Coast sugar producers. In 1885, Spreckels refused to join the East Coast sugar trust, which sought to create a national sugar monopoly on the scale of Standard Oil. After Spreckels's rejection, the East Coast trust bought American Sugar Refining, sparking a bitter war with Spreckels.

A fierce fighter, Spreckels launched a frontal attack into the heart of the trust's East Coast stronghold. In 1889, the trust found a $3 million state-of-the-art Spreckels sugar plant in Philadelphia. The price wars that followed eroded the fortunes of the Sugar Trust and Spreckels. They called a truce in 1890, giving Spreckels control over the West Coast and the trust control over the East Coast.

To keep his products flowing to his factories and to market, Spreckels built railroad lines between San Francisco and Salinas, California. Then, with the same fighting spirit he showed against the Sugar Trust, he took on the railroad monopoly. He helped finance the San Francisco & San Joaquin Railway (which later was absorbed into the Santa Fe) to compete against the powerful Southern Pacific. Then, concerned about the dominance of San Francisco Gas & Electric, he organized his own power company, forcing his larger rival to improve service and reduce rates. Spreckels used the same tactics in the city transit business, undermining the strength of the transit monopoly and reducing fares.

Spreckels's sons inherited his fighting spirit. Claus Jr., who was in charge of the Philadelphia plant at the time of Spreckels's pact with the Sugar Trust, refused to go along with the arrangement. Spreckels dismissed him from the plant, leading to what would later become a family and business feud that threatened to undermine Spreckels's empire.

In 1893, Claus Jr. and another son, Rudolph, sued for control of the holding company that managed Spreckels's Hawaiian operations. After a year of bitter wrangling, Claus and Rudolph were given control of the land in an out-of-court settlement. The two renegade sons reorganized the company, but they were forced to sell shares over the years to raise money. A rival Hawaiian grower accumulated enough shares to throw out the Spreckels brothers in 1898. By 1905, the two renegade sons were back in the fold, and Rudolph was made the manager of his father's business. The elder Spreckels purchased a marble mansion on Fifth Avenue near Seventy-sixth Street in 1906. He died two years later at the age of eighty, leaving a fortune estimated by the *New York Times* at $50 million. His son Rudolph lost most of his $30 million fortune in the stock market crash of 1929 and died in modest circumstances three decades later in 1958.

41

George Peabody
(1795–1869)
Spanning the Atlantic
Est. wealth: $16 million

When George Peabody was born in 1795, in the town in Massachusetts that now bears his name, the Revolution was only a little more than a decade past and the War of 1812 was nearly two decades away. In a time of transition, Peabody became a financial bridge between England and America. He brought much-needed European capital into the new American republic and served as an unofficial U.S. ambassador to Europe. He was respected and beloved for his business acumen and generous philanthropy on both sides of the Atlantic.

Peabody was born in New England in extreme poverty and left school to work at age eleven. By 1814, he was serving as manager of a wholesale dry goods warehouse in Baltimore. He soon became a partner in the company and frequently traveled abroad on purchasing trips. In 1835, when the state of Maryland was on the brink of bankruptcy, he helped arrange for an $8 million loan in Europe to rescue the state. Unlike other gold diggers who benefited from the public misfortune, Peabody refused to take a commission for arranging the loan. It was the first of many such acts of generosity.

Two years later, he settled in London to build his financial firm, George Peabody & Company. Although he lived his life in England, Peabody was a strong supporter of American securities and businesses, helping to secure needed capital for the U.S. government and American firms. Peabody successfully competed with the powerful Rothschilds and Barings for sales of American securities. He also had the foresight to recruit Junius Spencer Morgan as a partner in 1854. Morgan would later help found one of the most powerful financial houses in the United States, run by his son, J. P. Morgan.

The Panic of 1837 and subsequent financial crises in the United States undermined investors' faith in American securities. Three U.S. banking houses in London suspended payments, and later nine U.S. states stopped payments on their European debts. Peabody, widely respected in London, stepped in to restore confidence in the creditworthiness of America. Peabody invested in U.S. companies and in the Bank of the United States at a time when few investors had confidence in the young nation's financial stability. His confidence proved well founded, and he sold his holdings at a large profit.

The serious and taciturn Peabody often worked ten-hour days, and frequently worked on Sundays. He rarely took a day off, until he was slowed down by gout and rheumatism. Although the blue-eyed, dark-haired millionaire may have been one of London's most eligible bachelor's, Peabody never married. When he was forty-three, he almost married a nineteen-year-old American, but she backed out of the wedding. He kept a mistress in Brighton, England, with whom he had a daughter.

Peabody was a pioneering philanthropist. Before Andrew Carnegie's "Gospel of Wealth" made philanthropy more popular, and before tax laws made it less painful, Peabody disposed of more than half of his $16 million fortune in acts of charity. Peabody was particularly interested in donating money for education. Perhaps this concern reflected his own regret over his interrupted schooling and his view of education; it was, as he once said, "a debt due from present to future generations."

His benefactions included small gifts, such as the $15,000 needed to ensure that American products appeared in the world exposition in 1851 or $10,000 to equip the *Advance* to search for lost Arctic explorer Sir John Franklin. His gifts also included such substantial donations as the $3.5 million Peabody Education Fund to support schooling in the South and a $1.5 million gift to found the Peabody Institute in Baltimore. On the other side of the Atlantic, he contributed $2.5 million toward creating clean, low-rent tenements for poor workmen and their families in London.

Although he spent much of his life in England, Peabody never gave up his U.S. citizenship or his fierce commitment to his native land. England and America fell over themselves to express their gratitude and respect for Peabody's contributions. He received a gold medal from Congress for establishing the Peabody Education Fund, and he was the first American to be honored with the Freedom of the City of London (later given to Dwight D. Eisenhower).

As a sign of how high Peabody was esteemed on both sides of the Atlantic, when he died in 1869 at the age of seventy-four, there were two funerals. First, his English friends packed into Westminster Abbey in London to grieve his passing. It was an unprecedented treatment for a non-British subject. Then his body was sent home on the British ship, HMS *Monarch.* By special order of President Grant, the transcontinental funeral procession was accompanied by the American ship, USS *Plymouth.* American friends attended his funeral at Harmony Grove Cemetery in Salem, Massachusetts.

Number 42 is Charles Crocker, one of the "Big Four" who built the Central Pacific Railroad (see page 111).

43

William Andrews Clark

(1839–1925)

Montana Copper King
Est. wealth: $150–$200 million

William Andrews Clark made his fortune in the Montana copper mines, finding value in the metal that many other miners had
overlooked in their search for gold. He became a U.S. senator, a
founder of the state of Montana, and one of its most prominent
citizens.

Clark was born on a farm in Fayette County, Pennsylvania,
and his family moved to Iowa when he was seventeen. After a stint
at Iowa Wesleyan, Clark left the farm to become a schoolteacher at
eighteen. A short time later, he left teaching, drawn to the gold
and silver mines of Colorado, where he went to work in 1862 at
the age of twenty-three. In 1863, he moved to the Montana Terri-

tory where he scraped $1,500 in gold dust from the rivers of Jeff Davis Gulch. He used his profits to establish a general store.

After taking a trip on horseback to the Pacific coast to buy goods, he obtained a contract to carry the mail on the trails between Missoula and Walla Walla, Washington. The mail route ran through hostile Indian territory. Usually Clark had an express rider who delivered the mails, but on more than one occasion he rode the route himself.

He used his growing fortune to buy a stake in several abandoned gold mines. Then he took a year off to study mining at the Columbia School of Mines in New York—learning about geology and mineralogy. What he learned made him realize that many of the Montana miners, in their quest for gold, were throwing away valuable copper and silver. Clark bought up discarded gold mines and soon was mining silver and copper out of them.

Using these earnings, he moved into banking, real estate, timber, water power, and cattle ranching. By the time he was thirty-four, he was a millionaire.

Clark became active in Montana politics and presided over the constitutional convention that achieved Montana statehood in 1889. Clark was one of the two leading figures in Montana politics. The other was his bitter rival, Marcus Daly, who had discovered the highly profitable Anaconda Mine. After Montana was admitted to the Union as a state, Clark thought he would easily win a seat in the Senate. But Daly put his substantial political and financial clout behind another candidate—an unknown by the name of Thomas H. Carter, who defeated Clark in the 1888 nomination.

The two fought again over the Senate seat in 1893, using some of the dirtiest campaigns in American political history. They passed out thousands of dollars in bribes, and finally in 1898 Clark achieved the prize he sought. Then, before he could take his seat in the Senate, the scandal over the bribery used by Clark and Daly in the election erupted—with charges that Clark had paid $430,000 to the Montana legislature (which made the Senate appointments in those days). With the seat almost in his grasp, Clark was forced to resign.

Later that year, Clark was appointed by Montana's acting governor to fill an unexpired term in the Senate, and he won reelection in 1901. Senator Clark was the richest of the twenty-six millionaires who served in the Senate at the time. He owned all of his properties outright. And at the height of his success, he was believed to be drawing in $1 million per month from his holdings.

Daly and Clark also clashed over the site for Montana's capital. Daly wanted it to be in the town of Anaconda, which he had founded. But Clark backed Helena, and he eventually won out.

Clark was known for his persistence and intense energy. While he was in Congress, he had almost no staff, responding to countless letters personally. At seventy, he still traveled down to Wall Street on the subway. He was refined and fastidious, and he usually worked independently, trusting his own judgment.

Like other men of his time, he moved to New York's Fifth Avenue, building a gaudy mansion that became known as "Clark's Folly." Clark declared that he would build the most expensive and beautiful mansion of all the extravagant homes on the avenue, spending more than $7 million on a house near the corner of Seventy-seventh Street. The structure incorporated every classical style of architecture, and one journalist sniffed that it would be "the ideal dwelling for the late Mr. Barnum." The mansion was soon filled with an expensive art collection, which included works by Rubens, Titian, Rembrandt, and Van Dyck as well as collections of rare Beauvais tapestries and antique lace and rugs, which were later bequeathed to the Corcoran Gallery of Art.

A year after his first wife died, Clark took in a "ward" at his New York mansion, a sixteen-year-old from Butte, Montana. It soon became apparent that his concern for Anna LaChapelle was more than paternalistic. He moved her to Paris where she bore him two children. Five years later, in 1901, he made her the second Mrs. Clark.

Clark left a fortune estimated at more than $150 million to his eight children. His son, William A. Clark, Jr., helped lead many of his father's enterprises and took over the business at the age of forty-eight after his father's death in 1925. Three years later, the younger Clark retired from business to devote himself to philanthropy.

Rich, but Not Rich Enough

P. T. Barnum

(1810–1891)

NOT QUITE THE GREATEST SHOW ON EARTH

Although William Andrews Clark's Fifth Avenue mansion may have been the perfect Barnum residence, Barnum couldn't have afforded it. Clark's home cost more than Barnum's entire $4 million fortune. There may have been a sucker born every minute, but there weren't quite enough to admit P. T. Barnum to the Wealthy 100. Barnum was one of the wealthiest men in New York, but the man who hawked the tallest and the shortest finds himself a tad shy of the superlative when it comes to comparisons of wealth. He left his estate to his grandson on the condition that the young man continue to use the Barnum name. For $4 million, his heir was more than happy to comply.

44

George Eastman

(1854–1932)

A Million-Dollar Smile

Est. wealth: $95 million

What Henry Ford did for automobiles George Eastman did for photography. He took cameras out of the hands of professionals and put them into the hands of average citizens. Millions of Americans bought his Kodak box cameras and film, making photography a part of everyday life and the Kodak company a household name.

Eastman, an only child, was born in Waterville, New York, in 1854. His father was a penmanship teacher who founded the first commercial college in Rochester, New York. He died when Eastman was eight, and his mother took in boarders to support the family. By seventh grade, Eastman had quit school to help the family by working at a variety of jobs. He went to work at a bank and became a junior bookkeeper at Rochester Savings Bank, where he rapidly advanced through the organization.

In 1877, at twenty-three, Eastman was planning a trip to Santo Domingo. A friend suggested he make a photographic record of the trip. Eastman was intrigued. He went out and bought $94 worth of equipment and chemicals he would need to take pictures. The trip fell through, but Eastman developed a life-long interest in photography.

The process of creating photos at that time was very cumbersome and expensive. Photos were produced using a "wet plate." A glass plate was dipped in chemicals and the picture had to be taken and developed before the chemicals dried. Eastman's first challenge was to create a dry plate. He worked through the night in his kitchen laboratory, mixing chemicals in his sink and going to work at the bank in the daytime. By 1880 his midnight experiments had produced a dry plate, using a surface protected by gelatin, for which he secured patents in the United States and England.

With this dry plate and just $3,000 in savings, he gave his notice at the bank and left to start the Eastman Dry Plate Company. With partner Henry Strong, a buggy whip manufacturer, Eastman opened his new business on January 1, 1881, in a small, rented third floor of a factory in Rochester.

The platemaking process was so sensitive that several times Eastman faced near disaster when the delicate chemicals failed to work. At one point, he could not produce a single good plate. Desperate to fulfill his orders, and unable to solve the problem, Eastman swallowed his pride and went to England, where he bought a formula from the leading British platemaker. He used this formula to restart his plant and to meet the growing demand for his products. (He later discovered the problem with his formula was that he had switched the type of gelatin used in the process.)

Eastman kept looking for ways to simplify the process of shooting and developing photos. By 1888, he had invented a film that could be rolled that replaced the fragile glass plates. Then he created a simple camera to use the film, which he called Kodak. (Eastman liked the letter *K*, and he made up the name for his new product.) The camera sold for $25 and was marketed with the slogan, "You Press the Button, We Do the Rest." Photographers shot their roll of one hundred shots, then sent the film—camera and all—back to the factory. There it was reloaded and sent back with the developed prints for a fee of $10.

Eastman continued to innovate. One of his chemists came up with a celluloid film to replace the old paper-backed rolls. Now the cameras didn't need to be sent back to the factory. Thomas Edison, working on motion pictures, sent for a sample of the new celluloid film, and began using this transparent film in his movie productions.

Eastman founded one of the most enduring and successful U.S. companies, which is still a leader in the film and camera industry to this day. The Eastman Kodak Company ultimately controlled more than 80 percent of the photography market. Eastman built the 480-acre Kodak Park headquarters in Rochester, New York, and by 1990 there were three thousand employees. At the time of Eastman's death in 1932, he had nearly ten thousand employees working at Kodak Park and another Rochester plant. He also had manufacturing operations in Tennessee as well as in England, France, Germany, Australia, and Hungary.

Eastman, a lifelong bachelor who had no heirs, gave away almost all of his $75 million fortune to charity, particularly to the city of Rochester, to MIT, and to the University of Rochester. He stepped down as president of his company in 1923 at the age of sixty-nine and served as chairman until his death. When he was stricken with a painful spinal ailment, he committed suicide in 1932 at the age of seventy-seven. In the note found beside his body, he wrote, "To my friends: My work is done. Why wait?"

45

Charles L. Tiffany

(1812–1902)

A Real Gem

Est. wealth: $35 million

In the movie *Breakfast at Tiffany's*, the character played by Audrey Hepburn explains that whenever she feels worried, she goes to Tiffany's. "It calms me down right away, the quietness and the proud look of it," says Holly Golightly. "Nothing very bad could happen to you there." Charles Tiffany, founder of the store, must have felt the same way when he looked at it more than a century before. The store he started at the age of twenty-five made him the leader of jewelry and fashion among New York's rising monied elite and made him a part of its ranks with a fortune estimated at $35 million.

Charles Tiffany's business did not have a very auspicious beginning. In the midst of a depression in 1837, he borrowed $1,000 from his father, a cotton manufacturer in Connecticut, to move to New York City. He and a friend set up a small store, stocking unusual "notions," including Chinese and Japanese items. After three days, they had earned a grand total of $4.98.

Soon, they began specializing in elegant glassware and jewelry. As a result of turmoil in Europe, Tiffany and his partners bought world-renowned jewelry at discount prices, including a necklace once owned by Marie Antoinette and the royal jewels of Hungarian Prince Esterhazy.

With its shelves stocked with diamonds and other European jewelry, Tiffany's soon found a ready market for its merchandise. A flood of gold-laden miners were streaming back to the city from California, and other wealthy citizens from across the nation were moving into rows of magnificent mansions lining Fifth Avenue.

Tiffany & Company rose to become the leading jewelry business in America, serving streams of foreign monarchs. Tiffany was commissioned by P. T. Barnum to build a tiny silver chariot as a wedding present for midgets General Tom Thumb and Lavinia Warren.

Tiffany had no experience in making jewelry, but he knew how to run a business. He instituted a policy of marking fixed prices on his items. By raising the standards for jewelry in America, Tiffany helped to establish the height of taste and fashion for generations of Americans.

Tiffany was a master of elegant and understated advertising. He also knew how to take advantage of an opportunity. When the trans-Atlantic cable was completed, Tiffany bought fragments of discarded cable from the project and turned it into commemorative paperweights and umbrella handles.

During the Civil War, Tiffany's craftsmanship shimmered on the jewel-encrusted hilt of the sword of General Ulysses S. Grant, and young women carried Tiffany lockets bearing the images of soldiers in the field. But the demands of the war ultimately forced Tiffany's factory to convert from producing jewelry to making military supplies. Tiffany was such a respected force in design that when the U.S. government redesigned its Great Seal in 1885, it commissioned Tiffany's for the project.

Tiffany's service to the wealthy and powerful of the world resulted in many honors. He received the Chevalier of the Legion of Honor from France and the medal Praemia Digno from the Czar of Russia. But one of the most lasting tributes came from Dr. George Frederick Kunz. Kunz, a world gem expert and longtime Tiffany employee, discovered a rare phosphorescent blue Brazilian diamond. In honor of the man whose name has become synonymous with fine gems, Kunz named his new find tiffanyite.

Tiffany's wife, Olivia, sister of his first partner, died in 1897. When Tiffany died in 1902 at the age of ninety, he was survived by four of his six children. Today, Tiffany & Company remains the premier jeweler in America. After a management buyout and public offering in 1984, Tiffany's began a phase of rapid expansion. By 1994, it had expanded to more than eighty-four stores in fourteen countries, with revenues of more than $682 million. The company that Tiffany founded is now in the hands of thousands of individual investors.

46

Thomas Fortune Ryan

(1851–1928)

New York Transit King

Est. wealth: $155–$200 million

The dominant force in New York transit and the creator of the first U.S. holding company, Thomas Fortune Ryan became one of the wealthiest and most powerful men in American business.

Ryan was born in 1851 on a small farm in Virginia. By the age of fourteen, he was orphaned and penniless. At seventeen, he made his way to Baltimore, where he wandered the streets looking for work. Ryan finally found a job as an errand boy at a dry-goods company owned by John S. Barry. In 1872, at the age of twenty-one, he moved to New York where he became a messenger in a Wall Street firm.

His fortune improved after he married Barry's daughter, a year later. With his father-in-law's help, Ryan became a partner in his own brokerage firm and bought a seat on the Stock Exchange. With the help of his corrupt Tammany Hall connections, Ryan was successful on Wall Street. Over six feet tall, the blue-eyed Ryan was a distinguished and imposing presence on the Street. He soon developed such power in New York that a journalist commented that "mayors are his office boys, governors come and go at his call . . . Tammany Hall is a dog for his hunting."

After his success in investment, Ryan built his empire in transit (or "traction" as it was called then). In 1883, at thirty-two, he joined with William Collins Whitney to seize control of one of the key city lines. Their rival, Jacob Sharp, had outbribed them for city approval to build new lines, distributing half a million dollars to the so-called "boodle" aldermen. After losing, Ryan and Whitney adopted a holier-than-thou attitude and exposed Sharp's bribery. City officials were ousted in disgrace. Then, the two upstarts bought the Broadway franchise from the ruined Sharp—for a twentieth of what Sharp had paid for it.

Ryan and Whitney continued to expand their transit empire, creating the Metropolitan Traction Company in 1886, the first holding company in U.S. history. Ryan described the company as a "tin box" to hold their various securities. He continued to fill up this box by acquiring new rail lines, watering stocks, and hiring his own companies as contractors at exorbitant prices. He added banking, public utilities, and industrial enterprises. In the late 1890s, he and Whitney also entered the tobacco industry, gaining a near monopoly.

In 1904, Ryan bought control of the Washington Life Insurance Company and then moved on to take control of Equitable. His most exotic adventure was heading into the Congo, where he was asked by King Leopold of Belgium to help reorganize and develop his African properties. Ryan helped establish diamond, gold, and copper mines, receiving a one-quarter share. Again Ryan was at the center of controversy, facing charges that he was profiting off human slavery. Ryan had no regrets. In response to a reporter, Ryan commented, "I sleep like a baby. I don't remember ever having been in better health or spirits."

Scandals and disaster followed Ryan at every turn, but he always seemed to wriggle free of any financial or criminal actions. An outcry occurred when it was revealed that Ryan invested millions of Washington Life's assets in his own banks. Ryan, well connected politically, helped calm the waters by appointing former President Grover Cleveland and other respected leaders to control the life insurance company.

In 1905, Ryan faced a new threat to his transit lines. Financier August Belmont had created a competing subway system in the city. After a prolonged battle, the two systems were merged into the $200 million Interborough-Metropolitan Company. A year later, Ryan cashed out of the transit business, just in time. The Metropolitan went into receivership in 1907. When the receiver picked through the wreckage, he found a trail of deceit, mismanagement, and outright theft. Of one $35 million bond issue, the receiver found that $15 million was unaccounted for and another $20 million had been spent recklessly. Whitney, who died in 1904, escaped the scandal, and Ryan, who lived, somehow managed to continue on unscathed.

So powerful was Ryan in American business and politics that at the 1912 Democratic Convention, candidate William Jennings Bryan openly accused Ryan of manipulating the presidential nomination process to get his candidates nominated. Bryan forced through a resolution opposing the nomination of any candidate backed by Ryan, August Belmont, or J. P. Morgan.

Ryan retired to his comfortable Fifth Avenue mansion in New York, bordered by a private statue garden that covered a third of a block. His mansion was filled with one of the finest collections of Limoges enamels, along with tapestries, bronzes, and other artwork.

Ryan was just as unconstrained in his personal life as he was in business. When his wife died in 1917 when he was sixty-six, he remarried just two weeks later. It earned him the lifelong animosity of his eldest son, Allan, who called his father's speedy remarriage "disgraceful." Allan, a successful broker and president of Stutz Motors, later lost his entire fortune when he tried to corner Stutz stock. Ryan offered no help as he watched his son declare bankruptcy. And, although Ryan divided his estate among his widow and other children at his death, Allan was cut off, left with only a pair of pearl shirt studs. (His brother and sister later gave him $50,000 per year from their own share of the inheritance.)

When he died in 1928 at the age of seventy-seven, Ryan's estate was appraised at $135 million, although his actual worth was estimated at $200 million or higher. An Irish Catholic, he had donated $20 million to the Roman Catholic Church (some said, to atone for his sins). With his six children and many grandchildren, Ryan's estate was carved into a total of fifty-four pieces and was soon widely dispersed among many heirs. Ryan, with typical contempt and control, provided in his will that any heir who complained about his inheritance would lose it.

47

Edward Stephen Harkness

(1874–1940)

Oil Fortune's Son

Est. wealth: $155 million

Edward Stephen Harkness's father was one of the founding partners of Standard Oil. Stephen V. Harkness was a whiskey tycoon whose daughter married Henry Flagler, one of the driving forces in Standard Oil's progress. Harkness invested $90,000 in Standard Oil, and the value of his share was mounting into the millions when he died in 1888. He left his holdings to his wife and sons, and they made over $100 million from Standard Oil, although none of them was active in the business.

Edward, the youngest of the four children, was fourteen when his father died. He became most closely identified with the Harkness fortune because he spent most of his life giving it away. His older brother, Charles, carefully managed the investments, and the family fortune continued to grow. When Charles died in 1916, when Edward was forty-two, Edward and his mother set up the Commonwealth Fund, with an initial endowment of $10 million. This fund supported children's health and child guidance programs, rural hospitals, and education, at first in Britain, and later around the world.

Harkness was a serious and orderly man who balanced a desire for careful use of his funds with a generous spirit. On one occasion, he held up a dollar, saying, "A dollar misspent is a dollar lost." But when a friend was advising him against a particularly generous donation, Harkness replied, "What's the use of having money if you can't have the fun of spending it?" Few of his dollars were misspent, but he certainly had fun spending them.

His gifts reflected his personal interests and insights. In addition to many gifts to the Presbyterian Church, children's health, and education, he also made at least two gifts that had a significant impact on medical schools and university life. He helped give us the teaching hospital and the residential college.

Harkness, who had long been interested in medicine, was one of the early proponents of the idea of a teaching hospital. He had offered the idea, and the cash to make it happen, to one institution that turned him down. Then Presbyterian Medical Center and Columbia University accepted the plan. In 1911, he gave $1.3 million to create the Columbia-Presbyterian Medical Center in New York City. He later donated a twenty-two-acre site in Washington Heights for the institution.

His next idea was to decentralize universities into smaller residential colleges to allow for more personal relationships between teachers and students. He knew from his own experience as a shy student at Yale how intimidating the large university could be. He offered the idea to Yale, but they weren't interested. Harvard took him up on the idea and the "house plan" was established there, with a gift of $13 million from Harkness. Yale later relented, and Harkness set up a similar system of colleges at Yale.

His contributions ranged from supporting the Shakespeare Memorial Theater in Stratford-on-Avon, England, to purchasing a collection of Egyptian treasures for the Metropolitan Museum of Art in New York. He also showed his love for Great Britain by establishing a $10 million trust fund for charitable purposes in the British Isles.

In all, Edward Stephen Harkness had given away $130 million of his fortune during his lifetime. His philanthropy was supported by his wife, Mary Emma Stillman, whom he married when he was thirty. They had no children. Harkness left the income from his remaining $55 million estate to Mary when he died in 1940 at the age of sixty-six. After her death in 1954, the Harkness estate was divided among the Commonwealth Fund, Presbyterian Hospital in New York City, and other charities. Her personal $20 million fortune was left to four heirs.

48

Henry M. Flagler
(1830–1913)
The Ponce de Leon of Florida Resorts
Est. wealth: $60 million

Henry M. Flager, the brains behind Rockefeller's Standard Oil empire, is perhaps best known for his vision of building an American Riviera on the Florida coast. He reshaped Florida into a playground for the wealthy and became one of its most colorful and wealthy citizens.

Flagler didn't start out throwing around millions or courting wealthy tourists in their private railway cars. The son of a poor Presbyterian minister, he headed out on the Erie Canal to seek his fortune when he was fourteen. It took him a few years, but he found it. He moved to Ohio with 9 cents to his name and started working at the L. G. Harkness Mercantile Shop for $5 per month. Within seven years, he had become the leading salesman in the company and a partner drawing a salary of $400 per year. At the age of twenty-three, he married the boss's daughter, Mary Harkness.

In 1850, Flagler entered the grain and liquor business in Bellevue, Ohio. By the time the Civil War broke out, he was wealthy enough to pay a "second" to serve in his place. He later took his $50,000 savings and made a disastrous investment in salt manufacturing in Michigan. He lost his entire fortune and went another $50,000 into the hole. He was destitute—even poorer than when he had started. He worked a menial job selling wood and went hungry all day to feed his wife and child at night. In 1866, he moved his family to Cleveland to look for opportunity. He found more opportunity than he could have dreamed of in the person of John D. Rockefeller, whom Flagler had met during his earlier work as a grain salesman.

Rockefeller was just entering the oil business, and Flagler had a lot of ideas for how they could gain control of the industry. He soon became Rockefeller's closest and most trusted adviser. They moved into homes near one another on Euclid Avenue in Cleveland, attended the same church, and walked together each morning to the office. Flagler used to say it was a good deal better to have a friendship founded on business than a business founded on friendship.

Together Flagler and Rockefeller built Standard Oil into the most ruthless, dominant, and successful player in the new oil industry, through backroom deals with railroads and strong-arm tactics against smaller rivals. In testimony before Congress, Rockefeller gave Flagler the credit for envisioning Standard Oil, saying, "I wish I'd had the brains to think of it."

In 1876, Flagler was already worth $6 million when he took his first trip to Florida. His wife of twenty-three years had fallen ill after the birth of their son, Henry. Flagler, a devoted husband, took her to St. Augustine to recuperate. During their two weeks there, Flagler noticed that land was cheap and the accommodations were not nearly as wonderful as the climate. It was the first germ of the idea that would bring him back to conquer Florida a decade later.

When his wife died in 1881, the fifty-one-year-old Flagler reentered society, accompanied by Ida Alice Shourds, the redheaded nurse who had cared for his ailing wife (and her lonely husband). Flagler and Shourds threw huge parties at his forty-room mansion on Long Island named Satan's Toe. To silence the gossips, Flagler married Ida, eighteen years his junior, in 1883. They returned to St. Augustine for their honeymoon, and Flagler once again was inspired to begin planning his southern empire. Five years later, Flagler opened his first hotel, the 540-room Ponce de Leon in St. Augustine.

Flagler was as ruthless in building his Florida empire as he was in establishing Standard Oil. In 1894, Flagler finished constructing the Royal Poinciana Hotel on Palm Beach Island—then an outpost in the Florida wilderness. Nearly a thousand workers had labored day and night to prepare the hotel for the winter tourist season. Eleven men died in the backbreaking work, but the hotel was completed. Flagler invited all the black laborers to a huge party on the mainland, but while they enjoyed the celebration, Flagler ordered their shanty town burned to the ground so that the millionaire guests at his luxury hotel wouldn't have to put up with the view of the thatched-roof village. Feigning concern after the accidental fire, Flagler offered to sell the laborers land on the mainland in what is now West Palm Beach, establishing a source of menial workers to serve his bustling hotel.

Flagler also built rail lines across the Everglades and across the ocean to his new Florida resorts. He laid tracks from Jacksonville, then extended them to Palm Beach, and finally to Miami. He was now below the frost line, so he could run oranges up the lines to the North at the same time he brought tourists to the South. In 1912, he stretched his rail lines across a string of islands in the Florida Keys. The rail line crossed fifty miles on the mainland, followed by more than one hundred miles of island hopping. The southward progress of the railroad was only stopped when he reached the last island, Key West. Even then, he dredged the Miami harbor and set up a steamship line to Nassau.

At each stop along the way, he built huge resorts. The Ponce de Leon hotel rose up in St. Augustine, the Breakers in Palm Beach, and the Royal Palm in Miami. As Florida's popularity rose, the flow of vacationers increased. Soon the "Florida Specials" were running down at high speed from New York, a thirty-hour trip. The private rail cars of the very wealthy were seen lined up at Flagler's new elegant winter resorts.

The Poinciana and Flagler's other resorts soon were the destination of the luxury cars of the very rich—the Rockefellers, the

Vanderbilts, and Carnegies arrived on the rail line Flagler constructed through the jungle. The Poinciana, with room for 1,750 guests and unheard of rates of $100 per night, became renowned for the no-holds-barred abandon of its parties. The Poinciana held drag costume parties and Flagler often showed up as Marie Antoinette. He once appeared during a "Washington Ball" dressed as Martha Washington, his walrus mustache and cigar blossoming from his otherwise matronly gown trimmed with tiny silk flags.

As Ida's behavior became increasingly bizarre, Flagler took a beautiful new mistress, Mary Lily Kenan, a classical singer and pianist from a well-to-do Southern family, who was thirty-seven years younger than Flagler. Increasingly delusional and antagonistic, Ida threatened to kill Henry and run off with her lover—"the czar of Russia." As her behavior grew increasingly violent, Flagler finally had her committed to the Choate Sanitorium outside of New York.

With his second wife tucked away comfortably in an asylum, Flagler then proposed to Mary Lily, with a $1 million string of Oriental pearls and diamonds as an engagement present. There was just one small problem: divorce was not legal in the state of New York.

Flagler began rounding up political, media, and business influence to get the divorce he needed. After changing his address to Florida (where divorce was legal only on grounds of adultery), Flagler passed out more than $125,000 in bribes to the governor and Florida legislature to pass a new law in 1901 allowing divorce on the grounds of "incurable insanity." The same afternoon, Flagler filed for divorce from Ida. (He also signed over $2.3 million in securities and property to provide for her throughout her life, as required by the law.) Just ten days later, after the divorce was finalized, the seventy-one-year-old Flagler married his thirty-four-year-old mistress.

Flagler gave his new bride $3 million in bonds and cash as a wedding gift, and they lived in Whitehall, the grand mansion of marble Flagler had built for Mary Lily on Palm Beach's Lake Worth. They threw parties that were again the talk of Palm Beach, and the extravagant Mary Lily made the *Guinness Book of World Records* for never wearing the same dress twice to her many parties.

Flagler died in 1913, five days after he was knocked down a flight of marble steps in their mansion by a set of newfangled pneumatic doors Mary Lily had installed. After his funeral, Mary Lily was heralded as the richest woman in America, inheriting a fortune estimated between $60 and $100 million. But the life of the richest widow was a lonely one, and three years later, Mary Lily married an old college flame, Kentucky lawyer Robert Bingham.

Bingham, deep in debt, was perceived by the Kenans as a golddigger. He had signed a prenuptial agreement giving up the rights to Mary Lily's fortune, but she gave him a gift with a trunk filled with $1 million, and he promptly wired the money out to his many creditors. Soon, Bingham virtually abandoned his new wife, spending most of his time out of town. Bingham hired a doctor to treat her for "heart disease" with morphine and cocaine injections. Mary Lily was found dead in her bath in 1917. A month before her death, Bingham had convinced her to sign a codicil to her will giving him $5 million of her estate. The bulk of her $150 million estate still went to her cousin, Louise Wise.

When the codicil to the will came to light, Mary Lily's family contested it and charged Bingham with murdering her. A long and bitter trial ensued, with the Kenans hiring investigators to ransack Bingham's office and exhume Mary Lily's body to prove that she had been poisoned. The results of the autopsy were never released, and Bingham received his $5 million. Some believed that the reason the family never released the autopsy was because Mary Lily died of syphilis, contracted during an affair with Bingham years earlier.

Bingham used his new fortune to buy the *Louisville Courier-Journal* and enhanced his position as a respected Kentucky business leader. Long after both Henry and Mary Lily were laid to rest, Ida continued to live with her delusions in a private mansion in a posh asylum. When she died in her sleep in 1930, her estate was worth $15 million. By 1995, the Flagler Co., still in the hands of the Kenan and Bingham heirs, was estimated by *Forbes* at $500 million.

49

James Buchanan Duke

(1856–1925)

Tobacco Tsar

Est. wealth: $140–$200 million

James B. Duke had inherited his hard drive and involvement in the tobacco business from his father, Washington Duke. Duke's mother died when he was an infant, and his father lost his tobacco farm near Durham, North Carolina, when they fled during the Civil War.

When Duke and his family returned to their farm, it belonged to someone else. His father, unwavering, returned to his old farm as a hired hand. Soon he had regained control of it. The young Duke got his start in the tobacco business driving "a pair of blind mules and a tumble-down wagon."

James, or Buck as he was called, had no interest in merely following his father's footsteps. He wanted to build something of his own. He was not a particularly bright student, but what he lacked in book smarts he made up for in hard work. The one area in which he did excel was math. And he knew how to make money.

The young Duke was very ambitious. Later he recalled that as a young man he had asked himself, "If John D. Rockefeller can do what he is doing in oil, why should not I do it in tobacco?" Why not? Maybe it was because there was no market for cigarettes in the United States at the time, although there was a large market for loose tobacco (used to roll cigarettes). Duke would create the cigarette market and significantly expand the industry in the United States and abroad. He would build a tobacco trust on a scale relative to the industry that would rival Rockefeller's Standard Oil.

As a teenager, Duke asked his father for $1,000 to set up his own tobacco business. His father made him a partner in the family firm instead. Despite his youth, Duke drove the company forward, handling the details of the factory and making sales visits across the country. By the time he was twenty-five, Duke was president of the company, which had become one of the major tobacco producers in the country.

Then Duke hit upon the idea of making cigarettes. Before the Civil War, cigarettes were virtually unheard of in the United States. Popular in Turkey and Russia, they came into Europe during the Crimean War and from there to America. Cigarette sales were still not very strong. By 1869, only about 2 million cigarettes were made in the United States each year. They were expensive and labor intensive to make. One expert roller could turn out only 2,500 per day.

Duke changed all this by buying and perfecting a machine that could produce 100,000 cigarettes per day. His production costs dropped from 80 cents per thousand to just 30 cents. He dropped his prices and launched a worldwide sales campaign. Within nine months, he had sold thirty million cigarettes. By 1899, the Dukes were producing nearly 1 billion cigarettes per year, half the output of the entire country.

With this victory under his belt, the twenty-seven-year-old

Duke headed to New York to take on the major players in the cigarette industry. His biggest rivals thought he would be broke within a year. But Duke built up a booming enterprise in New York. A bitter "cigarette war" ensued. In the end, Duke brought even the largest and most resistant companies to the bargaining table.

Finally, the large companies decided to merge into the American Tobacco Company. According to one story, there was a dispute over who should be named president. The companies agreed to put their sales statistics on the table and to let the company with the smallest loss appoint the president. Duke's company was the only one to show a profit. He became the head of the new company.

Now Duke faced a new threat. A group of investors led by Oliver H. Payne of Standard Oil began snatching up stock in the new company. Their intention was to seize control of the company but leave Duke as nominal head. Duke, who had never paid much attention to the stock market, traveled to see Payne in person. Duke said that if they followed through with the plan he would quit. "What will you do?" asked a shocked Payne. Duke replied without hesitation that he would sell all his stock and start a new company. Payne backed down. He didn't want to compete with Duke.

Duke then expanded into all kinds of tobacco products—snuff, cigars, and stogies—which he brought together under the banner of the American Tobacco Company. Duke then moved to England where he purchased the popular Ogden brand. His British rivals attempted to shut out Duke by offering exclusive distribution agreements with retailers. They thought it would be too late by the time Duke caught wind of the scheme, all the way across the Atlantic. But Duke heard about the plans by cable and made a very generous counteroffer for retailers that carried his products (and he did not require them to boycott other products). His rivals ultimately came to the table and joined forces with Duke. From his base in Britain, Duke then took his cigarettes to Japan, China, India, Australia, and other parts of the world.

In 1911, the government ordered Duke to break up the huge empire he had assembled. Duke then turned his attention to electric power. He helped found the Southern Power Company in 1905, which built numerous hydroelectric and steam generating plants.

Duke was a tall and striking figure with a head full of red

hair. He was known to be fair to his employees, once boasting that he had made more millionaires than any other man in the country. He was known for his frugality, traveling by freight trains at night in his early days of working for his father to save the cost of a hotel room. When he launched his operations in New York, he lived in a hallway bedroom and insisted that no member of the firm take more than $1,000 out of the business per year.

He pushed for efficiency wherever he could, paying attention to detail. When he started his New York factory, Duke had five women signing certificates to protect purchasers against fraud. One of the women produced half as many signed certificates as did her peers. Duke discovered the problem: Her name was Maggie McConichie. It was too long. Duke's solution: Change her name to a shorter one, A. B. Cox. She did, and soon doubled her output.

Through constantly building and expanding his tobacco empire, Duke had created a fortune of over $140 million. Shortly before his death, he gave $40 million to found the Duke Trust Fund, which was established to supply North Carolina with "preachers, teachers, lawyers, chemists, engineers, and doctors." The fund supported hospitals, orphans, the Methodist Episcopal church, and Trinity College, which changed its name to Duke University. When Duke died in 1925, his original $40 million gift was doubled, making Duke University the wealthiest university at the time. By 1934, the trust fund, largely funded by Duke Power Company stock, helped support 4 universities, 150 hospitals, 50 orphanages, and more than 1,000 Methodist churches.

Duke and his second wife, Nanaline, had one daughter, Doris. When she was born in 1912 at their mansion in New York, she was the sole heir to Duke's fortune of more than $100 million, and news reports described her as "probably the richest mite of humanity in all the world." (Her nearest rival was William K. Vanderbilt's son, heir to a fortune estimated at $60 million.) Doris became known as "the richest girl in the world," and the infant received bags of letters from people begging for gifts. Her doting father showered Doris with ponies, carts, toys, and pets. He bought the infant a marble-and-gold clock made in Switzerland so that she would awaken to soft chiming and bird sounds. He named his private railway car *Doris*.

Hounded by photographers and the public throughout her life, Doris Duke moved to Hawaii, where she was known as one of the best female surfers and an eccentric, reclusive heiress. She became friends with Philippines First Lady Imelda Marcos, who owned a house nearby. When Ferdinand and Imelda Marcos were forced to flee the Philippines and were later indicted on fraud and racketeering charges in the United States in 1988, Duke sprang into the headlines when she posted the $5.3 million bail. She said at the time that she believed in "loyalty to friends" and was ashamed of how the United States was treating Imelda "and her ailing husband."

50

Israel Thorndike
(1755–1832)
Massachusetts Privateer
Est. wealth: $1.8 million

Israel Thorndike was born in 1755 in Beverly, Massachusetts, where he became a cooper's apprentice. Thorndike was commissioned as a privateer in October 1776. He commanded or served on the *Tyrranicide* and other ships, prowling the harbors of Salem and Beverly looking for unsuspecting British merchant ships. He plundered a fortune at sea during the Revolutionary War, then took his loot home to Salem, Massachusetts, to build a large and profitable shipping, real estate, and manufacturing business. Thorndike left a fortune called at the time "the greatest that has ever been left in New England."

The British Navy never made it to Salem during the Revolutionary War, so privateers there found pretty easy pickings. A mix between pirates and patriots, privateers helped give the American colonies victory in the war, while retaining the war chests for themselves. Thorndike built a tidy fortune from the carcasses of British ships and became a war hero in the process.

After the war, Thorndike kept his ships so that they could engage in trade. Fortune again smiled on the port of Salem. The British warships had been kind enough to dispose of many merchant competitors in other ports, so once again Thorndike enjoyed clear sailing in building up his business in foreign trade.

He and his brother-in-law, Moses Brown, founded the shipping company of Brown and Thorndike. After Brown's retirement in 1800, Thorndike took the reins of the business. Brown and Thorndike set up a very profitable trade with the Orient. They shifted their base of operations from Salem to Boston and kept growing, moving into fisheries and real estate and then manufacturing. His "investments in real estate, shipping or factories were wonderfully judicious and hundreds watched his movements, believing his pathway was safe."

With his successes in war and politics, Thorndike became a prominent member of the New England community. He was soon a permanent fixture in the Massachusetts state government, serving for more than a quarter century in the legislature. He was elected more than a dozen times to the lower and upper branches of government. He also participated in the constitutional conventions of 1788 and 1820. After moving from Salem to a mansion in Boston, his home became a center of social activity.

He had a mansion in Beverly, which later became the city hall. He hosted President James Monroe for breakfast during a visit to Beverly in 1817, and Daniel Webster was there for dinner in 1830.

Thorndike was known for his generosity, contributing to a natural history professorship and donating a valuable collection of Americana from a German library to Harvard University. The library, which he bought for $6,500, was one of the most complete and valuable collections of works on American history. Thorndike died in 1832 at the age of seventy-five, "retaining to the last, great energy and activity." He left half a million dollars each to three sons as well as bequests to his widow and other children.

Number 51 is William S. O'Brien, who was one of the Silver Kings (see page 71).

Number 52 is Isaac Merritt Singer, the designer of the sewing machine (see page 133).

53

George Hearst
(1820–1891)
A Miner Who Founded a Media Empire

Est. wealth: $19 million

George Hearst was a miner and U.S. senator who picked up the *San Francisco Examiner* as payment for a gambling debt. His son, William Randolph Hearst, built the newspaper into the nation's largest newspaper chain and became one of the most lavish and colorful media moguls.

The fortune that launched the media empire came from mining. George Hearst, born on a Missouri farm in 1820, was running a small merchandise store when his father died, leaving a pile of debts. The twenty-six-year-old Hearst discovered rich lead ore deposits and used this new revenue to pay his debts. Four years later, in 1850, he left the family farm and, walking next to an oxcart, headed to California to look for gold. For nine years, he worked in placer mines without success. For a time, he also started a store in Sacramento, but with tough competition, he barely did better. Then in 1859, his luck turned when he invested in the Nevada silver mines. But again, his Nevada Ophir mine failed, and Hearst was broke once more. In 1875, he and his wife, Phoebe Apperson Hearst, had to give up their home in San Francisco.

A year later, undaunted, the fifty-six-year-old Hearst headed to the Black Hills of South Dakota to look for gold. When he left, his wife told him, "George, if you find a good mine, let us have a home stake." So when he bought a gold mine, he called it the Homestake Mine. The mine became legendary, producing more than $160 million in dividends.

Hearst continued to go wherever the mining prospects were rich. He had one success after another. His holdings included the San Luis mine in Mexico and the Anaconda in Montana, one of the biggest copper strikes ever. He and his partners eventually owned or controlled more than one hundred North American mines.

With a bushy beard, Hearst looked and acted the part of the prospector. George and Phoebe Hearst became well known for their lavish lifestyle as well as their generous philanthropy.

In 1882, at sixty-two, Hearst launched his political career, running an unsuccessful campaign for governor of California. Hearst was a vocal opponent of the domination of politics (and everything else) by the railroad interests. This battle against the railroad giants came to a head in his contest against Leland Stanford for a Senate seat in 1885. Stanford won the election, but when Senator John Miller died in 1886 Hearst was appointed to fill his unexpired term. Two years later, he won his own seat.

Hearst called himself "the silent man of the Senate" because he spoke so little. But he is remembered for his extensive knowledge of the western United States and his warm humor and his honesty. He died in 1891, within a week of the close of the 51st Congress.

Before his death, Hearst transferred the *Examiner* to his only son, William Randolph Hearst, who was twenty-eight at the time of his father's death. The younger Hearst, whose life inspired Orson

Welles's famous 1941 film *Citizen Kane*, built the paper into a powerful publishing empire worth more than $160 million by the time of his death in 1951. It included eighteen newspapers, nine magazines, and other news-related businesses. By then, however, much of the media empire was no longer owned by Hearst.

William Randolph Hearst was one of the biggest spenders of American history, doling out money at the rate of about $15 million per year. At a dinner party, Henry Ford once asked Hearst if he had saved any money. Hearst joked that he spent it faster than it came in. Ford told him he really ought to put away $200 or $300 million for a rainy day. Hearst obviously didn't take Ford's advice.

Hearst built the monumental mansion of San Simeon, a garish mixture of art and architecture from different styles and periods. The pool alone in this pleasure dome cost more than $1 million. He owned seven castles around the world. He was a multimillionaire who lived hand to mouth, but he enjoyed his money.

Despite his best efforts to completely deplete his fortune, Hearst still had an estate estimated at more than $59 million when he died in 1951 at the age of eighty-eight—not enough to earn a place of his own among the Wealthy 100. The Hearst media empire, bought back by Hearst heirs in 1974, continued to expand after Hearst's death. By 1995, the family trust, whose income was shared by five branches of the family, had reached a value of more than $4.5 billion, according to *Forbes* estimates.

54

John Hancock

(1736–1793)

Poor Little Revolutionary Rich Boy

Est. wealth: $350,000

John Hancock is remembered for his oversized signature on the Declaration of Independence and an equally large ego, but it was the size of his fortune that first brought him into the rebel cause. Hancock, who had inherited a very successful business from his uncle, was one of the wealthiest merchants in New England

Born in Braintree, Massachusetts, in 1736, Hancock was sent

as a young boy to live with his uncle after his father died. Uncle Thomas, who had no children, was the richest merchant in Boston (because he died before the Revolution, he is not included among the Wealthy 100.) Thomas Hancock was the son of a poor minister, who was apprenticed for seven years to learn the bookbinding trade. He then launched his own book-selling and publishing business in Boston. He married the daughter of one of the wealthiest merchants in the city and, following his father-in-law's example, Thomas expanded his investments in exporting and shipping. Through trade in whale oil and investments in shipping, Thomas Hancock became one of the most successful merchants in New England.

When Thomas adopted his nephew, John, he sent the young boy to Harvard. After his graduation in 1754, John Hancock was sent to London to learn about the British side of the shipping business. He returned to Boston in 1761, where he was made a partner in his uncle's firm. When his uncle Thomas died in 1764, the twenty-seven-year-old John Hancock found himself at the head of the largest and most profitable mercantile house in Boston.

The business did not fare well under Hancock's leadership. Within eleven years, the thriving firm went out of business in 1775. The failure was due in part to the declining relationship between Britain and the colonies. The Stamp Act went into effect just as Hancock took over the firm. But he accelerated its decline. He tried to gain a monopoly on whale oil, but when prices dropped rapidly he took a large loss. He blamed British rules rather than his own business mistakes for the decline of his business.

This business drew Hancock directly into the cause of the Revolution in 1768. One of his ships, aptly named the *Liberty*, had arrived in port with a cargo of Madeira wine. Some of the cargo was stolen from Hancock and smuggled ashore. The British authorities, combatting rampant smuggling by many merchants, decided to make an example of Hancock. They seized the *Liberty* and filed suit against him. The seizure of the vessel by the unpopular British authorities sparked rioting on the shore. (The feelings of ill will toward the British over the incident were so high that when the *Liberty* was later converted to a coast guard boat, it was captured and burned by a mob.)

Hancock was defended in his legal case by Samuel Adams, who managed to have the charges dropped. Hancock found himself a cause célèbre among those moving the country toward the Revolution. Recognizing the importance of Hancock and his fortune to the patriot cause, Adams continued to cultivate him as a supporter of the movement for independence. Hancock became active in Boston politics. He was later appointed president of the Provincial Congress and was elected president of the Continental Congress.

Hancock, who always had an exaggerated sense of his own abilities, expected to be named commander-in-chief of the Continental Army. But he was not the equal of George Washington, who ultimately won the appointment. Hancock was so upset when Washington was named to lead the army, that he resigned as president of the Congress in 1777.

Hancock's actual military and political career was less than distinguished. During the Revolution, he commanded a Massachusetts contingent in the unsuccessful attack on the British at Rhode Island in 1778.

Hancock enjoyed wide popularity in his native state of Massachusetts. He was elected to nine terms as governor and played an important role in the convention to ratify the U.S. Constitution. Frequently when Hancock would find himself in a political crisis in state politics, he would conveniently acquire an attack of the gout. He resigned as governor in 1785 in the face of civil unrest, claiming that the disease had flared up. When the rebellion was put down by James Bowdoin, Hancock, his gout miraculously cured, ran for election as governor and was returned to power. Despite his failures in business, Hancock still owned large expanses of Massachusetts land. He died in office in 1793, leaving a fortune estimated at $350,000.

55

John W. Garrett

(1820–1884)

The General of the Baltimore & Ohio

Est. wealth: $15 million

The Baltimore & Ohio Railroad had depleted its initial $3 million capitalization but still had not completed its span from Baltimore to the Ohio River. There was dissention on the board of directors. A young merchant named John Work Garrett, who owned stock in the railroad and served as chairman of its financial subcommittee, stepped forward. He crafted an impressive financial plan and, with the backing of Johns Hopkins, the B & O's major shareholder, was named president of the railroad in 1858.

Garrett was born in Baltimore in 1820 and learned about

business as a partner in his father's commission house. After attending junior college, Garrett, nineteen, joined his father's firm where he spent seventeen years as a partner before taking over the Baltimore & Ohio.

As leader of the struggling railroad, Garrett introduced tough new fiscal discipline. By the time he issued his first annual report, he was showing a gain in earnings during a time when other businesses were losing money.

Just when Garrett had the rail line on a firm financial footing, he found himself in the middle of the Civil War. The Baltimore & Ohio crossed in and out of Confederate territory, and it became a key target of the South as it tried to disrupt northern supply lines. While generals were leading men into battle, Garrett was fighting a war of his own to keep the railroad running.

Garrett often visited reconstruction crews and narrowly missed being captured on several occasions. He also helped provide information to the Union troops. In 1863, he transported twenty-thousand soldiers from Washington to Chattanooga, the first time large numbers of troops traveled to battle by rail.

When the war ended, Garrett rebuilt and extended his railway system. The Baltimore & Ohio stretched west to Pittsburgh and Chicago, and north to New York. He also established wharves in Baltimore to transfer cargo from his trains. He built railroad cars, hotels, and telegraph lines. Garrett and Hopkins wrested control of the railway away from the politicians who had built it. Garrett also launched aggressive rate wars against rival rail lines.

Amidst increasing competitive pressure, Garrett implemented two successive 10 percent wage cuts. At the same time, the railroad began running "double headers," trains twice the normal length with the same size crew. Workers revolted. In 1877, Garrett found himself in the middle of a new war—the first great railroad strike. The walkout on the Baltimore & Ohio soon spread to the Pennsylvania Railroad. Rail traffic was shut down on the East Coast. The Pennsylvania militia was called out to put down the strike, but the violence escalated until President Rutherford Hayes sent in the army. With troops protecting strikebreakers, the strike diffused.

Shortly after the strike, Garrett became tired of the battles with other railroads and employees, and he finally retired. He had built the Baltimore & Ohio from 514 miles of track before the Civil War, to more than 1,711 miles when he retired. Garrett, a large and forceful man, died in 1884 at the age of sixty-four. He left a fortune of $15 million to his two sons.

His son Robert Garrett II took charge of the railroad. During the Civil War, Robert had run away to join the Confederate Army, putting himself and his father on opposite sides of the conflict. His father later convinced him to return home. After the war, Robert graduated from Princeton and returned home to help his father run the railroad and other business enterprises. The younger Garrett led the Valley Railroad in Virginia, which eventually was connected to the Baltimore and Ohio system. At that point, Garrett was elected third vice president of the railroad. He became president when his father died. During his tenure, he built the $14 million extension of the line into Philadelphia, and he extended the Baltimore and Ohio telegraph system. He had no children.

While Robert led the railroad, his brother, Thomas, ran the family banking business. Thomas's son, Robert Garrett III, became a general partner in the Robert Garrett and Sons investment banking firm. He also is credited with bringing the Boy Scouts to Baltimore in 1910.

Number 56 is John W. Mackay, who was one of the Silver Kings (see page 71).

Julius Rosenwald

(1862–1932)

Est. wealth: $80 million

Richard Warren Sears

(1863–1914)

Est. wealth: $25 million

A Mail-Order Fortune

Richard Sears was a young station agent in Redwood Falls, Minnesota, when an unclaimed shipment of watches caught his attention. It would become the basis for a catalog business that would change American retailing and life. It would also make Sears and his partner Julius Rosenwald among the richest men in America.

Sears was born in Minnesota in 1863, the son of a blacksmith and wagon maker who lost his entire fortune in a stock deal when Richard was fifteen. After his father's death two years later, the seventeen-year-old Sears went to work at the Minneapolis and St. Louis Railroad in Minneapolis. He slept in a loft above the station, selling coal and lumber on the side. In 1886, a local jeweler refused to accept the shipment of watches from a wholesaler. No freight had been paid, so the watches sat in the station.

Sears, who processed freight, learned the wholesale price of watches when they came in on the trains. And he knew what they sold for in the jewelers' shops. He obtained permission to sell the watches. He drafted letters describing the merchandise and sent them to railroad agents up and down the line. Sears—later called "the Barnum of advertising"—was a brilliant advertiser and promoter. As a child, he had been fascinated with mail order and often sent away for free booklets or bought trinkets by mail, which he sold to railroad agents, who could then resell them at a profit.

His approach to advertising was often very direct and down-to-earth. It wasn't flashy, which appealed to the skeptical farmers and townspeople who became his core customers. He promised "satisfaction guaranteed or your money back." One of his descriptions of a harness in the 1894 catalog read:

> $3.98 buys this harness. No harness concern on earth can beat this price. CASH IN FULL must accompany all orders. We send all other grades C.O.D., subject to examination, but on this our cheapest harness there is but a very few cents profit, and we believe you will agree, we are not at all unreasonable when we ask you to send cash in full with your order.

Sears also created club plans, in which groups of men would contribute $1 per week to a pool. Each week, one of the men would receive a watch—drawn by lottery—and by the end of thirty-eight weeks, they would all have watches.

The retail price for each of his original watches was $25, but Sears bought them wholesale for $12 and sold them for $14. He sold the entire shipment, paid the cost to the wholesaler, and made a tidy profit. In six months, he had netted $5,000 in the watch business, the most money he had ever had in his life.

The twenty-three-year-old Sears then bought more watches and soon left the railroad to found the R. W. Sears Watch Company. He soon launched national advertising and moved to

Chicago. When the watches came back for repair, he enlisted the help of watchmaker A. C. Roebuck, and their names would be forever linked with retailing. By the time he had made $100,000, at age twenty-six, Sears was ready to retire. He sold the business and set out for Iowa to become a country banker.

Bored by the quiet life, Sears again returned to retailing. Because he was barred from using his own name for three years after the sale of the old business, the new company was called A. C. Roebuck, and later became Sears, Roebuck, & Co. The first Sears, Roebuck catalog listed just twenty-five watches, but would later become the "Big Book," running thousands of pages with everything from wood stoves and kitchen utensils to automobiles. (The expression "horseless carriages" to describe cars was Sears's idea, one of an endless stream of inspirations added to the book.)

While Sears was a master of advertising, his partner Julius Rosenwald was an operational genius who could deliver on the high level of orders Sears generated and still maintain the standards of efficiency and honesty that Sears promised in his ads. Rosenwald expanded the company until it ultimately counted one-quarter of the U.S. population among its customers.

Rosenwald was born on a street in Springfield, Illinois, where Abraham Lincoln had once lived. He worked in the clothing business in New York before setting up his own retail store when he was twenty-one. He then built a manufacturing plant in Chicago to make his own clothing. One of his customers was Richard Sears.

When Sears expanded his direct mail business, Rosenwald bought a one-fourth interest for $37,500, using borrowed money. Sears, impressed with Rosenwald's skill as a manager, appointed him vice president of the company in 1895.

The company opened a one-hundred-acre plant in 1906, the size of a small city, with its own postal stations and switching tracks. Automatic letter openers, an innovation at the plant, tore through 2,700 letters per hour. Gravity-fed conveyor belts kept merchandise moving to the shipping platforms. An order that arrived in the morning was filled by night.

In 1907, the styles of Sears and Rosenwald clashed. Facing an economic downturn, Sears wanted to boost advertising while Rosenwald wanted to cut expenses. Rosenwald had the backing of the company's directors, and Sears, who had threatened to quit before, retired as president in 1908. Sears remained chairman of the board for the next five years, but he rarely attended meetings.

In 1913, he sold his Sears, Roebuck stock for $10 million. He died a year later, at the age of fifty, leaving an estate estimated at $25 million to his widow and four children.

After Sears left the firm, Rosenwald became president, a position he held until his death in 1932. Rosenwald set new standards for honesty and fairness in an industry known for slick sales pitches and deception. Customers got exactly what was described in detail in the catalog. The company also offered one of the first money-back guarantees and initiated "send no money" advertisements. By 1920, the company was selling 100,000 different items to 6 million customers.

Rosenwald offered his employees profit-sharing plans and stock options. All employees who earned less than $1,500 received an "Anniversary Check" for 5 percent of their salary on their fifth anniversary with Sears. During the Depression, Rosenwald stepped in with $20 million of his own funds to carry the company stock through hard times and to protect shareholders, many of whom were employees.

Soon people thought they could get *anything* from Sears. Children wrote to Rosenwald asking for baby brothers or sisters. Bachelors on the frontiers wrote seeking wives. They described themselves in detail and trusted the company to pick out the right mate.

Rosenwald would have been the last to brag about his substantial achievements. He ate at the company cafeteria, turned down honorary degrees, and refused to wear an insignia on his military uniform when he was called into service by the secretary of war in World War I. (He once jokingly introduced himself in a group of high-level generals as "General Merchandise.") When asked about the source of his accomplishments, he replied, "Ninety-five percent luck and five percent ability."

Since his name was not included in the Sears, Roebuck Company name, he is perhaps best known for his philanthropies, totaling more than $63 million. Rosenwald once said, "Charity is one pleasure that never wears out." He established the Museum of Science and Industry in Chicago. Although he was Jewish, his philanthropy cut across all lines. As Dr. John Mott, the president of the World Alliance of Young Men's Christian Association (YMCA) organizations, commented after Rosenwald's death, "He transcended all barriers of race, religion and nationality." Rosenwald used challenge grants to leverage his gifts with local contributions, helping to build thousands of schools for black students in the rural South and several dozen YMCAs across the United States.

As a result of his generosity and his steadfast support of the company during the Depression, his estate—once as large as $200 million—was reduced to just $17 million at his death in 1932 at the age of sixty-nine. After his death, Rosenwald's son Lessing served as chairman of the company until 1938. Lessing's son, Julius II, became a director of the company along with Lessing's nephew, Edgar B. Stern, Jr. The company continued to expand under the leadership of General Robert E. Wood (a non–family member), who led the company until 1954 and is credited with moving it from a catalog company to the nation's largest retailer.

Richard Sears's heirs inherited an estate that was spread across many small farms and other real estate holdings, as well as nearly $2 million in uncollected debts. Sears's widow and children had little experience or talent for business. As a result of waste and mismanagement, the estate was further eroded until his grandchildren shared a fortune estimated at no more than a few million dollars. Sears's grandson, Carroll Sears, said that when he takes his sons to Sears to shop and they say, "Look, Dad, that's our store," he replies, "That's our name, but it's not our store."

The company Sears and Rosenwald founded became the largest in the country, ultimately employing almost a half million people, or about one out of every two hundred U.S. citizens. The Sears catalog, which started with a shipment of watches, reached a circulation of 50 million at its peak, making it the most widely distributed publication in the nation except for the Bible.

58

George F. Baker
(1840–1931)
The Sphinx of Wall Street
Est. wealth: $100 million

GeORGE F. Baker built the First National Bank into the most successful and powerful bank of its time—and perhaps of any time. With J. P. Morgan, he was one of the most powerful financial leaders of his time. His stern and taciturn demeanor earned him the nickname "the sphinx of Wall Street."

Baker, born in Troy, New York, was the son of a shoe merchant who had served as a state legislator and private secretary to New York governor William H. Seward. After completing studies at Seward University in Florida, New York, Baker began work as a clerk in the state banking department. In 1863, Baker helped found the First National Bank, the first bank established in New

York under the national bank act. Baker started at the bank as a cashier. In 1877, he was elected president of the bank at the age of thirty-seven and was appointed chairman in 1901.

Baker was a tough and silent leader who kept to himself about his business and his personal life. During Congressional hearings, he told legislators who were prying into his affairs, "It is none of the public's business what I do." A friend once said, "The Almighty could not draw a word out of Baker about his early days." His cold and impervious image and his financial success earned him the characterization of "a moneymaking machine."

If Baker himself was not a moneymaking machine, his bank was. First National became the nation's largest underwriter of government bonds. The bank and its shadow company, First Securities, which handled the securities the bank was not permitted to deal in, both produced huge returns for shareholders. During Baker's tenure at the bank, it paid out dividends of more than 2,500 percent, including 1,900 percent in one year.

Baker also held shares and directorships in a wide range of companies, including Guaranty Trust and Mutual Life Insurance. He served as director of so many railroads that the U.S. Interstate Commerce Commission, concerned about interlocking directorates, ordered him to step down from some of them. Baker also served on the Finance Committee of U.S. Steel, owned by his friend J. P. Morgan.

Concern was so great about the concentration of power in the hands of Baker and a few other business leaders that Congress launched an investigation into the "money trust" that Baker led. The hearings concluded that four men—Baker, Morgan, James Stillman, and John D. Rockefeller—held a total of 341 directorships and controlled 112 companies with assets of more than $22 billion. Although the men claimed they did not use these interlocks to work in concert, U.S. banking regulations were ultimately changed to avoid such concentration.

What is perhaps most remarkable, given the millions of dollars that he controlled, was that Baker personally escaped the scandals that followed so many of his peers. And he lived so simply that B. C. Forbes, founder of *Forbes* magazine, commented, "even the rankest Socialist would not quarrel with Mr. Baker's mode of living."

Although Baker had a cold public image, he was actively engaged in philanthropy. He was called "the man with the hardest shell and the softest heart in America." As with his business dealings, Baker didn't like to talk about his donations. He quietly contributed to the Metropolitan Museum of Art, the Red Cross, Cornell, Columbia, and other charities. He made substantial contributions for the buildings of Harvard University's business school bearing his name.

Baker's wealth was estimated at $200 million before the stock market crash in 1929. By the time he died in 1931 at the age of ninety-one, the value of his estate had dropped to about $73 million. (He had given an additional $22 million to philanthropies.)

His son, George F., Jr., one of three children, succeeded Baker as chairman of First National after his death. The younger Baker, who had worked at the bank since shortly after his graduation from Harvard in 1899, led the bank for the next six years until his own death in a yachting accident in 1937. The younger Baker had set up a $15 million foundation and left another $45 million to his four children. One of his sons, Grenville, died of gunshot wounds on the Baker family estate in Florida in 1949. The second son, George F. III, committed suicide on the same estate twenty-eight years later in 1977.

George Washington

(1732–1799)

The Father of Our Country Estates

Est. wealth: $530,000

George Washington isn't usually thought of as a shrewd businessman. He was a great general and a courageous political leader. He was "first in war, first in peace, and first in the hearts of his countrymen." But he was also among the richest Americans of his time, with a fortune that he himself valued at $530,000 at the time of his death in 1799.

Washington was more wealthy than his colleague Benjamin Franklin, who is much more widely associated with thriftiness and business success. In fact, Washington was about three times as wealthy as "Poor Richard." Washington was much wealthier than his treasury secretary, Alexander Hamilton. And shortly before his death, Washington visited financier Robert Morris in debtor's prison in Philadelphia. How did this leader, who had risked everything to found a new democracy, end up with a fortune greater than all these early wizards of business and finance?

Washington didn't gain his wealth by leading the American army in the Revolution. He refused to accept pay for his services as commander-in-chief during the war. He turned down the $500 per month salary he was voted to receive as leader of the Continental Army, vowing to keep only enough to cover his expenses. Afterward, he submitted a record of his expenses to Congress. In fact, he reportedly offered to personally finance an army to fight England.

Washington, the former surveyor, built his wealth by accumulating land and marrying one of the wealthiest widows in the nation, Martha Custis. In a time when the great fortunes were largely land fortunes, Washington held enough acreage to be among the richest. Some he inherited, some he bought, and some were given to him in gratitude for his service to the country. He accumulated 9,744 acres valued at $10 an acre on the Ohio River in Virginia; 3,075 acres, worth $200,000, in the Great Kenawa; along with other parcels in Virginia, Maryland, Pennsylvania, New York, Kentucky, and other places. As a young surveyor, Washington had invested his earnings by purchasing land in the Shenandoah Valley. By the time he was twenty-eight, he owned nearly 1,500 acres.

But his future security was assured when he married Martha Custis in 1759. The twenty-seven-year-old widow's first husband, Virginia planter Daniel Parke Custis, left her a 17,000-acre estate, worth $360,000, which she shared with her two children. She was perhaps the wealthiest woman in Virginia, with a total estate valued at $600,000 or more. George and Martha Washington had no children of their own, and Washington's two stepchildren died before he became president.

Although Washington was land rich, it was rumored that he was cash poor. He reportedly had to borrow $500 to travel from Mount Vernon to New York to be inaugurated as president. The new position carried a $25,000 annual salary. Washington was skilled with numbers and kept careful accounts of the gains and losses of his estate.

When he died in 1799 at the age of sixty-seven, George Washington left his estate to Martha, along with his slaves, with the instruction that they should be set free after her death. He was buried on his 8,000-acre estate at Mount Vernon. Martha joined him there just three years later. In his will, Washington also gave away his most liquid assets, $50,000 in stock, to several schools. His twenty-three residual beneficiaries were left with a share of investments in stock that amounted to just $1,500 each, further proof that Washington was cash poor.

Just a half century later, Mount Vernon, which could not be sustained as a self-supporting farm, had fallen into disrepair. As Gustavus Myers writes, "It was only by the persistent gathering of public contributions that his very home was saved to the nation, so had his estate become divided and run down." In 1853, concerned that this national landmark would be lost to the nation, a citizens group began raising funds to purchase and restore the home of the first president. The Mount Vernon Ladies' Association raised $200,000 to buy Mount Vernon and restore the buildings and grounds. The association also recovered much of the original furniture and other possessions of the first president. It now operates the estate as a national memorial to Washington.

Although there is some controversy about the exact dimensions of Washington's estate and his position in society, one commentator said Washington's financial affairs were the equivalent of those of J. Paul Getty and Nelson Rockefeller combined. Whatever his status, biographer Paul Leicester Ford wrote that no fortune "was more honestly acquired or more thoroughly deserved." Maybe it is no coincidence that his visage now appears on more U.S. currency than any other individual.

Prominent but Poor

Robert Morris

(1734–1806)

Haym Solomon

(1740–1785)

FINANCIERS OF THE AMERICAN REVOLUTION

It is perhaps ironic that the two men who did the most to keep the delicate finances of the nation together during the Revolutionary War both died virtually penniless. Robert Morris, after an unfortunate investment scheme after the war, ended up in debtor's prison a few blocks away from the grand mansion he was once building in Philadelphia. Haym Solomon's heirs petitioned the government for the hundreds of thousands that Solomon advanced to the war effort, but they never received a cent.

Morris's name has long been synonymous with the founding of the nation. Morris had built a large shipping and banking business in Philadelphia before the Revolution. A staunch patriot, he became the "financier" of the Revolution, raising hundreds of thousands of dollars to support the Continental Army. He stabilized the faltering finances of the young nation and made a comfortable living. With a few bad business deals after the war, he ended his life millions of dollars in debt.

Solomon, virtually ignored in early histories of the Revolution, is said to have contributed as much as $800,000 of his own funds to the war effort. Other researchers have concluded that it is more likely that he served as a broker for others' funds. A devout patriot, the British sentenced him to be hanged in New York. He fled to Philadelphia in 1778, leaving behind his entire fortune and his young family. Using his connections with European financial markets, he saved the Continental Army and the fledgling government on more than one occasion. For example, according to one story, he received an urgent request from Washington at the synagogue on Yom Kippur. Washington needed $400,000 to keep the Army afloat. In one night, it is said, Solomon raised the funds.

(continued)

(continued)

The financier also supported many leading individuals of the young republic, including James Madison, Thomas Jefferson, Baron von Steuben, and James Monroe, before the government could afford to pay pensions. It is unlikely, arriving penniless in Philadelphia, that he could have assembled a large enough personal fortune to make the contributions he did to the war effort from his own funds. Whether these were his own funds or he was merely an agent, Solomon played a crucial role in the success of the Revolution.

In 1941, a monument was erected in Chicago, showing George Washington flanked by Solomon and Morris. Their personal and financial sacrifices kept the struggling colonies financially afloat. In part due to their boundless generosity to the cause, they both died poor.

60

Anthony N. Brady
(1843–1913)
The Great Consolidator
Est. wealth: $50–$100 million

Anthony Nicholas Brady, a New York tea merchant, built his fortune by consolidating transit systems and utility companies in New York and other areas. He created New York Edison from a group of utility companies (which later became Consolidated Edison) and founded the Brooklyn Rapid Transit Company from a group of city transit systems.

Brady was born in Lille, France, in 1843 and immigrated to Troy, New York, as a child. At fifteen, he left school to go to work, and by the time he was nineteen he decided to start his own business. He opened a tea store in Albany, which was so successful he started a chain of stores throughout New York, including one in New York City. It was one of the first chain stores in American history, but Brady soon tired of the business.

A heavyset man with a ruddy complexion, Brady moved from one business to the next, continually extending his empire by using government contacts to expand his scope of operations. He had a keen eye for opportunities—whether in construction, gas and oil contracts, or city transit. Every time he entered an industry, he would consolidate small players into a large company. In the process, he improved operations and became a dominant force in utilities and other fields.

After leaving the tea business, Brady next founded a building materials company, attracted by the building boom in New York. He then moved to general contracting, including sewers and pavements. Then he gained control of large New York granite quarries to supply his construction projects.

His municipal construction work led to an interest in public utilities. He invested in the gas business and later became an early participant in the oil business. He took on Standard Oil as a fierce competitor, using his contacts from his other interests to control oil contracts in the Chicago area. Ultimately, like almost all of Standard's other competitors, Brady became an ally of the monopolistic oil company. He joined the Standard Oil gang in investments in tobacco, rubber, and other areas.

Having tried his hand at gas and oil, Brady turned his attention to electricity. He made significant investments in public electrical utilities and became a driving force in the New York Edison Company.

Brady became a major player in the rapidly growing city transit systems, or traction, as it was known then. He bought transit lines in Providence and New York City. He helped organize the Metropolitan Traction Company and was involved in the reorganization of the Brooklyn Rapid Transit Company.

The opportunities above ground were attractive, but there were still greater opportunities beneath the streets. Brady was instrumental in spearheading the development of the New York subway systems. He also extended his transit interests to Washington and Philadelphia.

Brady was a director in dozens of enterprises. When he died in 1913 at the age of sixty-nine, his investments were so diversified that estimates of his wealth varied widely, ranging from $50 million to $100 million. Brady and his wife, Marcia, the daughter of a Vermont lawyer, had two sons who inherited most of Brady's fortune. His son Nicholas served as president of New York Edison and Brooklyn Rapid Transit before his death in 1930. The second son, James, who founded the Maxwell Motor Car Company, handled the family business interests after his father's death. Active in Catholic charities, he left $60 million to his wife, Genevieve. When she died in 1938, she instructed that her estate be divided into a hundred parts, so the "consolidated" fortune of Nicholas Brady was ultimately diffused among many relatives and charities.

61

Adolphus Busch

(1839–1913)

The Baron of Beer

Est. wealth: $50 million

Adolphus Busch, a founder of the modern U.S. brewing industry, established one of the leading beer companies. He built a family fortune and corporate dynasty that continues to this day.

Busch was born in Mainz-on-the-Rhine, Germany, the
youngest of twenty-one children. His father was a dealer in wines
and brewing supplies. In 1857, at the age of eighteen, Busch made
a fateful decision to come to America, moving with relatives to St.
Louis. Two years later, when his father died and left him a small
inheritance, Busch set up his own store to sell brewer's supplies
with his brother Ulrich.

One of the his customers was the owner of a Bavarian brewery, Eberhard Anheuser. In 1861, Adolphus and Ulrich were married to Anheuser's two daughters, Lilly and Anna, in a double ceremony. When his father-in-law died in 1879, the forty-year-old Adolphus became the president of the company. Busch built the company from a local brewery to an international leader in beer production and sales. His laboratories developed a new pasteurization process that allowed beer to be shipped across the country without refrigeration, expanding sales and driving down the cost of distribution.

Busch was a brilliant marketer. The first and longest-running success of Anheuser-Busch was the creation of Budweiser beer. It was lighter and sweeter than most of the beers at the time. There are a variety of stories about the origins of the beer that made the company a national leader. According to legend, the recipe came from European monks. Some said the yeast for the beer was originally smuggled over in an ice cream container. Others have said the concept for the beer came in a flash of inspiration by Busch. The less flattering story is that it was "borrowed" from a small brewery in Bohemia that was making a similar brew, called Budweiser. Whatever its origins, it became immensely popular, along with Anheuser-Busch's more expensive Michelob brand.

Busch became an evangelist of beer, once stating, "It is my aim to win the American people over to our side, to make them all lovers of beer." He was a master salesman. Busch, a vibrant and distinguished-looking man, was described by biographers Peter Hernon and Terry Ganey as "P. T. Barnum, Buffalo Bill, and Cornelius Vanderbilt rolled into one." Busch set up representatives across the United States and he focused on building his brands.

Busch, who became a naturalized U.S. citizen in 1867, also contributed in some small way to the national culture. He was taken by a painting called *Custer's Last Fight* hanging in a St. Louis saloon. The saloon, about to go out of business, owed Busch money, so he accepted the painting as payment. He presented the original to the 7th Cavalry, but first he had it turned into brilliant lithographic posters that eventually were a common sight in barrooms across the country. It became one of the most recognizable scenes of American history.

St. Louis, where the first lager beer in the U.S. may have been served, was ideally situated for making beer. There was a ready supply of water and grain, good transportation, and miles of underground caverns that could be used for storing the product.

Soon what began as a local company making mediocre beer was now serving the entire nation and winning international awards. The Anheuser-Busch plant grew to the size of a small city, with 110 buildings, 6,000 employees, a $10 million payroll, and production of more than 1.6 million barrels of beer per year.

Using his capital to buy into the upstream and downstream businesses that were involved in beer making, Busch bought glass bottle plants, ice-making businesses, refrigerated railroad cars, and eventually the railroads themselves. He acquired sole rights to manufacture the first diesel railroad engines in America. He invested in real estate and banking. His grandson later recalled that "everything he touched turned to gold."

Busch lived lavishly, his pockets always filled with gold coins, which he passed out liberally. Presidents came to visit him, and he traveled by ship or in his private railroad car, shuttling between four mansions, including one in Germany. Before the days of income tax, he was earning an estimated $2 million per year. When he died at age seventy-five, his $50 million estate was the largest ever probated in the state of Missouri.

Busch gave generously to education and other charities, and he built a family brewing dynasty that remains strong to this day. His eldest son, August Anheuser Busch, began working at the family business when he was twenty-four and became a vice-president in 1894, at the age of twenty-nine. August ran the business after his father's death in 1913, leading the company through the Depression and Prohibition—during which he developed a non-alcoholic beer and moved into other businesses such as corn products and malt products.

His son, August A. Busch, Jr., took over the company when his father died in 1934 and led the firm until his own death in 1989. August Jr. became the owner of the St. Louis Cardinals and launched the "Bud Bowl" and other marketing innovations. Today, the firm is led by August III, and the fifth-generation Busch, August IV, is a vice president in brand management. *Forbes* estimated that the total family fortune was $1.3 billion in 1995.

62

John T. Dorrance

(1873–1930)

Sultan of Soup

Est. wealth: $115 million

Dr. John T. Dorrance was a chemist whose innovations in developing condensed soup and advertising alchemy made Campbell's Soups a fixture of American life.

Dorrance was born in Bristol, Pennsylvania. His family owned a successful timber and flour business and were comfortable enough to send him to college at the Massachusetts Institute of Technology. After graduating from MIT in 1895, Dorrance went on to earn his Ph.D. in chemistry from the University of Goettingen in Germany in just two years.

A brilliant chemist, he was courted by Columbia and Cornell universities, but he turned down those offers to join the Joseph Campbell Preserve Company, where his uncle was a partner. Shortly after graduation, Dorrance was sailing on the Delaware River when he stopped at his uncle's company in Camden, New Jersey, to stock his larder. He asked his uncle for soup and was surprised to find that among the 200 canned products the company made, there was no soup.

Dorrance, who had turned down a university faculty position, went to work for his uncle at a salary of just $7.50 per week. During his first year with the firm, Campbell's posted a loss of $60,000. But Dorrance saw opportunities in canning, and thanks to his efforts, it would be the company's last unprofitable year.

Dorrance had been impressed with the flavorful soups in Europe during his studies there. He thought soup could be a popular product to market to Americans. There were two other companies that were producing soup in the United States, but because of the high water content in soups, the bulky cans were expensive to ship.

Just two years later, in 1899, the twenty-six-year-old Dorrance had developed a process for removing the water from soup, creating the first condensed soup. The chemist created a process of making a thicker more flavorful soup that would retain its flavor when diluted with water. He also studied cookbooks and sent to Europe for soup recipes. The first varieties were Tomato, Consomme, Vegetable, Chicken, and Oxtail.

Although Dorrance understood the science of soup making, he also wanted to become an expert at the art. He spent three months of every year working in some of the most famous kitchens in the world, including the Café de Paris and the Waldorf in New York. He was named an honorary member of the elite French chef's association, *Société de Secours Mutuels et de Retraite des Cuisiniers de Paris*, and his soup earned a gold medal at the Paris Exhibition in 1900 (an image of which was added to the soup's label).

Although eating soup was popular in Europe, it was a challenge to convince Americans to adopt the custom. Dorrance personally took to the road, demonstrating the soups in grocers' windows. His soups, which were priced at 10 cents a can compared to 35 cents for uncondensed varieties, became an instant success. With the new process and extensive advertising—including the introduction of the Campbell Kids—Dorrance's company was selling sixteen million cans of soup per year by 1904. By 1911, it had extended its sales into California, making it one of the first national brands. The familiar red and white labels, borrowed from the uniforms of the Cornell football team by a Campbell's executive, became a familiar sight in American grocery stores and larders.

Dorrance was named president and general manager of the company in 1914, a position he held until his death in 1930. In 1915, when his uncle decided to retire, he sold John Dorrance his share of the business for $755,720. Less than 20 years after starting at the company, John Dorrance was sole owner.

The business continued to grow. During tomato season in the mid-1920s, the Campbell assembly line produced ten million cans of soup per day. In 1927, the company grossed $50 million in sales.

Despite his large fortune, Dorrance lived modestly in his $100,000 mansion in Radnor, Pennsylvania. He spent summers in rented homes in Bar Harbor, Maine. His biggest extravagance was hosting large parties for his four daughters. On one occasion, he rented three floors of the Belvue-Stratford Hotel in Philadelphia and decorated them with exotic flowers and cages of tropical birds.

He died in 1930, at the age of 56, apparently exhausted from his unremitting drive to build his business as well as, reportedly, from heavy bouts of drinking. He left a fortune estimated at $115 million, which made him the third richest man in America at the time, after Payne Whitney and Thomas Fortune Ryan. Dorrance's estate was divided into eight equal parts. He left two parts each to his widow and his son, and one each to his four daughters.

Dorrance's younger brother, Arthur, a vice president in the company at the time of Dorrance's death, took charge of the company. He served as president until his death in 1946. He was succeeded as head of the company by John Dorrance's only son, John T. Dorrance, Jr. Although the younger Dorrance stayed out of the spotlight, he continued to expand the business, adding C. A. Swanson Company in 1955, Pepperidge Farm in 1961, and Vlasic Foods. By 1979, the company was seventeenth among food processors, with $2 million in sales, and the leading manufacturer of soup. Two of the senior Dorrance grandchildren appeared among the *Forbes 400* in 1995, Bennett Dorrance and Mary Alice Dorrance Malone, with fortunes estimated at $1.2 billion apiece.

63

George M. Pullman

(1831–1897)

A Sleeping Giant
Est. wealth: $17.5 million

It was an idea that kept George Pullman awake at night. The mechanic's son might have thought of it during the long ride from his native state of New York to Chicago, Illinois, as he tossed and turned restlessly while sleeping upright on the uncomfortable train seats. He held on to the idea for three years in Chicago, as he worked as a contractor leveling the city's streets. Pullman's idea for improving the sleeping conditions on railroad trains would transform rail travel forever.

But first, he needed to prove it could be done. In 1858, at the age of twenty-seven, he convinced the Chicago & Alton Railroad to allow him to remodel three of their coaches into sleeping cars.

The cars, with fold-down upper berths, were very popular with sleep-starved travelers when they were put into service in the Chicago area. But they were not so popular with the railroads, who wouldn't pay extra for the comfort of passengers. So, Pullman left for the Colorado mining fields, where he opened a general store.

While he ran his general store, he began planning an even better sleeping car. Four years later he returned to Chicago with his patent in hand and began working with a partner on the railroad car—the first true Pullman sleeper. In addition to the upper berth, they added a lower berth, created by sliding the seats together, essentially the design that is used in sleepers to this day. It took them an entire year and $20,000 to build the first car, the *Pioneer.*

Travelers loved the new train, but the railroads were even more reluctant to buy this new car. Pullman's sleepers were too high to fit under standard bridges and too wide to pull up to some platforms. The railroads would have to rebuild bridges and platforms to accommodate the new sleeper. To encourage railroads to make these changes, Pullman arranged to have one of his sleepers attached to President Lincoln's funeral train in April 1865 and to President Grant's official train a few years later. With public pressure for the new cars, the railroads eventually raised their bridges and redesigned their platforms. Soon every railroad in the country began adding Pullman sleepers.

At the age of thirty-six, Pullman and his partner, Ben Field, organized the Pullman Palace Car Company in 1867. It became the biggest railroad car manufacturer in the world. The inventive Pullman continued to add more types of cars. In 1867, he created the first combination sleeping and restaurant car, and then a freestanding dining car. To allow passengers to move from their sleeping cars to the dining car, Pullman next created a "vestibule car," with elastic diaphragms to seal the two cars together, even on sharp curves. He also began building the luxurious private "palace cars" that became the new status symbols of the very rich. In place of the horse-drawn carriages of the old days, the wealthy purchased custom railroad cars with stained glass and chandeliers, mahogany, observation lounges, and pipe organs. As one of the wealthiest citizens of his age, Pullman himself had his own palace car, the *Monitor.*

Commodore Cornelius Vanderbilt refused to use Pullman's cars on his New York Central line. So Pullman challenged his powerful rival by erecting his own rail line across the Hudson River to compete with Vanderbilt. The West Shore Railroad paralleled Vanderbilt's line all the way to Buffalo. After Pullman sold his interest in the railroad, the existence of the two roads later led to bitter railroad wars until the lines were ultimately consolidated.

Vanderbilt had backed a rival sleep car manufacturer (Webster Wagner) and Andrew Carnegie had supported another rival (Theodore Woodruff). But Pullman, with only the support of his shareholders, built the leading company in the industry.

Pullman established plants across the country, creating a whole town for building railroad cars—Pullman, Illinois. Completed in 1881, the city of Pullman was designed as a model industrial town. In stark contrast to the crime and slums of most industrial areas, Pullman offered sturdy brick houses on paved streets with modern gas, sewer, water, and electric. The town boasted a movie theater, library, school, church, and shopping center. Residents of the company town would sometimes complain that they were baptized in a Pullman church, and when they died they would probably go to a Pullman heaven or a Pullman hell.

The paternalistic town was designed to provide Pullman with a contented and captive workforce, but it was actually the site of some of the most bitter labor disputes in the nation's history. In 1894, the depression led Pullman to slash wages, but rents in the town of Pullman remained the same. The result was a bitter strike at the Pullman plant. Members of the American Railway Union, in sympathy, refused to work on all railway trains that carried Pullman cars, tying up rail traffic across the United States. Rioters in Chicago burned millions of dollars in railroad property before the strike was quelled by National Guardsmen who stormed into Pullman's workers' paradise with machine guns. In 1898, the Illinois Supreme Court ruled that the company had no right to build a city of its own, and Pullman was absorbed into Chicago.

When he died in 1897, just three years after the Pullman Strike, Pullman was a bitter and broken man. He was generous in private life, but in business he was often described as cold, arrogant, and autocratic. His fortune, once as high as $40 million, had been depleted by the labor strife. Although it was rumored that his estate had fallen below $8 million, when his will was probated in 1900, the estate was valued at $17.5 million. He gave several large gifts, including $1.2 million for the establishment of a free vocational training school in Pullman, Illinois.

Robert Todd Lincoln, son of the president whose body was transported to his grave in a Pullman car, succeeded Pullman as head of the company.

Paranoid about his former workers, Pullman ordered that his grave be lined with concrete to foil grave robbers. His casket was placed on an 18-inch concrete floor, and eight heavy iron T-rails were placed on top. These rails were covered with another layer of concrete.

Pullman didn't trust his wife or four children much more than his former employees. He left his twin sons an annual income of just $3,000 each, commenting that neither had talents "requisite for wise use of large properties." His wife, who successfully sued to claim the principal, became prominent in society and philanthropy in Chicago, particularly in assisting destitute children, before her death in 1921.

64

Robert Wood Johnson, Jr.
(1893–1968)

Billion-Dollar Band-Aids

Est. wealth: $1 billion or more

Robert Wood Johnson, Jr.—known as General Johnson after his service in World War II—expanded and built the surgical dressings company founded by his father and uncles into an international powerhouse, manufacturing pharmaceuticals, personal-care products, and other goods.

The wiry, blond-haired Johnson was known for his take-charge attitude. When he was mayor of Highland Park, New Jersey, he once received a call during a formal dinner party from an irate resident. The woman said her trash hadn't been picked up and that he was a lousy mayor. Johnson left his twenty guests and, still dressed in his formal wear, hopped in his station wagon and drove to the woman's house. When the astonished woman pointed out the garbage can, Johnson picked it up, put it in the back of his car and hauled it to the dump.

Johnson's father, Robert Wood Johnson, Sr., had been a New England pharmacist when he began developing and manufacturing antiseptic bandages. He set up the Johnson & Johnson Company with his brothers James and Edward Mead. The elder Johnson was a pioneer in applying the teachings of Joseph Lister, who advocated antiseptic surgery and protecting wounds to prevent infection. Johnson worked on the practical application of these theories, developing a surgical dressing that would be as germfree as possible.

Robert Wood Johnson, Jr., was born in 1893 in New Brunswick, New Jersey, where Johnson & Johnson had established its corporate headquarters just a few years before. Johnson did not attend college, and at seventeen, he joined his father's firm as a mill hand. He moved rapidly up the organization. By twenty-five, he was named vice president, by thirty-nine, he was president, and he became chairman of the board at forty-five. When Johnson took the helm of the company, it was primarily a domestic firm, with sales of about $11 million per year. He expanded the product line and extended its geographic reach to 120 countries. When he died, the company was the world's largest manufacturer of surgical dressings, medical aids, and baby products. It had annual sales of $750 million.

A respected corporate leader, Johnson earned the title of general during World War II, when he rose to the rank of brigadier general. He served in a variety of capacities, including captain of the Medical Corps and chief of the New York Ordnance District. Finally he was named vice chairman of the War Production Board.

Johnson applied that same discipline and spirit of service to running the company. For him, creating a model organization was every bit as important as building profits. He once said, "We are building not only frameworks of stone and steel but frameworks of ideas and ideals." He advocated decentralizing the business, raising minimum wages, and improving working conditions. He encouraged his employees to take risks.

James Burke, who later became chairman and CEO of Johnson & Johnson, recalled Johnson's reaction to a failure early in Burke's career. Burke, who was then director of new products, had tried to market a new chest rub designed like modern stick deodorants. It was a flop, and the General called him to his office. Burke thought he was surely going to be fired.

"I understand that your product failed," Johnson said.

"Yes, sir. That's true," a nervous Burke replied.

"I understand it cost this corporation $865,000."

"Yes, sir. That's right."

Then Johnson stood up and extended his hand to the startled Burke. "I just want to congratulate you," he told Burke. "Nothing happens unless people are willing to make decisions, and you can't make decisions without making mistakes."

Johnson also was an outspoken corporate advocate for the rights of workers, and he promoted fair wages. He also took care of his managers, saying, "Make your top managers rich and they will make you richer." The J&J credo became a model for corporate social responsibility.

In his youth, the energetic Johnson enjoyed yachting, playing tennis, hunting, and flying airplanes. He won several yachting cups and participated in a race across the Atlantic Ocean to Spain. He also explored near the Arctic. He enjoyed flying planes and helicopters and fox hunting near his Revolutionary-era home, Morven, in Princeton, New Jersey. He was known as a polished speaker with a keen sense of humor.

Johnson said that "to ignore the conditions of the many underpaid people in the United States is as foolish as it would be to ignore public health, crime, and the need for education."

General Johnson and his brother, John Seward, had inherited 84 percent interest in Johnson & Johnson. They took the firm public in 1944, retaining about 70 percent of the company. When he died in 1968 at the age of 74, Johnson carried his spirit of social concern into his personal bequest, giving nearly $1 billion in J&J stock to establish the Robert Wood Johnson Foundation, the second-largest foundation in the nation and the largest one devoted to health care. It ensured that the concern Johnson showed throughout his lifetime will be carried on for years to come. Johnson was survived by his widow and two children.

His brother, John Seward, who died in 1983, left an estate to his widow and six children that would grow to an estimated $1.6 billion by 1995. By 1990, Johnson & Johnson had grown to more than $9 billion in sales with more than 82,000 employees.

John Francis Dodge
(1864–1920)

Horace Elgin Dodge
(1868–1920)

Twin Engines of the Auto Industry
Est. wealth: more than $100 million each

The friendship and the business partnership between brothers John and Horace Dodge were as dependable as a Dodge automobile. They began life, in John's words, as "the poorest little urchins ever born," and rose together to become legendary master automakers. They were the muscle behind Henry Ford's success, and then went on to create their own car company, building a joint fortune of more than $200 million. For years the two redheaded brothers worked side by side, day and night. Coincidentally, at the height of their careers, they died months apart in 1920.

The Dodge brothers, who grew up in Detroit, Michigan, were so inseparable that they often refused to respond to mail unless it was sent to "the Dodge Brothers" with a capital *B*. When their family arrived in Detroit in 1886, the young Dodges worked in a boiler factory at salaries of less than $20 per week. When John Dodge came down with tuberculosis, they both realized that John needed to do less strenuous work. According to one story, John talked to a company about a job, but the owner said he had only one opening. "Either both of us come to work, or neither of us will," said Horace. They ate lunches together and spent weekends together. They were known to finish each other's sentences, wore identical suits and derby hats, and worked side by side throughout their careers.

The first vehicle they produced was a bicycle. Every day when Horace rode his bicycle to work, he thought about how hard bikes were to maintain because dirt from the unpaved roads got into the bearings. Horace, a keen mechanic and inventor, began tinkering in his workshop at home and came up with a dirt-resistant ball bearing. John saw the business possibilities, and they started a bicycle company. They built a successful company, which they ultimately sold for $7,500 in cash.

The brothers used their newfound capital to set up Dodge Brothers machine shop in Detroit. They worked sixteen to eighteen hours a day, snatching a few hours of sleep on a tool bench. Horace worked on the designs while John worked on the books and the business. When they started, they earned less than the skilled machinists who worked for them.

The Dodge Brothers first made automobile engines for Oldsmobile cars. Ransom Olds liked the engines so much, he ordered 3,000 transmissions as well, making the Dodge Brothers one of the largest automotive suppliers of the day. By the time Henry Ford came to the Dodge Brothers in 1903, they were a large and highly successful enterprise. Ford was a small, poorly funded startup company. The Dodge Brothers decided to take a gamble on this unproven car company and became instrumental in Ford's success. They did most of the manufacturing of the first Ford cars based on his designs. They also became two of the biggest shareholders in the new company, which would soon dominate the automotive industry.

The Dodges then set out to build their own car company.

The first Dodge Brothers car was meticulously crafted. Every part was surveyed by Horace's keen mechanical eye. The Dodges, distrustful of the welded metal body that had been subcontracted, added many rivets to it, "just in case." They dropped the tires off the top of the four-story plant, and John personally crash-tested the car by driving it at twenty miles per hour into a brick wall.

The first Dodge car was built in 1914, one of 120 new makes of cars to enter the market that year. While it was a bit more pricey than the low-budget Fords, the Dodge set new standards for honest value and reliability. It even came with a sixty-one-page owners' manual, the first of its kind.

Dodge automobiles soon were legendary. A Dodge carried Lieutenant George S. Patton, Jr., on a daring assault on the Mexican headquarters of one of Pancho Villa's commanders in 1916. After the forty-mile-per-hour raid, Patton proclaimed the motorcar "the modern warhorse."

The reputation of the Dodge brothers themselves proved no less glowing. During World War I, two companies had tried and failed to make the delicate recoil mechanism for the French 155mm field artillery, which was constantly jamming. The big brass in Washington turned to the Dodge brothers. Horace redesigned the mechanism and it worked perfectly. The patriotic Dodge Brothers refused to accept any profit from the product.

Dodge continued to gain on Ford, ultimately moving into the number two position in the industry by 1921, with more than 150,000 cars per year. Their success as rivals drew Henry Ford's wrath. Ford ultimately got tired of the Dodge brothers' control of his company, and they tired of "being carried around in Henry Ford's vest pocket," as John Dodge once commented. Ford announced that he would no longer pay dividends to shareholders, but would instead invest the money back into the company. The move was clearly designed to hurt his largest shareholders, the Dodges, who relied on the Ford capital for their own business. The Dodges protested and forced Ford in court to pay $2 million in dividends to the brothers. Ford then bought out the Dodges' share of the company.

John Dodge died on January 14, 1920, stricken with influenza or pneumonia. After his brother's death, the robust health of Horace began to deteriorate. In November, the day before Horace made his last trip to Palm Beach, Florida, he visited his brother's Woodlawn tomb. Two weeks later, Horace died in Florida of cirrhosis of the liver. The sudden deaths of the two brothers, both in their fifties, led to rumors they had been poisoned, perhaps even by arch rival Henry Ford. There seemed to be little merit to this speculation. They died of natural illnesses, and in Horace's case, perhaps of a broken heart at the loss of his brother.

Unfortunately, the Dodges had not prepared their children to take over the business. The family sold Dodge Brothers in 1925. The huge inheritance brought the family nothing but grief, in their personal and professional lives, with strings of financial losses, failed marriages, and premature deaths. Horace's widow, Anna Dodge, later commented that "wealth is a curse."

Their families, which the brothers spent little time on, collapsed under the pressures of the massive inheritance. The Dodge business, however, on which they lavished most of their attention, continued to succeed. In 1928, the Dodge Brothers company was bought by a small firm called the Chrysler Corporation, which overnight became the third largest car company in the world. Chrysler rode the Dodge reputation to success. Although the two brothers may not be as well remembered as Ford and other automotive pioneers, their name continues to stand for quality in the industry they helped to create.

Prominent but Poor

William Durant

(1861–1947)

FOUNDED GENERAL MOTORS, BUT FOUND NO FORTUNE

William Crapo Durant founded General Motors Corporation, but it didn't make him a wealthy man. He started out manufacturing Buicks, then brought together a group of manufacturers into General Motors in 1908. Financial problems eventually cost him control of the company. Then he founded the Chevrolet Motor Company and used this vehicle to take back control of General Motors in 1915. During World War I, he was again forced out. Finally, he formed a new firm, Durant Motors, in 1921. But Durant Motors and later business ventures were generally unsuccessful. By 1935, he was bankrupt. Durant may not have built a large personal fortune, but he did establish a corporation that would become the largest in the world.

67

J. Paul Getty

(1892–1976)

Rockefeller Redux

Est. wealth: $2 billion

When Vice President Nelson Rockefeller once compared J. Paul Getty's success to that of John D. Rockefeller, Sr., Getty blanched at the comparison. Getty said it was like comparing "a sparrow to an eagle." Whereas the senior Rockefeller had begun his life in poverty, Getty was heir to a multimillion-dollar fortune. Getty also pointed out that his company was much smaller than Rockefeller's Standard Oil mega-empire. Exxon Corp., a spin-off of Standard Oil, earned twice as much in profits as Getty's total sales for 1973.

But there were striking similarities between the two giants. Both men had made their success through the growth of the oil industry—one during its infancy and the other during its international expansion. Both were declared America's richest man. Although Getty never contended, as Rockefeller did, that his fortune was a divine gift, he wrote that he had no trouble comparing himself to a "Caesar." By the time he died in 1976, his estate was at least $2 billion.

Young Jean Paul learned about the oil business from this father, George F. Getty, a successful oil man who ran the Minnehoma Oil company in Tulsa, Oklahoma. With his father's backing, J. Paul began investing in oil leases in what were believed to be worthless oil fields in Oklahoma, but that turned out to be rich in oil. J. Paul had earned his first million from these investments by the time he was twenty-four in 1916. He then moved to California, where he spent the next two years living as a playboy in Los Angeles. In 1919 he returned to business with his father, speculating on oil leases and drilling wildcat wells.

The younger Getty's wild lifestyle—including a series of marriages and divorces—and his risky investments made his father wary about turning his fortune over to him. When he died in 1930, George Getty left J. Paul only $500,000 of his $10 million estate, and half of that bequest went for taxes. Most of the elder Getty's oil business passed on to J. Paul's mother, Sarah Getty.

J. Paul's dreams of building an oil empire soon outstripped his own resources, and he wanted access to his father's estate. So he fought his own mother in court for her stake in George F. Getty, Inc. She finally sold her share of the business to J. Paul for $4.5 million, which he paid in promissory notes. He confided to his publicist, "I just fleeced my mother." But Sarah may have had the last laugh. To protect her son and family from his own speculations, she established the $2.5 million Sarah Getty Trust to provide for J. Paul and his sons. The trust became a dominant force in Getty Oil. When Getty Oil was sold to Texaco in 1984, Sarah Getty's trust was worth over $4 billion.

Getty had a combination of skill in investments and financial maneuvering and an ability to spot long-shot bets that would pay off. He was either very shrewd or very lucky—placing bets on land that others had written off and somehow managing to strike it big. He was often a tiny David who took on the Goliaths of the oil industry through financial maneuvers.

One of his biggest successes was his investment in the Middle East. In 1949, he achieved a coup by obtaining a sixty-year concession from Saudi Arabia for oil in a no-man's-land between

Saudi Arabia and Kuwait. He took the fields right out from under the noses of the major oil companies because they didn't consider the fields valuable. Getty paid an unprecedented price for the rights to the oil fields, and he spent more than four years drilling without much to show for it. Then he made a strike that *Fortune* declared was "somewhere between colossal and history making."

Getty could get money from a stone. Others had written off the low-grade "garbage oil" that was in abundant supply in his neutral zone in the Middle East. Getty saw its value and systematically began turning it into gasoline and selling it on the world market. He built a refinery in Delaware and put together a fleet of tankers.

His Middle East successes helped propel him into billionaire status and made his company the "eighth sister" in the oil industry. (The "seven sisters" were British Petroleum, Royal Dutch Shell, Standard Oil of New Jersey, Standard Oil of California, Mobil, Texaco, and Gulf.) With the addition of Tidewater and Skelly oil companies—wrested by Getty out of the hands of Standard Oil—the Getty Oil Company had total assets of $3 billion by 1967.

At the age of sixty-four, Getty was hoisted out of obscurity by a 1957 *Fortune* article that declared him to be America's richest man. They listed his wealth as $700 million to $1 billion. He commented wryly to Art Buchwald, "It looks like I'll have to change my name if I expect to get any peace."

Getty was a complex personality. He was America's richest man but spent the last quarter century of his life living outside the United States (although he never gave up his citizenship). During World War II, he was a suspected Nazi sympathizer, yet he personally ran an aircraft company that built parts for Liberator bombers. His life revolved around building a family business, yet he was married and divorced five times.

Getty, who had no qualms about being called a Caesar, also had no reservations about living like one. He constructed a $17 million re-creation of a Roman villa on his property in Malibu, which eventually became the museum housing his art collection. Getty also invested in real estate. In 1938 he bought the Hotel Pierre in New York City for $2.3 million, and he built the Getty Building on Madison Avenue. In 1959 Getty purchased the sixty-acre Sutton Place estate in England and lived the rest of his life there amid British nobility. (Even in purchasing this distinguished country estate, Getty was ever the bargain hunter. He bragged that his purchase price of $140,000 was estimated to be just one-twentieth of its replacement value.)

Getty also was known as a skinflint, saving bits of string to tie up packages. He had his secretary check every item on his grocery bill before he would pay it. He also washed his own underwear—not, he contended, to save money but because he didn't like the detergent the laundry used.

Even when he died in 1976 at the age of 83, the expatriate did not find peace. He had left instructions for his remains to be buried near his museum in California. But state laws did not permit burial on private property. So his remains spent more than two years floating around the Forest Lawn cemetery until he was finally allowed to be laid to rest on the Pacific coast.

After a succession of five failed marriages between 1923 and 1939, Getty gave up on matrimony. But he was always surrounded by a harem of beautiful women, attracted by his wealth and, reportedly, his sexual prowess. At the age of sixty-one, Getty reportedly had compiled a list of a hundred lovers whom he remembered fondly.

He had a stormy relationship with his five sons, and changed his will twenty-one times in an effort to control his heirs. His youngest son, Timmy, died of a brain tumor at the age of twelve. His eldest son, George, died from an overdose of assorted pills, in what was believed to be a suicide. Getty didn't return to the United States to attend either of the funerals. Getty fired his namesake, Jean Paul Jr., and didn't consider any of his children worthy to follow him in business. Biographer Robert Lenzner describes the family as "an alienated group." After Getty's death, his company was sold to Texaco for more than $10 billion.

The money and fame of the Getty fortune continued to haunt his heirs. His grandson Jean Paul Getty III was kidnapped in 1973 and held for ransom, and the kidnappers cut off his right ear and sent it to an Italian newspaper. His family paid the ransom and he was released. Aileen Getty, daughter of Jean Paul, Jr., conducted an interview with NBC's *Dateline* in February 1996, in which she said, "I hate being a Getty," and complained that her family had cut her off financially. She later retracted her statements, saying they were a result of drug abuse.

Several Getty heirs remained on the *Forbes* 400 list in 1995. Son Gordon Peter Getty orchestrated the 1984 sale of Getty to

Texaco and is credited with doubling the family fortune to $3 billion. His fortune was estimated at $1.6 billion in 1995. Jean Paul Jr. (Eugene Paul), had an estimated estate of $840 million in addition to partial control of the $1.2 billion trust. Three daughters of George Getty possessed fortunes estimated at $570 million apiece.

68

William H. Aspinwall
(1807–1875)
Spanned the Isthmus of Panama
Est. wealth: $4 million

Before the Panama Canal, before the California Gold Rush, William Aspinwall was one of the first businessmen to see the potential of Panama. He had started a steamship line that sailed from the East Coast to the West on the long and perilous route around Cape Horn. Then he decided to cross the isthmus of Panama, a move that made him one of the leading steamship operators in the world.

The son of a merchant and grandson of a sea captain, Aspinwall grew up around shipping. After attending public school, he was apprenticed to his uncles, who were merchants in New York. In 1832 Aspinwall became a partner in the firm, and five years later, his uncles turned the business over to Aspinwall and William Howland. They developed strong ties with Venezuela's president and gained a near monopoly on trade with the republic. They also had strong trading ties with Mexico, the Indies, and the Pacific. Aspinwall became one of the leading merchants in New York.

Then he came up with his scheme to span Panama. He received a charter for the Panama Railroad from the New York legislature and gained approval to build from New Granada officials. For five long years, the crews traced their difficult route across the jungles of the isthmus, covering less than ten miles per year. They laid forty-nine miles of track through the pest-infested strip of land dividing the Atlantic from the Pacific.

Aspinwall and partners also set up the Pacific Mail Steamship Company, running ships from New York to the east coast of Panama, and then ships to California from the Pacific side. It cut the length of the sea voyage to California from eight months around the Horn to just two months across Panama.

It still didn't look like a very good bet when the Pacific Mail company was established in 1848. By then, only six thousand people had traveled to California by land or sea. Aspinwall had always been viewed as a very conservative investor. Could he have lost his touch?

Then came the Gold Rush of 1849. Soon the prospectors were streaming to the West Coast and hauling back their gold to the East. Aspinwall and his Pacific Mail line could hardly keep up with the traffic. In 1849, more than 35,000 people came to California by sea alone. By 1850, California's population had grown from a handful of scattered farmers to more than 96,000. Its population was larger than the state of Delaware. Many of the citizens came on the Pacific Mail.

Aspinwall later faced competition from Vanderbilt's route across Lake Nicaragua, and finally lost most of his passengers to the Union Pacific Railroad when the transcontinental tracks were completed in 1869. But Aspinwall had already made his millions. The railroad alone had netted about $6 million for its investors by 1859.

Aspinwall resigned as president of the steamship company in 1856. During the Civil War, he served the United States as a secret emissary for Abraham Lincoln in England. There, he petitioned the British government not to sell iron-clads to the Confederates.

Between his success in trade and transcontinental travel, Aspinwall had become one of the richest men in New York. He helped found the Society for the Prevention of Cruelty to Animals and became a civic leader. But perhaps the best tribute to his vision and accomplishments came at the completion of the Panama railroad. For the thousands of settlers and traders who arrived on the Atlantic Coast of Panama by steamship, their first sight was a terminal named Aspinwall, in honor of the man who had driven the project to its completion.

Aspinwall's Pacific Mail Line was absorbed into Dollar Steamship in 1925, and later became American President Lines. The current company, American President Companies, Ltd., is the leading company in trans-Pacific shipping. And as a result of their acquisition of Aspinwall's line, the company claims to be "the oldest continuously operated steamship company in the United States."

69

Johns Hopkins
(1795–1873)
Builder of Baltimore
Est. wealth: $10 million

The city of Baltimore was officially incorporated just one year after Johns Hopkins was born, and the man and the city grew up together. In 1800, when Hopkins was a young child, Baltimore had a population of just 35,000. By 1860 Baltimore had become the nation's third largest city, with a population of more than 200,000, and Hopkins was one of its most prominent and wealthy citizens.

Hopkins was born on his family's Maryland tobacco plantation in 1795. He received his unusual first name in honor of his great-grandmother, Margaret Johns, daughter of the owner of a 4,000-acre estate in Calvert County, Maryland. Her son was the first to receive the name Johns Hopkins, and the name was then passed on to his grandson.

The younger Johns Hopkins's parents were prominent Quakers. When they freed their slaves in 1807, twelve-year-old Hopkins and siblings were pulled out of school to work on the plantation. At seventeen, he joined his uncle's wholesale grocery and commission business in Baltimore. The uncle, Gerard Hopkins, was a wholesale grocer and commission merchant.

Hopkins fell in love with his cousin Elizabeth, but his uncle forbade their marriage. Both of them remained close friends throughout their lives and neither married. It led to a falling out between Hopkins and his uncle.

Throughout his career, Johns Hopkins balanced a desire for success in business against his Quaker heritage. The former drove him to build a fortune of nearly $10 million. The latter led him to give most of it away.

Hopkins also faced a conflict between his business sense and religious values over the issue of whiskey. During the hard times of 1819, many customers wanted to pay for their goods in whiskey. His uncle refused to trade in alcohol, vowing that he would not "sell souls into perdition." This and the differences over Elizabeth drove Johns Hopkins out on his own. He set up his own business when he was twenty-four, with the help of a $10,000 loan from his uncle.

Johns Hopkins's traffic in whiskey led to his expulsion from the Society of Friends meetings, although he was later reinstated. It turned out, however, to be the basis for a very profitable business. He expanded into Virginia, North Carolina, and Ohio. He later shifted from dealing in hard goods to banking. He financed projects and invested in property in Baltimore and other areas.

His most significant investment was the Baltimore & Ohio Railroad. The construction of the Erie Canal threatened to undermine Baltimore's position as a commercial center. The railroad, the first U.S. railroad to carry passengers, gave the city a new lease on life. Hopkins became director of the railroad in 1855. During the panic of 1873, he lent the railroad $900,000 to carry it through the crisis.

Hopkins also became a guardian angel of Baltimore. He loaned the city half a million dollars to take it through the turmoil of the Civil War. During the panic of 1873, he shored up city finances and kept the local economy from collapsing.

Although Hopkins had always wanted to travel, his business and personal life revolved around Baltimore. There he made his success in business, and he established one of the world's leading universities, which bears his name.

Although he counted his pennies when it came to his personal spending, he was very generous in giving away his fortune. Shortly before his death, he decided to devote his fortune to the service of humanity. He was perhaps influenced by his good friend George Peabody, who founded Baltimore's Peabody Institute. After making provisions for his family, Hopkins bequeathed the bulk of his fortune to charity when he died on Christmas Eve in 1873. Having lived through epidemics of cholera and yellow fever, he decided to found a medical school. He gave a total of $7 million equally divided between the Johns Hopkins University and the Johns Hopkins Hospital. It was the largest philanthropic bequest in U.S. history. Thus, Johns Hopkins would always remain at the heart of the city that was at the center of his life, and the millionaire who left school when he was twelve would forever be associated with one of the world's leading universities.

70

John Werner Kluge

(1914–   )

High-Tech High Roller

Est. wealth: $6.7 billion

"*K*lug" means *clever* in German, and John Werner Kluge has certainly lived up to his name. He used his innate cleverness and gambler's instincts to build a huge communications empire—spanning radio, television, and cellular phones. His successes placed him at the top of the *Forbes 400* list for three years in a row, before his $6.7 billion fortune was outpaced by Bill Gates and Warren Buffett.

Kluge's father, an engineer in Germany, died in 1922 when Kluge was only eight, and he and his mother immigrated to the United States. They settled in Detroit, where Kluge worked on a Ford assembly line. He later left for New York to study economics at Columbia on scholarship. To pay for his expenses, he sold shoes and did secretarial work.

Kluge's most lucrative college job, however, was sitting at the card table. He may have majored in economics in college, but he minored in poker playing, raking in $7,000 in winnings by the time he graduated in 1937 (worth about $70,000 in 1990 dollars). He

has applied the same gambling spirit to the business world. "Taking a business risk is where I get my kicks," he told the *Washington Post* in a 1987 interview.

Kluge always played against the odds, building his fortune

from almost nothing through a series of successively larger bets—often against the advice of his financial advisers. Kluge invested in the unproven technology of television in the 1950s. He later took on dying stations that others had abandoned and turned them around, and when the world was tuned to AM radio, he bought FM. More recently, while television viewers were watching the new sitcoms, he was returning to the golden oldies like *I Love Lucy, The Dick Van Dyke Show,* and *Father Knows Best.* He also was among the first to roll the dice in cellular phones and paging devices, by investing in these markets when many investors thought they were unlikely to develop.

Kluge's first bet was a small one. After working as an executive in wholesale food distribution, he had saved enough to pay $15,000 to purchase his first radio station in 1946. From this little outpost in Silver Spring, Maryland, he moved on to buy a controlling interest in the Metropolitan Broadcasting Corporation in 1959. The company, which later became Metromedia, owned WNEW-TV in New York and WTTG-TV in Washington along with a Cleveland radio station. By 1961, Metromedia was the fastest growing group broadcaster in the United States, and by the early 1980s it was the largest independent operator of radio and television stations. Kluge continued to expand his empire. He made Metromedia the biggest outdoor advertising company, with 35,000 billboards. He bought the Ice Capades, the Harlem Globetrotters, and picked up Jacques Cousteau documentaries. He also spent more than $270 million to purchase small paging companies that held local cellular licences, soon becoming a leader in cellular telephones and paging.

Kluge has had his share of bad hands, but he usually knows when to fold. He purchased World Wide Broadcasting in 1960, the only commercial short-wave radio station in the United States. It was a private version of Voice of America. The station was failing when he picked it up, and it continued to bleed red ink. Still he managed to sell it at a million-dollar profit to the Church of Jesus Christ of Latter Day Saints two years later. He wasn't as lucky when he made an unsuccessful attempt to found a magazine covering the lives of diplomats around the world. He suffered considerable losses before the magazine folded. His luck in business also didn't extend to his personal life. He has been married three times. In 1981 he married his third wife, a former magazine model, and he converted to Catholicism.

In 1984, he took on his highest stakes game in his life. He launched a leveraged buyout to take Metromedia private. With the help of Michael Milken, Kluge raised $1.2 billion in junk bonds, but then had to sell off parts of the company to pay back the debt. Some observers thought he couldn't possibly liquidate enough assets in time to meet his payments. But he did. He sold off television and radio stations. He sent the Globetrotters trotting and put the Ice Capades on ice. And finally, much to the surprise of the business world, he sold off his cellular telephone and paging operations. He ended up with $2.5 billion in cash.

He has since bought stakes in long-distance telecommunications, food chains (Ponderosa, Bonanza, Steak & Ale, Bennigan's), and motion pictures (Orion Pictures). After his successful leveraged buyout of his own company, he also participated in several other LBOs. Since the end of the Cold War, he has expanded his television and telephone business in Eastern Europe.

Kluge has shown his gratitude to his alma mater, Columbia University, giving more than $100 million to the school. He has particularly supported minority scholarships. He wants to ensure that others will have the same opportunities he had. And maybe he is also grateful because it was at Columbia that he learned two lessons that have helped him build his fortune: the importance of economics, and the value of a good poker hand.

He doesn't revel in the attention his fame and fortune has brought him. As he once said, "If I had my choice, I'd stay in the woodwork all my life." The five-foot-seven Kluge, compact as a linebacker, is known for his good humor and down-to-earth style. *Vogue* called his eighth-floor apartment in the Metromedia building in New York the "satin citadel" and his primary home is the $250 million Morven Farm in Charlottesville, Virginia, which includes a huge mansion, a golf course designed by Arnold Palmer, and a working cattle ranch. He ranked third on the October 1995 *Forbes 400* list, with a fortune estimated at $6.7 billion.

71

Samuel Colt
(1814–1862)
The Gunslinger
Est. wealth: $5 million

Samuel Colt, the inventor of the multifiring Colt revolver, was so much trouble as a young man that his father sent him to sea at the age of sixteen. A year as a sailor was expected to help the fiery young man settle a bit.

Colt had a lot of time to think during the sea voyage to India. But he wasn't thinking about how he could become an upstanding citizen or help run his father's silk and cotton manufacturing business in Connecticut. During a stop in London, Colt was impressed by several repeating firearms he saw on display in the Tower of London. A sharp inventor with a quick mind, Colt started thinking about his own weapon. On the ship, he whittled a wooden model of a gun with a revolving barrel. (An alternative to the Tower of London story is that he developed the idea for his revolver's action from watching the ship's wheel turning.)

Colt returned with the desire to build his new invention, but he had no funds. He spent a year working in his father's dyeing and bleaching business in Ware, Massachusetts. He took particular interest in the chemical work at the plant. Then, the nineteen-year-old told his father he wanted "to paddle his own canoe." For the next three years, he used his knowledge of chemistry to raise funds to develop his new invention. He hit the lecture circuit— under the name of "the celebrated Dr. S. Coult [*sic*] of New York, London, and Calcutta"—giving demonstrations on chemistry with a particular emphasis on the effects of laughing gas.

Soon he had raised enough funds to build a prototype of his revolver. He built a pistol and rifle in 1833, and obtained patents in England and France. In 1836, he secured a U.S. patent for his five-shooter. It was the first practical multifiring weapon. He started the Patent Arms Manufacturing Company in Paterson, New Jersey, with $200,000 from his cousin and other investors. Colt couldn't convince the U.S. Army to buy his new weapons. They didn't perform well in tests at West Point, and the head purchaser for the army considered them too bulky. The Patent Arms company failed in 1842, and he lost his patent rights to other companies.

Colt's friends suggested he give up his quest to create a revolver company and use his connections to find a comfortable government job. He wasn't interested. He wrote defiantly to a relative: "However inferior in wealth I may be to the many who surround me, I would not exchange for their treasures the satisfaction I have in knowing I have done what has never before been accomplished by man . . . I would rather be at the head of a louse than at the tail of a lyon!"

Colt continued to invent, working on underwater cartridges and batteries for submarines and mines for blowing up enemy ships. The mines were effective but were considered by military and political leaders of the time to be too brutal. John Quincy Adams, then a U.S. Congressman, called them "an unChristian contraption." Colt also helped Samuel B. Morse, the inventor of the telegraph, develop his first telegraph line between Washington, D.C., and Baltimore. Colt also developed an underwater telegraph line between New York and Coney Island.

But then, even though he had folded his company, Colt began receiving requests for his revolvers. These orders came not from the military but from Texas Rangers and other western frontiersmen. The Rangers, battling Indians who could shoot arrow after arrow while riding at full speed, had no time to stop and reload. The revolvers allowed mounted Rangers to return fire repeatedly without stopping. Ranger Captain Samuel Walker said Colt's weapon, with a few modifications, could be "the most perfect weapon in the world for light mounted troops." The Texas Rangers were demanding a bigger .44 caliber six-shooter, which Colt designed and built. More orders streamed in from the California gold fields, where the Colt became the law of the land.

Colt was back in the arms business, but he struggled along until the Mexican War broke out in 1846. He was so financially strapped that he tried to enlist in an army rifle regiment, but he was rejected. A short time later, however, he received a massive order from the U.S. government for 1,000 revolvers to fight the war. Colt bought back his patent rights and set up a plant in Connecticut.

Still, Colt would have remained a small manufacturer of weapons if he had not developed a system for meeting the increased demand for his revolvers. He initially subcontracted the work to Eli Whitney, Jr., who had inherited his father's gun-making factory. Then Colt brought in talented machinists and managers who built the first equipment and processes for mass production. While they may not have achieved truly interchangeable parts (as Colt sometimes advertised), they did achieve an unprecedented level of efficiency and uniformity. This "American system" became world renowned.

By the time he died, Colt had more than 1,500 men working in his Hartford, Connecticut, factory. His revolvers had become the symbol of both outlaws and order in the Wild West. Colt himself was a frontiersman of a different sort. He had tamed the business of mass production of weapons and built himself a fortune of more than $5 million.

Prominent but Poor

Eli Whitney

(1756–1825)

COTTON GIN KING DETHRONED

Eli Whitney should have been set for life with the invention of the cotton gin in 1793. But the invention, which transformed agriculture in the South, was snatched from his hands by the cotton spinning industry. It took him a year to patent the machine, and by that time rivals had already sprung up to meet the overwhelming demand for the machine that could do the work of fifty laborers. Whitney finally won a bitter court battle to protect his rights to the machine, but by then his patent protection had almost expired. He petitioned Congress for an extension of the patent but was turned down. As Gustavus Myers notes, "He had given millions upon millions of dollars to the cotton-growing states, he had opened the way for the establishment of the vast cotton-spinning interests of his own country and Europe, and yet, after fourteen years of hard labor, he was a poor man, the victim of wealthy, powerful, and, in his case, a dishonest class." Whitney later partially rebuilt a bit of his fortunes with a government contract to make rifles. It was here that he began to apply the principles of the assembly line and the idea of interchangeable parts that would later become the basis for American manufacturing. Overall, despite his efforts to make a fortune in business, he contributed much more to the economic success of the nation than he did to his own pocket.

72

James Stillman
(1850–1918)
The Invisible Hand
Est. wealth: $77 million

When James Stillman was a child, he and his siblings used to enjoy playing banker. They kept their play money in a tin box marked "City Bank." Stillman's father was a successful cotton merchant in New York, and Moses Taylor, president of the *real* (National) City Bank, was a frequent visitor to their home. It was no wonder they made his bank the center of their play.

Before long, Stillman would replace the play money with real money. And the tin box would become the National City Bank building. As president of the bank, Stillman would wield power and influence over the development of the nation that must have exceeded anything in his childhood fantasies. He was, according to

B. C. Forbes, "second only to Morgan in shaping the financial destinies of the United States during the last years of the nineteenth and the first decade of the twentieth century."

Stillman was far less visible in his dealings than J. P. Morgan, but he was just as omnipresent. Many of the large conglomerates of the time owe their success to the financial skill and deep pockets of James Stillman and his National City Bank.

Before Stillman came to National City Bank, he had already made a comfortable fortune. When his father was forced to step down from his cotton business because of ill health, Stillman took over and ran the mercantile firm. He widened his investments. He served as a director of the Chicago, Milwaukee & St. Paul Railroad, where he met William Rockefeller (John D.'s younger brother). Rockefeller became a lifelong friend and both of Stillman's daughters married Rockefeller sons.

In 1884, at the age of thirty-four, Stillman was appointed director of the National City Bank, and he was named president in 1891, at the urging of William Rockefeller. Stillman learned well from Moses Taylor, who had been his financial mentor. He knew the value of keeping up high reserves, and the bank's deposits and gold reserves far surpassed those of rivals. Stillman even bought gold from Europe during the Panic of 1893 to demonstrate to investors that the bank was on solid financial footing. The bank soon became the leading institution on Wall Street. The bank's reserves were also instrumental in helping restore stability during the Panic of 1907. Stillman was a vocal advocate for the stronger banks coming to the aid of the weaker ones.

The primary source of Stillman's fortune, and the bank's success, was his use of his large war chest to help the "Rockefeller gang" build the major conglomerates that were to dominate business at the turn of the century. He bankrolled Standard Oil, Amalgamated Copper, and Consolidated Gas. He shocked Wall Street by handling sales of stocks in these new companies, which was not usually part of the work of a national bank. He lined up with E. H. Harriman in the railroad battle for control of the Northern Pacific against James J. Hill and J. P. Morgan. He built the bank from a successful commercial bank to a major investment bank.

Stillman took the job of banking very seriously. He once compared the work of a bank to the heart pumping blood out into the body. He believed this infusion of capital flowing through bloodstreams of the nation made the country successful.

Perhaps this seriousness about banking was why the shy Stillman was known as a cold, austere man. Friends who saw him during his off hours, however, found him to be warm, energetic, and generous. Even in his philanthropy, Stillman worked quietly and without notice. He did attract some attention in World War I when he came to the aid of French families and children after the war. The gift combined two of his loves—France and children. He traveled frequently to France, which he considered his adopted second country. And, as for children, he once said that if he ever neglected his banking interests, it would be because of his love of children. (He had five children of his own.)

In 1909, Stillman retired as president and spent much of his time at his villa in France. During World War I, he gave generously from his personal fortune to support the Allied cause. Stillman remained chairman of the bank and in 1917 returned to the United States to play a more active role at the bank. When he died in 1918 at the age of 68, he left a fortune estimated at $77 million, along with an even more personal treasure—the small metal City Bank box he had kept from his youth.

National City Bank, later Citibank, became a pioneer in retail banking. Until the 1920s, most banks concentrated on large corporate and individual accounts. In the 1920s, National City began building branches and promoting individual checking and savings accounts. In 1928, National City was the first commercial bank to offer personal loans. Citibank remains one of the leading financial institutions in the world. By 1978 it held $1 of every $25 on deposit in U.S. banks.

One of Stillman's five children, James Alexander Stillman, served as chairman and president of the bank until 1921. Grandson James Stillman Rockefeller served as president of Citibank during the 1950s and 1960s.

73

William Collins Whitney

(1841–1904)

A Gentleman Bandit

Est. wealth: $23 million

William Collins Whitney was born with grace and breeding, but he lacked money. Whitney's ambition was to build a fortune of $50 million and gain a place on Fifth Avenue. He would ultimately do both, and then proceed to squander half his fortune on houses and horses.

In a financial world dominated by rough-hewn and uncultured men, he was a rare and polished stone. He had "a tall, handsome grace that is the despair of men and the admiration of women" and a "careless air of culture." He could dazzle the town with elegant balls, but he could also engage in tough, no-holds-barred business battles for control of New York's transit system. It was his successes in transit, with partner Thomas Fortune Ryan, that made Whitney's fortune.

Whitney studied at Yale and then completed his law degree at Harvard. His well-to-do family was endowed with more culture than cash. His friends from school expected him to head to Congress or maybe even the White House. He would ultimately serve in Washington, but he turned his back on political office to pursue his business interests.

As a corporation counsel for the city of New York, Whitney first made his mark by helping to lead the corruption cases that broke the Tweed Ring, which controlled the city's politics and purse strings. He later worked for the Vanderbilts as a corporate lawyer.

In 1869, he married Flora Payne, daughter of Standard Oil partner Henry B. Payne. His marriage and his own family contacts placed Whitney at the center of the nation's most powerful financial and political circles.

In the early 1880s, his political and business connections brought him into the center of a battle for control of New York City's transit system. Whitney joined with his brother-in-law Oliver H. Payne, Ryan, and other investors in seeking to seize control of the Broadway railway franchise from its owner, Jacob Sharp. Whitney, who was leader of the city's Democratic party and counsel for the city, used his influence to get Mayor Franklin Edison to veto Sharp's request for a franchise. Sharp countered by bribing city aldermen to override the veto. Ryan and Whitney exposed Sharp's bribery payments, and the bad publicity ultimately led Sharp to sell his franchise to Whitney and his partners.

Whitney, through his extensive political connections, helped elect Grover Cleveland as president in 1884. His friend called Whitney to Washington to serve as secretary of the navy. Whitney reluctantly left behind his enterprises in New York to answer the call. In addition to earning a reputation as one of the finest navy secretaries, Whitney and his wife were credited with sparking a renaissance in Washington social life. It was said they entertained 65,000 people during their four years of lavish balls at their sumptuous Washington mansion. Whitney also indulged in his hobby of breeding and racing horses that was to be a lifelong passion.

When Whitney returned to New York, there were rumors that he would make a run for president. Whitney had other ideas. When asked if he was planning a "Whitney for President" campaign, he replied: "Oh, no. I am done with politics. I must make some money. Mrs. Whitney has money; I have none. I am going into New York City street railroads."

Whitney and Ryan continued to expand their city transit network. Between 1888 and 1893, they gained control of most of the trolley and elevated railway franchises in Manhattan and large parts of Brooklyn. Their Metropolitan Street Railway Company carried almost a third of the city's annual $500 million in fares, with more than a half-million passengers daily. In a little over five years, he and Ryan had each made over $40 million.

They used their resources to launch a raid on James Buchanan Duke's tobacco company, eventually joining with him to create the American Tobacco Company. Whitney helped the Guggenheim family fend off a bid by Henry H. Rogers for control of the copper smelting industry.

Whitney liked the pomp and the power of wealth. He built ten mansions—including one next to the home of his former employer, Cornelius Vanderbilt—assembled art collections, and purchased private railroad cars. But his greatest passion was racing horses, a hobby he pursued with the same intense ambition that he displayed in his business life. He spent millions acquiring the best horses and building the best stables. His thoroughbred Volodyovski won the English Derby.

Horses were not his only indulgence. As Henry Adams commented, Whitney "had gratified every ambition, and swung the country almost at his will; he had thrown away the object of political ambition like the ashes of smoked cigarettes . . . New York no longer knew what most to envy, his horses or his houses." His extravagances, even as they enhanced his reputation, depleted his fortunes by an estimated $28 million. He left a fortune of about $23 million when he died in 1904, which pales in comparison to the $155 million of his partner, Thomas Fortune Ryan.

His eldest son, Harry Payne Whitney, was active in managing the Whitney copper interest with the Guggenheims. He personally led Daniel Guggenheim through the western United States, acquiring valuable mineral rights for the Guggenheim Exploration Company. He married sculptor Gertrude Vanderbilt, daughter of Cornelius Vanderbilt II.

74

William Thaw
(1818–1889)

Father of the Trial of the Century

Est. wealth: $12 million

Wiliam Thaw tended to avoid the limelight, quietly building a $12 million fortune in the canal, railroad, and coke businesses. He became one of Pittsburgh's leading citizens. The same could not be said for his son. The sordid details of Harry K. Thaw's life were emblazoned in newspaper headlines in 1906, after the younger Thaw shot and killed architect Stanford White, his wife's former lover. His trial was the O. J. Simpson trial of the early 1900s.

His father, William Thaw, was a quiet and deliberate builder. He started out in the canal business. With his brother-in-law, he became involved in the Pennsylvania & Ohio Canal Line. Their company received and forwarded merchandise on the canal. They also bought interests in 150 steamboat lines. When the days of the canal faded, Thaw moved into railroads, helping lay the tracks west from Pittsburgh to St. Louis. He drew together a mishmash of small lines into a coherent freight network, and ran the Pennsylvania Railroad lines north and west of Pittsburgh. He invested in coke and also kept his hand in the shipping business, helping to establish the Red Star Line.

Other than his significant fortune and business success, he is primarily noted for his interest in science. Among other projects, he supported the work of Samuel Pierpont Langley in building an observatory and studying the laws of flight.

The Thaw fortune might be little known outside of Pittsburgh, except for the exploits of one of his ten children. The insane millionaire Harry K. Thaw perpetrated what became known as "the murder of the century."

Harry, who had inherited $3 million from his father, dropped out of Harvard and used his fortune to cultivate a playboy lifestyle. He had an eye for actresses and showgirls. In New York City, he became enamored with chorus girl Evelyn Nesbit who was performing in the hit Broadway musical *Floradora*. She was just seventeen, but very experienced.

The attractive Nesbit had already had a passionate affair with Stanford White, one of the most prominent architects of the time, who had designed many of the great mansions and public buildings of New York. During the affair, White gave Nesbit a Little Red Riding Hood cloak and a red swing on which he would push her stark naked. The relationship, which shocked the nation, was later immortalized in the 1955 Hollywood film *The Girl on the Red Velvet Swing*.

Thaw took Nesbit away to Pittsburgh, where he thought they would have a fresh start when they were married in 1905. On June 25, 1906, the couple was back in New York at Madison Square Garden. They walked into the rooftop garden of the building, where the curtain was just rising on a show. There was Stanford White, sitting alone at a table, in the building which he had designed. Without warning or provocation, Thaw drew a revolver and shot White dead.

During the two trials that followed, Thaw said he was driven to rage by the stories of his wife's earlier relationship with White. There were no television cameras in the courtrooms back then, but the journalists and sketch artists of the day gave blow-by-blow descriptions of the lurid details of the case. President Theodore Roosevelt decried the trial reporting as "filth," but the controversy just fueled public fascination with the case.

The defense attorneys painted the murder as an act of chivalry, but ultimately fell back on an insanity plea. After one hung jury, a second jury in 1908 found Thaw innocent by reason of temporary insanity. He was sent to a mental institution from which he escaped to Canada in 1913. When he was extradited to New York two years later, he was released because the jury concluded he was now sane. His subsequent actions proved otherwise. He returned to court for horsewhipping a youth, attempted suicide, and then became entangled with a string of actresses and showgirls.

And what became of his love for Evelyn Nesbit, the woman for whom he was willing to kill? After his return from Canada, Thaw accused her of infidelity, denied paternity of her son born in 1909, and filed for divorce.

Number 75 is Paul Allen, cofounder of Microsoft (see page 127).

76

Cyrus H. McCormick

(1809–1884)

Reaping a Fortune
Est. wealth: $10 million

Cyrus McCormick inherited the dream of creating a mechanical reaper from his father. Robert McCormick, a Virginia farmer, had worked for years in his shop on his farm to create a workable reaper. He first came up with a strange contraption with sickles on the ends of sticks. Then, he built a new model. It cut the wheat, but it tossed grain all over the field.

The young Cyrus decided to try his hand. He developed a reciprocating blade, mounted around a cylinder, and a variety of other innovations in 1831. The new reaper worked. The next year, he was set to give a demonstration on a six-acre field of wheat. The field was very hilly and rocky, and McCormick's reaper struggled across it. Farm laborers who had gathered to watch jeered from the sidelines at this rattling machine designed to replace them. Then a neighbor took pity on McCormick, inviting him to demonstrate the reaper on his more level field. McCormick cut six acres with two horses in the time it would have taken six men with scythes.

Cyrus McCormick now had a great machine, but he still did not have a business. It took him nine years to find the first buyer. The reaper, advertised at $50, just didn't sell in an age when all farm work was done by manual labor. To keep alive, McCormick turned to iron mining, but in the panic of 1837 he went bankrupt. He lost everything, except the reaper. The bank didn't think it was worth repossessing.

McCormick continued to give demonstrations while trying to sell his strange machines. It wasn't until 1840, nine years after his original invention, that McCormick sold his first reaper. Word of the machine spread as farmers began to use it, and McCormick continued to demonstrate it. By 1844, he had sold fifty reapers.

Two years later, at thirty-seven, McCormick took $300 and left the farm to set up a factory to build his reapers in Chicago. He chose the city to reach the growing market among farmers in the West. At the time, Chicago was a small hamlet without even a railroad, but McCormick accurately perceived that the nation's wheat-belt would continue its westward movement, and Chicago would be a prime location for the sale of farm implements.

McCormick tried everything as he attempted to sell his reapers. He created marketing innovations such as money-back guarantees, fixed prices, and payment options that aided his sales to struggling farmers. He also was among the first to use advertising effectively, featuring testimonials from satisfied farmers and the slogan that the reaper would pay for itself in a year. McCormick fended off rivals, patent attacks, and even challenges from his own brothers and sisters. The business kept growing. By 1850, there were 3,000 reapers working in America.

After conquering the United States, McCormick brought his reaper to the Great Exhibition in London in 1851. At first, it was thought to be the most ridiculous thing in the show. What was this strange-looking contraption? Then McCormick was given a chance to demonstrate the machine on a local field. In just seventy seconds, he mowed down seventy-four yards of wheat. The crowd was stunned. Then it burst into cheers. The machine won the first prize at the exposition. "The reaping machine," gushed the London *Times*, "is worth the whole cost of the exposition." McCormick went on to take gold medals in exhibitions in France and Germany. And his business became a worldwide success.

McCormick was a skilled inventor, but it was his persistence and optimism that made him millions. He turned every obstacle into an opportunity. When the Great Chicago Fire destroyed his entire plant and most of the city in 1871, it appeared he might leave the business. After all, he was sixty-two years old and had millions in the bank. Before the embers had cooled, McCormick began building an even larger factory. In 1877, when he was defeated in a race for the U.S. Senate, he commented, "Well, that's over, what next?"

At the time of his death in 1884, at the age of seventy-five, he was the richest man in Illinois and the largest landlord in the city. He passed on his fortune of at least $10 million (some estimates place it as high as $100 million or more) and his business to his son, Cyrus H. McCormick II.

The younger McCormick continued to build the McCormick Harvesting Machine Co. and led it into the merger, financed by J. P. Morgan, to form International Harvester in 1902. Cyrus Jr. became the head of the new enterprise, and International Harvester was run by a virtually uninterrupted succession of McCormick descendants until 1979. Then Cyrus's great-grand-nephew Brooks McCormick stepped down as chairman and named outsider Archie McCardell, a former Xerox executive, to lead the $8 billion company.

The McCormick family also became a prominent name in Chicago publishing. The nephew of the elder Cyrus married the daughter of Joseph Medill, editor and primary owner of the *Chicago Tribune*. Their son, Colonel Robert R. McCormick, developed the small midwestern paper into one of the nation's leading papers. He also created a $40 million empire in newspapers, television and radio stations, paper mills, steamships, and real estate. In 1941, the McCormicks entered a bitter competition with another of Chicago's most prominent families when Marshall Field III, grandson of the family patriarch, established the *Chicago Sun*.

In 1984, the farm machinery company McCormick founded was absorbed into Tenneco's J I Case farm equipment company. As International Harvester's chairman Donald D. Lennox commented at the time, "You can only pay so much for tradition and history, and you have to let your emotions stand aside and let your good business judgment take over."

Rich, but Not Rich Enough

John Deere

(1804–1886)

PLOWED UNDER BY MCCORMICK

John Deere, inventor of the steel plow, had built a better plow, and the world beat a path to his door. He shipped his plows to every corner of the Earth. Deere plows were used by Australian bushmen and moujiks of Russia. His invention made the lives of farmers easier and built him a small fortune—much smaller than that of McCormick. Deere's wealth at the time of his death in 1886 (two years after McCormick), was estimated at just half a million. Yet while McCormick's name dropped from his company within a few decades of his death, John Deere & Co., with its familiar green and yellow colors, carries the name of its founder into fields around the world to the present day.

77

Arthur Vining Davis
(1867–1962)
The Emperor of Aluminum
Est. wealth: $400 million

Arthur Vining Davis, the man who built the Aluminum Company of America and made himself hundreds of millions of dollars in the process, was driving through his growing Florida real estate empire. As he headed along a dusty back road, he passed some workmen on one of his projects. He ordered the chauffeur to stop next to a man who was leaning on his shovel.

"Are you supposed to be working for me?" barked Davis, a short, stocky bulldog of a man.

"Yes, sir. I sure am," the startled man replied.

"No, you're not," roared Davis. "You're not sweating."

Throughout his life, Davis drove those who worked for him without mercy, and drove himself every bit as hard. At ninety he retired as chairman of the Aluminum Company of America (ALCOA), which he had built from scratch into the dominant player in the new industry. He then turned his full attention to his extensive projects in Florida and the Caribbean—building luxury resorts, homes, and a variety of businesses.

When he was asked at age eighty-eight when he would take a day off, he replied, "That day will never come." He was restless and impatient, an inveterate builder. He once bought an old minesweeper to use as a yacht, but turned it into a banana boat instead. He was soon shipping more than a million tons of produce per month from Caribbean ports to Florida.

He was so busy building, he didn't even have time to discuss his enterprises. A reporter once asked Davis about his plans in Florida. The tycoon replied curtly: "Making money. What else? Now go away and let me get on with it."

Davis was born in 1867, the son of a Congregational minister in a town near Boston. When Davis graduated from Amherst in 1888, his father helped him get a job in Pittsburgh, through a former parishioner. The company where Davis first worked was a start-up venture called the Pittsburgh Reduction Company. He earned $60 per month when there was enough money to pay salaries. The young founder, Charles Martin Hall, had invented a new production process for manufacturing aluminum cheaply. Aluminum offered a lighter alternative to iron, steel, and other metals, but it was very expensive until Hall developed his new manufacturing process. Hall was still trying to prove his idea was commercially viable, and the company consisted of four people, including Davis and Hall. The aluminum plant required constant supervision, and Davis and Hall alternated twelve-hour shifts. On Thanksgiving Day, in 1888, they had something to be thankful for. They had produced their first batch of commercial aluminum.

There was just one problem: No one wanted to buy it. Davis, showing vision and determination, concentrated on building a broad market for this metal. When he couldn't convince other manufacturers to use aluminum, he cast his own aluminum kettles and kitchen utensils. He hired college students each spring to sell Alcoa's Wear-Ever line of cookwear. The company also manufactured aluminum wire for electrical work, aluminum horseshoes, bicycles, and even parts for the Wright Brothers' airplane engine.

Davis had at least one set of powerful backers in his court. Andrew and Richard Mellon also believed in the future of aluminum and poured in cash to keep the fledgling business afloat. (Ultimately, Davis and the two Mellon brothers would jointly control more than 51 percent of the shares of the company.) Davis became a close friend and adviser of the Mellons, and they were involved in other ventures together.

When Hall died in 1914, Davis assumed control of the company. He was involved in every aspect of the business and was said to have known every new hire above the level of foreman. He drove his staff and the business relentlessly. When he was in his office, one executive later recalled, "there was a tension in the air—you could sense it even in the girl at the reception desk." Alcoa's dominance in the aluminum industry brought the company into conflict with federal regulators. But Davis also received a Presidential Certificate of Merit for helping supply aluminum to the U.S. Air Force during World War II.

When he retired as chairman of Alcoa in 1957, Davis was the third richest individual in the world. At the age of ninety, Davis quietly exited from Pittsburgh and began the second act of his career. Like Henry Flagler before him, Davis headed to Florida to build resorts, an interest he had already begun to cultivate during his time at Alcoa. He became such a powerful financial force in the region that a *Miami Herald* reporter once described him as a "large body of money surrounded by Dade County." His interests included owning more than one-eighth of Dade County along with luxury resorts on a smattering of islands in the Caribbean. He also had investments in banking, the biggest ice cream plant in the Southeast, the world's largest tropical nurseries, and the largest shipping line in Miami.

Davis even built a paradise for the ultra rich on the island of Eleuthera, for multimillionaires who didn't want to rub elbows with ordinary millionaires at his Boca Raton resort. Davis himself fell into this uncommonly rich category. He built a massive estate of his own on the island, including an air strip, eighteen-hole golf course, and thirty guest houses. But he didn't spend a whole lot of time enjoying it or his other mansions.

In 1957, *Fortune* estimated the wealth of this penniless preacher's son at more than $400 million. Davis had no comment. He resented the public attention to his personal finances, pounding his fist on the table and shouting that a man's wealth was his own damn business. Besides, who had time to add it up? As *U.S. News & World Report* commented in 1957, "No one but Mr. Davis knows the extent of his wealth. And, even in the tropics, he's presumably too busy to count it."

78

Thomas Handasyd Perkins

(1764–1854)

Bigger Than the U.S. Navy

Est. wealth: $3 million

The shipping business of Thomas Handasyd Perkins was so big that when George Washington asked him to serve as secretary of the navy, Perkins turned down his commander-in-chief. It wasn't because he was unpatriotic. It was just that Perkins owned more ships than the navy, so he felt his talents were needed more at home.

Born in 1764, Perkins grew up in the years leading up to the Revolutionary War. At five, he witnessed the Boston Massacre, near where his father ran a profitable wine business in Boston. Perkins's father died in 1773, and Perkins's mother opened a store that sold china, glass, wine, and other imports. She was so successful, with the help of her three sons, that she became a prominent figure in Boston business and philanthropy before her death in 1807.

Perkins was sent to school in Boston but was forced to flee during the British siege of the city. He was later preparing for Harvard, but decided on a business career instead. He and his two brothers became successful merchants, setting up a brisk trade with Santo Domingo, which included trade in slaves, although it was never a large part of the business.

In 1788, Thomas, suffering from ill health, returned to Boston from Santo Domingo to marry Sarah Elliot, daughter of a prominent Boston tobacconist. His wife's uncle, James Magee, was a captain on a ship owned by Elias Hasket Derby. The young Perkins joined Magee on several voyages to Canton, trading butter, rum, and iron, returning with a cargo full of teas and other imports from the East. On later voyages, Perkins crossed alligator-infested creeks in Java and was among the first Western visitors to Batavia.

Perkins soon established his own profitable trade in the Orient, the West Indies, Europe, and other parts of the world. He eventually set up a Perkins & Co. trading house in Canton. Among other goods, Perkins engaged in a brisk trade in opium, even though the trade had been outlawed by the emperor of China in 1800. He made a fortune importing the drug into China to trade for Chinese goods.

Always alert for new opportunities, Perkins traveled to Bordeaux during the French Revolution in 1794, thinking the unrest in France would create a ready market. It gives some indication of Perkins's attention to detail that, during one public execution, he timed how long it took to behead sixteen people. Sixteen people in just fourteen minutes! he marveled in a letter to his children. And he pointed out that if they hadn't needed to bring in a second basket to dispose of the remains, the act could have been completed in just twelve minutes. Perkins, while personally shocked by this "horrid" display, nonetheless was impressed by its efficiency.

While he was in Paris, Perkins was asked by the U.S. government to help arrange for George Washington Lafayette, the fourteen-year-old son of the Marquis de Lafayette, to escape the bloody French Revolution. Perkins arranged passage to the United States on a ship in which he had part interest. The young Lafayette went to live with his namesake at Mount Vernon.

In 1796, when Perkins visited the future site of the nation's capital in Washington, D.C., he met General Washington. Washington, grateful for Perkins's role in arranging Lafayette's passage to America, invited the merchant to Mount Vernon to visit. "I consider the visit to Mount Vernon as one of the most interesting in my life," Perkins later wrote. "It was the only opportunity which I should have ever had of conversing familiarly with this great and good man." Two years later, Washington died.

Perkins was active in civic and military life. He was a colonel in the Massachusetts militia, and was known throughout the country as "Colonel Perkins." He also served as president of the Boston branch of the first United Sates Bank and was elected to the Massachusetts legislature between 1805 and 1832.

When he needed to find a way to transport rock from a quarry he owned to the ocean, he built what may have been the first railroad in the nation. He never became a railroad mogul, however. His Granite Railway Company only stretched two miles from the quarry to the shore.

In 1838 Perkins dissolved his commercial firm and retired. He contributed generously to the Massachusetts General Hospital, the Boston Athenaeum, and the Perkins Institution for the Blind in Boston. He died at the age of ninety.

Perkins was known for his sharp mind and his remarkable foresight. A colleague once suggested Perkins might want to invest in coffee after the price had plummeted from 25 cents a pound to just 15 cents. Perkins replied that he wasn't interested. He explained that the price would continue to fall because there were more productive coffee trees than needed to meet demand "by a proportion I could state with some precision if necessary."

Perkins then proceeded to lay out his view of fluctuations in coffee prices for the next decade. He said he expected that coffee prices would continue to drop to 10 cents. At that point, plantations would fold. Given the five to six years it takes to bring a coffee tree to full bearing, there would follow a period of rising prices. Investing at that point twelve to fifteen years out,

Perkins said, would be a very wise investment. The subsequent events in the coffee industry unfolded very much the way Perkins had predicted.

It was this forward thinking and preparation that made him such a success in business. He was a noble and dignified-looking man, known for his terseness. Daniel Webster once described Perkins "as a man without spot or blemish; as a merchant, known and honored over the whole world . . . and as an unwavering and determined supporter of the constitution of the country."

79

Joseph Pulitzer

(1847–1911)

The Pauper Who Became a Publishing Prince

Est. wealth: $30 million

When Joseph Pulitzer arrived in the United States from Budapest as a teenager, he couldn't speak English, had no money, and had poor vision. He slept on park benches in Madison Square, awakening to the tap of a policeman's nightstick. By the time he died in 1911, he owned the leading New York daily newspaper and had a fortune estimated at $30 million.

As a teenager, he had left Budapest seeking military adventure. He was rejected from the Austrian army, the French Foreign Legion, and the British military. He had terrible vision and was in less than fighting form. Not to be discouraged, he signed up with an American recruiter for the Union army, and he came to the United States to fight in the Civil War. He participated in four skirmishes

Pulitzer may not have been a great soldier, but he was a fighter. By the end of the war, he had earned enough money to buy a ticket to St. Louis to find work. There was not much opportunity for a young immigrant who spoke little English, but Pulitzer found a job as a reporter for a German-language newspaper.

Pulitzer forged ahead with his boundless energy, vision, and tenacity. He became a naturalized U.S. citizen in 1867. He then became part owner of the German-language paper and bought another newspaper. While writing in German, he continued to study English and law. Soon he had mastered his adopted tongue so well that he became a forceful and popular political speaker. He served as a representative to the Missouri legislature in 1869 and a representative at the Missouri constitutional convention in 1875. Shortly after he was admitted to the bar in Washington, D.C., but before he set up practice, journalism called him back.

He bought the *St. Louis Dispatch* in 1878 for only $2,500, just about what the struggling paper was worth. Pulitzer poured his small fortune and his heart and soul into the paper. He merged the paper with a struggling rival, the *Post*, and within a year the *Post-Dispatch* had doubled its circulation. By 1881, the paper was producing profits of $45,000 per year.

Pulitzer became a crusader against political corruption in St. Louis, which made him many enemies. In 1882, Pulitzer's chief editorial writer shot and killed a prominent attorney in a fight over an editorial criticizing the attorney. In the resulting uproar against Pulitzer and his paper, Pulitzer left town. Suffering from ill health, he planned to head to Europe to take a break from the news business. During a stop in New York, however, financier Jay Gould offered to sell him the *World*, a New York daily, for $346,000, payable in installments.

Pulitzer built the *World* into one of the leading metropolitan dailies, using a combination of crusading zeal for political causes and sensational writing and stunts. In the process, Pulitzer created mass circulation journalism with an understanding that papers had to be entertaining as well as informative. Within three years of his purchase, the paper was generating a half-million dollars per year in profits. Pulitzer was passionate, aggressive, relentless, crusading—but he was never dull. He was a strong supporter of the Democratic party and a promoter of the concept of an "aristocracy of labor."

Pulitzer's ill health took him out of active control of the *World* in 1887. During a bitter newspaper war with William Randolph Hearst, the paper slipped into the depths of yellow journalism. It was banned from clubs and libraries for its sensationalist stories of crimes and other scandals. But later, Pulitzer returned to active management of the paper and set new standards for journalistic resourcefulness and integrity. By the time of Pulitzer's death, its circulation had climbed to 300,000 daily and 600,000 Sunday. In addition, an evening paper he started, the *Evening World*, sold another 400,000 copies per day. The papers were housed in the $2.5 million World Building.

Pulitzer had a gift for the newspaper business, from headlines to the details of finances. He pushed for the highest standards with signs posted in the newsroom: "Accuracy, Terseness, Accuracy." He challenged his reporters to find "what is original, distinctive, dramatic, romantic ... without shocking good taste or lowering the general tone." Even after he retired from active control of the newspapers—and had virtually lost his eyesight—he badgered his editors with detailed suggestions and criticisms to make his pages better.

Pulitzer's aggressive style naturally made him a few enemies. For a scathing editorial about President Theodore Roosevelt's handling of finances and politics in Panama, Pulitzer was publicly denounced by Roosevelt in Congress. For his attacks, Pulitzer was taken to court by Roosevelt, J. P. Morgan, and other towering opponents, but the cases were later dropped. At his death, there were no less than seventy-three libel suits pending against the *World* and eighteen against the *St. Louis Post-Dispatch*.

Pulitzer was generous in life and even more generous in death. When he died in 1911 at the age of sixty-four, he left most of his $30 million estate to his family. But he also distributed some of his fortune among charities and former employees. He bequeathed a total of $100,000 to his employees, including his valet, his secretary, and a fund for executors to distribute to faithful employees at lower levels of his news organizations. He also left $2 million to set up a journalism school at Columbia University.

Pulitzer is best known, however, for establishing the Pulitzer Prizes for literature and journalism, funded by $500,000 of his gift to Columbia. These prizes have become the most sought after awards by writers, identifying examples of the highest standards of "accuracy, terseness, and accomplishment." They embody the high standards and idealism that Pulitzer tried to promote in his own papers.

Pulitzer also decreed in his will that his three dailies could not be sold. After his death, his eldest son, Ralph, ran the *World*, but the struggling paper proved unprofitable. In 1931, the family obtained a court decree that allowed them to break the patriarch's will and sold the paper to Scripps-Howard. The *World* merged with the *New York World-Telegram*. Another son, Joseph Jr., ran the *Post-Dispatch*. He was also active in the early development of radio and became a pioneer in television in St. Louis. His son, Joseph III, continued the tradition, succeeding his father as editor and publisher of the *Post-Dispatch* in 1955. The family company went public in 1986, although family members retain 96 percent of voting power. *Forbes* estimated the total family wealth at $930 million in October 1995.

80

Daniel Willis James
(1832–1907)
Following in His Father's Footsteps
Est. wealth: $26 million

Daniel Willis James followed in his father's footsteps as a member of Phelps, Dodge & Company, leading it to successes in Arizona copper mining and Western railroads. His father, a native of New York, had been a founding partner of the American metals firm Phelps, Dodge & Company, and represented it in Liverpool, England. At his death in 1879, he was the oldest and most respected merchant in England engaged in Anglo-American trade. James's mother, Elizabeth Woodridge Phelps, was daughter of the head of the family-owned firm.

Born in England, Daniel James attended boarding schools and studied at the University of Edinburgh. In 1849, at the age of seventeen, he left for New York to establish his career. Within five years, he became a junior partner in Phelps, Dodge and helped make the company a major player by building copper holdings in the Southwest and Mexico. The mining operations then led to investments in railroads.

One of James's most profitable railroad investments was in the St. Paul, Minneapolis & Manitoba Railroad, where he served as director. The railroad became part of the Great Northern Railroad, and James worked closely with railroad giant James J. Hill at Great Northern and on other projects.

One of the most generous philanthropists of his generation, James was known for his personal concern for all people, "from God down to the newsboy." He served as a trustee of the Children's Aid Society of New York and founded the Society's "Health Home" for mothers of sick children. For the most part, however, he was very quiet about his contributions to both business and society.

His son, Arthur Curtiss James, inherited the family fortune along with the lion's share of the Phelps, Dodge business. Although he was the largest shareholder of the company, he did not play an active role in its governance. He, instead, focused on running railroads. He went on to double the family wealth through financial investments, particularly in railroads. Arthur Curtiss appeared among the thirty wealthiest Americans in *Forbes* in 1918, with an estimated fortune of $60 million.

Despite the substantial power he wielded in the country, the younger James also was virtually unknown. The younger James continued his father's commitment to philanthropy. With no close heirs, when he and his wife died three weeks apart, they donated their fortune to charity. They had given away an estimated $20 million during their lifetimes and willed another $25 million to set up the James Foundation. Before the fund was liquidated twenty-five years later, according to the specification of the will, it had distributed more than $144 million to a variety of educational, religious, and social causes.

81

Howard Hughes
(1905–1976)
Hell's Angel
Est. wealth: $1.5 billion

He was one of the most secretive yet controversial billionaires in American history. His life stretched from public ticker-tape parades celebrating his around-the-world flight to sealed hotel rooms in Nevada where the germ-phobic billionaire walled himself off from society. He started out making movies and ended up with a life story of his own that was more bizarre than any Hollywood plot. Even the exact size of his fortune is a subject of speculation.

The basis of Howard Hughes's original fortune was simple enough. His father had developed a superior bit for drilling oil wells. From this invention, the elder Hughes founded the Hughes Tool company, which he passed on to his son. After his father's death, Hughes bought out relatives to gain complete control of the business, and then paid little attention to its operations. (Some speculate that this may be why it performed so well.)

Hughes then set out to make his own mark on the world. He had a lifelong interest in movies and aviation, and these two inter-

ests came together to produce an early film, *Hell's Angels*, a World War I aviation story. Hughes spent three years to make the movie, and it cost $500,000, not to mention the lives of four stunt fliers. Hughes, a pilot himself, crashed a plane when he was trying to demonstrate to the stuntmen how they should perform a particularly dangerous maneuver.

Hughes produced and directed a string of lowbrow but commercially successful pictures in the 1930s. In *Hell's Angels*, he introduced the world to the unknown Jean Harlow, whom he paid $125 per week. He later also discovered a dental receptionist named Jane Russell, who starred in his Western *The Outlaw*. Hughes bought his way into the big-time motion picture business with the purchase of shares of RKO in 1948. He sold out after seven years, with just a $1 million profit to show for the investment.

Hughes's interest in aviation led to the founding of Hughes Aircraft in 1932, but it never achieved success as an airplane manufacturer. The company did find a strong second life and great success as a producer of aircraft equipment, including radar and weapons guidance systems. Hughes's aviation interests also led him to buy a struggling airline in 1937, which he renamed Trans World Airways. Hughes's domination and insistence on total control of TWA led it to the brink of bankruptcy. He was stripped of his voting rights because of mismanagement, and then sold off his 78 percent share for $546 million.

Hughes was an accomplished pilot and designer. He set several records for speed. In 1935, he designed a plane that broke the existing speed record, clocking 352 miles per hour. He then proceeded to set a new speed record for coast-to-coast flight, 9 hours and 27 minutes. Finally, in 1938, he set a new around-the-world record of just under four days. He returned to ticker-tape parades in New York. Although he was a master of speed, Hughes did not do quite as well when he turned his attention to setting records for size. He did succeed in building the largest plane in the world, but his *Spruce Goose*, an eight-engine flying boat that could hold seven hundred people, flew only one mile at an altitude of seventy feet before it was put in mothballs.

If Hughes was intriguing when he was in the public eye, he was even more fascinating when he disappeared. Starting in the 1950s, Hughes spent his later years in seclusion, first in Las Vegas hotels, where he speculated in Nevada casinos and land. Then he hopped from the Bahamas to London to Managua to Acapulco.

He avoided photographers. The few people he trusted to see him had to pass him his mail wrapped in tissues to avoid germs.

His fortune was as tangled as his life. In 1968, *Fortune* magazine estimated that he was worth as much as $1.4 billion, in a dead heat with J. Paul Getty for the title of America's richest man. But when Hughes died in 1976, he left an estate estimated at only between $600 million to $900 million. What happened?

In 1953, Hughes had dumped all his valuable Hughes Aircraft holdings into a medical research "charity" (the Howard Hughes Medical Institute). Because Hughes retained absolute control of these holdings, the move was apparently to avoid taxes and soften Air Force criticism of the company's performance. (The move was so blatant that Hughes was challenged by the IRS, but he apparently used his political connections to maintain its tax-exempt status.) With the addition of the value of Hughes Aircraft, sold to General Motors for $5.2 billion just nine years after his death, it is probably safe to say that the total fortune Hughes controlled was worth well over $1.5 billion.

Howard Hughes was more successful in building his own reputation than he was in building business enterprises. Throughout most of his career, the tool company he inherited was among the most profitable of his businesses. As biographers Donald Barlett and James Steele comment, "If he had invested the profits of the tool company, left to him by his father, in a passbook savings account, he would have died a much richer man." (Although this discounts the true value of Hughes Aircraft.)

Hughes didn't leave a will, so the intrigue and haggling over his estate continued for many years after he died. A group of twenty-one cousins and an aunt, along with three hundred other descendants, came forward, amid many pretenders, to claim the fortune. As of 1995, nearly two decades after his death, they were still working on selling off the last of Hughes's huge Nevada land holdings.

Meanwhile Hughes Aircraft, now Hughes Electronics, which was struggling when General Motors purchased it in 1985, became a phenomenal success when it moved away from aviation. Hit with defense cuts in the 1980s and 1990s, the company moved into new markets such as direct broadcast satellite television, cellular and digital wireless systems, and high-tech automotive features. The $15 billion giant became one of the leading companies in consumer electronics and communications.

Perhaps the most enduring legacy of Howard Hughes (besides the fights over his will) is the Howard Hughes Medical Institute. Court decisions ultimately made this apparent tax shelter a true research foundation. With an infusion of billions from the sale of Hughes Aircraft, it became the largest private U.S. source of funds for biomedical research, spending $280 million per year on research projects.

82

Frank W. Woolworth

(1852–1919)

Nickeled and Dimed His Way to Wealth

Est. wealth: $65 million

It seemed that Frank W. Woolworth couldn't sell his way out of a paper bag. He had dreamed of entering the mercantile business since he was a child growing up on a farm in Great Bend, New York. He and his brother used to play at running a store, using the dining room table as a counter. But young Frank just didn't seem to be cut out for it.

He spent two years working for no salary as a clerk at a small grocery store, just for the experience. At twenty-one, he took another job working for a store owned by W. H. Moore. Woolworth received no salary for the first three months. After that, he drew $3.50 a week, barely enough to pay his room and board. In two years, he had worked his way up to $6 per week.

Then came what appeared to be his big break. He joined one of the early "ninety-nine cent stores" in Michigan, in which all merchandise was priced at 99 cents. Young Woolworth was brought in as a clerk at a whopping $10 per week. He was elated. He felt secure enough in his fortunes to get married.

But he was such a poor salesman, the owner cut Woolworth's salary to $8.50, telling him there were salesmen paid $6 per week who were selling much more. Woolworth was devastated. When he wrote to his mother about his troubles, she replied, "Some day, my son, you will be a rich man." Not even Woolworth himself believed it at that point. His failure as a salesman eroded his health. He came down with nervous prostration and fever that nearly took his life, and he spent a year at home on his father's farm recuperating. It looked like he would never go back to retailing.

He set up a small farm in New York, but then in 1877 he received a call from his old employer, W. H. Moore. They wanted the twenty-five-year-old Woolworth back as a clerk at $10 per week. Moore knew Woolworth wasn't much of a salesman, but he did have a talent for setting up stores and dressing shop windows. Woolworth had another chance at retailing, and he was determined to make it work. He worked from 7 A.M. to 10 P.M., year in and year out without vacations.

Woolworth had heard about a store that had set up a five-cent counter. He talked Moore into trying the scheme, and it was a great success. His employer then backed Woolworth in setting up an entire store of five-cent items in Utica, New York, in 1879. It was a failure. Woolworth had struck out again.

Still he was not defeated. He realized that the five-cent cutoff was too limiting. The twenty-seven-year-old Woolworth, with the backing of Moore, opened another store in Lancaster, Pennsylvania. This time they added a ten-cent line to the five-cent items. It was just the margin they needed for success. This new five-and-ten took off and became a model for a whole chain of stores across the country. Three of his first five stores were failures, but Woolworth didn't turn back. With his brother and other partners, Woolworth began covering the nation with the familiar five-and-ten-cent stores, founding the F. W. Woolworth Company.

He launched his first five-and-ten in 1879 and within just over fifteen years, he had twenty-eight stores and sales of more than $1 million. By 1912, Woolworth's stores—under his name and other chains—had grown to nearly 600 stores, and the $65 million company was the largest merchandising firm in the nation. In 1913, Woolworth celebrated his success by building the tallest building in New York City, the fifty-five-story Woolworth Building. He called the $13.5 million skyscraper "the Cathedral of Commerce."

In an interview in *American Magazine,* Woolworth shared some of his secrets to business success. At the top of the list was: "Of course you will be discouraged. But keep on." These words took Woolworth through defeat after defeat, through failure after failure, and then to stunning success.

By the time of his death in 1919, he owned more than a thousand stores in North America, and their familiar red signs with gold letters became the center of towns across America. His stores were selling more than $100 million in goods per year. No one questioned his ability as a salesman now. He had built a personal fortune of more than $65 million. When he died at the age of sixty-seven, his estate was left to his three daughters. One of his daughters married Franklyn Hutton and their daughter, Barbara Hutton, made headlines for a succession of high-profile marriages, including European princes and playboys, as well as movie star Cary Grant. By the 1970s, Woolworth's empire had been overshadowed by Kmart and other rivals, and none of the Woolworth family has any direct control over the company.

83

John McDonogh
(1779–1850)
The King of the Merchant's Mardi Gras

Est. wealth: $2 million

When John McDonogh started trading in New Orleans, it was a foreign country. First it was controlled by France, then by Spain, and finally—with the Louisiana Purchase—by the United States. But no matter who was formally in charge of the government, most of the city and surrounding territory was soon under the control of John McDonogh.

McDonogh came to the city in his early twenties as an agent for the Baltimore mercantile house of William Taylor at the turn of the century. After establishing a very successful trading business in Louisiana and Florida, McDonogh began to make his own "Louisiana Purchase." He bought up so much land in western Florida that, at one point, he was believed to be the largest landowner in the world. His estate was valued at more than $2 million shortly after his death.

McDonogh became the John Jacob Astor of New Orleans. He bought huge tracts of undeveloped land; most of it was just wastes and wilds at the time, but he always had his eye on the distant future. He bought lands around the small towns and villages of Louisiana, confident that these areas would soon be the suburbs of bustling cities. His coup de grace was the assembly of a belt of swampland that completely encircled the city of New Orleans. He also purchased tracts on the outskirts of new plantations, confident that the plantations and towns would continue to expand.

McDonogh was less successful in love than in business. He proposed to the lovely and wealthy Michaela Leonarda in 1810. His suit was rejected because he refused to convert from Protestantism to Leonarda's Roman Catholicism. Four years later, he fell in love with another woman and asked her to marry him. Her father, a strict Catholic, would allow the match only if McDonogh converted. Again, McDonogh refused. They waited for her father to change his mind, but he didn't. Distraught over the decision, she became a nun in the Ursuline Order. McDonogh visited her at the convent every year until his death in 1850. When he died, they found among his possessions a lady's slipper and a piece of faded ribbon believed to have belonged to the woman. It is likely the two carried their affection to the grave.

There was some speculation that this lost love drove McDonogh to leave his home in New Orleans and move to a secluded plantation across the Mississippi. There were also indications that he was advised by a doctor to give up drinking, smoking, and his busy life for health reasons. He may have just wanted to have peace and quiet to better attend to his extensive business investments.

Whatever the motivation, he became a Howard Hughes of his day. His disappearance from the daily life of the city fueled speculation about him. He was known as a miser and an eccentric. He lived and dressed so simply that one contemporary said he looked more like a poor country preacher than a wealthy landowner.

McDonogh was a bit quirky, but usually in a benevolent way. For example, he decided to allow his slaves half of Saturday to work for themselves. The slaves had been working to earn extra money on Sundays, a practice that McDonogh, a devout Protestant, sought to discourage. So in 1822, he gave them half of Saturday to work for him or outside his plantations for pay.

A few years later, he developed an even more dramatic plan. He set up a scheme whereby the slaves could purchase their own freedom—on a sort of installment plan—stretched out over about fifteen years. It would take them seven years to purchase the other half of Saturday. Then, using that time, they could continue to buy back their freedom one day at a time. After earning their own freedom, it would only take about a year of work to free all of their children. In all, some eighty slaves earned their freedom through this plan and set sail for Liberia.

McDonogh was not an abolitionist any more than Henry Ford was a friend of workers. After these slaves departed, McDonogh bought more. McDonogh called the plan "one of simple honesty." Others marveled at how zealously McDonogh's slaves seemed to work. It was only later that his secret pact with the slaves to gain their freedom was disclosed.

It seemed clear, however, that McDonogh's plan was a bit more than a way of motivating his workforce. He took a personal interest in the success of the colony in Liberia. He sent two former young slaves to Lafayette College in Pennsylvania to train to become a preacher and a physician so they could contribute to life in Liberia. In his will, he also instructed that almost all his slaves be freed.

What was the secret of his success? The millionaire said there were three key principles he followed. The first was that he understood the need to spend money to make money. Early in his career, after fulfilling a $10,000 army contract for the Spanish government of New Orleans, he gave a big party for the governor and army officers. The affair was expensive, but the result was a second contract from which he earned $30,000. It also illustrated McDonogh's second rule—to take advantage of the talents and power of those who may be less wealthy. No individual by himself could create a substantial fortune alone. The third rule? "Prayer," McDonogh maintained. "I have never prayed sincerely to God in all my life without having my prayers answered satisfactorily. Follow my advice and you will become a rich man."

By 1855, following these principles, McDonogh had built an estate valued at $2.2 million, mostly in real estate. At his death, the value of his land had been significantly eroded by the Civil War. Most of his estate was bequeathed to support a plan to establish free schools for poor students in New Orleans and Baltimore. Nearly twenty McDonogh schools were established in the New Orleans area, and an 835-acre McDonogh Farm School for poor boys was built outside Baltimore.

84

Samuel Slater

(1768–1835)

Industrial Spy

Est. wealth: $1.2 million

Samuel Slater is credited with establishing the American textile industry. His fortune was based on an act of industrial espionage that was perhaps as great a blow to England as the loss of the Revolution. Slater arrived in the United States with almost nothing— except the knowledge he carried in his head about textile manufacturing. It was enough to establish the American textile business and his own personal fortune.

Born the son of a prosperous British farmer and timber merchant, Slater excelled early in mathematics. At the age of fourteen, his father was killed in an accident and Slater was sent to work as an apprentice for a stocking manufacturer. His bosses, Jediah

Strutt in partnership with Richard Arkwright, were pioneers in the textile industry. They had built the world's first automated mill for spinning yarn and the first water-powered spinning mill in 1771. Slater, who had a natural aptitude for mechanical work, spent every day at the plant, even going to work after church services on Sunday. Strutt took an early interest in the ambitious young Slater and personally taught him about the cotton-spinning machinery.

Slater wanted to start his own company when he completed his indenture at twenty-one, but Britain was already crowded with hundreds of textile factories. He came across an advertisement by the Pennsylvania legislature offering a bounty to experienced textile workers who came to the United States. He decided to move to the United States and establish a yarn factory there.

The knowledge of textile machinery was considered so valuable to Britain that it was against the law for machinery or plans to be exported. It was even illegal for experienced textile workers to leave England. Slater began memorizing the blueprints of the Arkwright factory. When the twenty-one-year-old Slater left for America in September 1789, he faced a stiff fine and imprisonment merely for setting sail from Britain, but, identifying himself as a farm laborer at the port, he made it safely to the United States.

He was heading for Philadelphia to respond to the Pennsylvania Legislature's offer, but when his ship docked in New York he heard about textile-manufacturing opportunities there. Working in an outdated plant in New York, Slater heard about a Rhode Island merchant who wanted to build a cotton spinning plant. Moses Brown, a wealthy retired Quaker merchant, wanted to build an Arkwright-style plant. Slater wrote to Brown, who needed good yarn for his weaving plants and offered Slater all profits on the venture, after deducting the costs of capital and machinery.

Brown had built a small spinning frame, but it didn't work well. He asked Slater to set up a new British-style textile machine, which allowed for continuous spinning rather than the stop-and-start motion of the older machines. Using the plans he had memorized, Slater designed an Arkwright-style machine. It took nearly a year to build the first machine. Slater didn't have the right parts or tools or mechanics who understood the business. But, using his own extensive knowledge of all parts of the spinning business, he painstakingly designed and built the first modern American spinning machine. At the end of 1790, the new machines produced their first cotton yarn.

In 1791, Brown and Slater built the nation's first cotton-spinning mill in Pawtucket. In its first ten months of operations, it produced 8,000 yards of American-made cotton cloth. It was so successful that the American market could not absorb such high volumes of cloth, and the mill had to be shut down temporarily until they could find new markets.

Slater then struck out on his own, building the Samuel Slater & Company factory and another plant in Smithfield, Rhode Island, the town that would later be known as Slatersville. Slater cotton mills on the Merrimac River in New Hampshire became the foundation for the extensive industrial development of Manchester. Slater also established the Manufacturer's Bank in Pawtucket.

Slater's early mills were operated by children, and he later used whole families to work in the mills. Immigrant families flocked to the mills. In 1892, Slater changed the company name to Samuel Slater and Sons, when his sons, George, John, and Horatio, became his partners.

Slater had firmly established the American cotton industry and had created a personal fortune estimated at $1.2 million. (His wealth might have been higher. In 1899, the heirs of just one branch of Slater's family shared $9 million in stocks, bonds, real estate, and other investments.)

Slater's sons continued to build the empire, and son John Slater would later contribute $1 million to an education fund for the newly emancipated slaves of the South after the Civil War. The fund, created in 1882, generated nearly $4 million during the next fifty years.

85

August Belmont
(1816–1890)
Belmont Stakes
Est. wealth: $10–$50 million

August Belmont, the representative of the Rothschild banking family in the United States, became one of the most powerful financiers in the nation. An active force in both business and politics, he brought valuable European capital that was crucial to building the young American republic.

Born to a poor family in Prussia, Belmont's first job was sweeping the floors of the Rothschild Brothers' Frankfurt banking house at the age of fourteen. Belmont proved he had other talents. He was a sharp financial negotiator and dealmaker, and he was soon sent out to the Naples office. After completing successful negotiations with the Papal Court, he was then shipped off to Havana, Cuba.

While crossing the Atlantic, Belmont heard about the financial panic of 1837 in the United States. Where there was financial panic, he knew, there was also financial opportunity. After completing his mission in Havana, he took the next ship to New York and notified his employer that he was establishing his own banking house.

Again, he followed his intuition. He had no capital, but he set up a small Wall Street office in 1837, at the age of twenty-one. His only asset was the backing of the huge Rothschild empire in Europe. With the Rothschild name behind him—even if he didn't at first have Rothschild capital—he secured credit from panic-shy American investors and then issued loans to other struggling banks on the brink of bankruptcy. The tiny August Belmont & Company thrived. Within four years, Belmont had joined J. P. Morgan as one of the leading bankers in the nation.

Belmont, a short, stout man with dark eyes, was known for his sharp wit and European polish. He was left with a permanent limp from a duel he had fought in Indiana in 1841 "over a subject too trite to be mentioned." Most of his friends and partners didn't know he was Jewish, since he hid his heritage during a time when Jews were looked down upon. His family name was Schönberg, which meant "beautiful mountain," but he changed it to its French equivalent, Belmont.

Belmont was a regular fixture in New York society. After becoming a U.S. citizen, he became active in politics and was appointed consul-general for Austria in the United States, in 1844. In 1849 he married the daughter of Commodore Matthew Perry, who had opened Western trade with Japan. This marriage, and his substantial wealth, helped propel him into the leadership of the Democratic party.

Fiercely devoted to his adopted country, which he valued more than his wealth, he was a strong supporter of the Union during the Civil War, and he outfitted one of the first German regiments to join the Union cause. He wrote to a friend, "I prefer to leave my children, instead of the gilded prospects of New York merchant princes, the more enviable title of American citizen."

Given his extensive contacts and stature in Europe, Belmont's support of the Northern cause was instrumental in persuading England not to support the Confederacy. He traveled to London in 1861 and Paris in 1863 to make the Union's case and obtain European funding for the war effort.

Belmont also was an avid horse breeder and racer, and he helped found the first polo club in the nation. He hosted a popular racing event that became known as the Belmont Stakes. The tradition continues to this day as part of the Triple Crown with the Preakness and the Kentucky Derby.

In addition to horses, he spent lavishly on entertainment and paintings. As one obituary writer noted, puritans might frown that Belmont "got out of life too much pleasure himself and gave too much to others." The nonpuritans, the obituary continued, would remember him as "a man who, combining solid business qualities with a noteworthy aptitude for the less serious affairs of life, contributed certainly in as large a measure as any other of its citizens, to make the city of New York an agreeable place of residence."

When he died in 1890, Belmont had lived to see his hopes of Union victory fulfilled. He had helped to ensure that his children would be able to call themselves American citizens, and had left enough of a fortune behind to see that his widow and children could live as "merchant princes." His estate was estimated at between $10 million and $50 million.

Belmont's three sons took over the banking house. His eldest son, Perry, served four terms in Congress, and his middle son, August Jr., took control of the firm when his father died in 1890. The younger August was instrumental in developing New York's transit system. The family continued to be involved in banking, but August Jr. lost money in his subway ventures, and in 1924, when his will was probated, most of the Belmont fortune was gone. Author John Trebbel asks, "Where had the money gone? Aside from what was lost in business, substantial in itself, most of it appeared to have gone to high living." By the third generation, Belmont's rags-to-riches ascent had largely reversed itself.

86

Benjamin Franklin
(1706–1790)
Lived Usefully and Died Rich
Est. wealth: $150,000

Benjamin Franklin arrived in Philadelphia with one Dutch dollar in his pocket and a loaf of bread under each arm, while munching on a third loaf. He was seventeen and had run away from an apprenticeship with his brother, a Boston printer. Franklin didn't have any assets, except his native wit and intelligence.

He became one of the most prominent men of his time—a critical force in the establishment of the nation, a successful printer, and a pioneer in science, education, and government.

Although the inventive man wasn't the Bill Gates of his time—his friend George Washington actually had an estate worth more than three times as much—the business-savvy Franklin was among the wealthiest citizens of Philadelphia.

His $150,000 estate wasn't from his invention of bifocals or the Franklin stove. It didn't come from a booming lightning rod business. Nor did it rest primarily in his successful printing business. Had Franklin been born in an age of mass production, he might well have found millions from producing his useful inventions for mass markets. At the dawn of the American nation, his fortune "did not come from manufacture or invention, which he did so much to encourage, but from land." He owned several large houses in Philadelphia, along with other land in the city, and holdings in Boston, Nova Scotia, Georgia, and Ohio. He had bought land in Philadelphia before the Revolution that appreciated rapidly after the city became the capital of the new nation.

Born in 1706, Franklin was the son of a Boston soap and candle maker, the youngest of ten children. His father had hoped to provide Ben with a full education, but, short on funds, his family pulled him out of school after one year. Franklin, then ten, wanted to go to sea, but his father set him to work at candle making. Franklin tolerated the profession for two years before his older brother James invited him to work in his new printing business. Franklin was indentured at twelve to serve until he was twenty. He was an avid reader, and when he became a vegetarian at sixteen, he used his food savings to augment his library. After several years of a turbulent relationship, James released Ben from his indenture, and the young Franklin headed for Philadelphia.

After working for various printers in Philadelphia and London, Franklin became part owner of a print shop in 1728. With his *Pennsylvania Gazette* newspaper and *Poor Richard's Almanac*, he established a profitable printing business. His publications reflected his common sense and humor. Franklin became deputy postmaster general and turned around the postal service in 1753. He built the first fire company, free library, insurance company, university, and hospital. If wealth were in any way related to influence and inventiveness, Franklin would have been not only one of the most prominent but also the wealthiest man of his time. But his discoveries in electricity and other fields, along with his stoves, bifocals, and other inventions, did more to burnish his reputation than to feather his nest.

When he served as governor of Pennsylvania after the Revolution, Franklin refused to accept any salary for his work. He represented the American colonies in London before the Revolution from 1757 to 1762 and from 1764 to 1775. He later was sent to win French support for the Revolution and the diplomatic visit brought about the alliance with the French in 1778 that ultimately led to victory for the Americans. Franklin considered himself underpaid for his services as minister to France. His pay was just 500 pounds per year, plus expenses. During the last of his six years in France, Congress increased his pay to 2,500 pounds. But when he returned to the United States, Franklin felt Congress should recognize his service with a land grant, as was often the custom in other nations. The new Congress never acted on his claims.

Franklin, with his high forehead and flowing locks, was known for his abounding curiosity, disarming humor, and patient diplomacy. He had a keen intellect and a disciplined and practical attitude toward work and life.

Even in his philanthropy, the man who said "a penny saved is a penny earned" used his cleverness to achieve the most impact from his money. At his death, he left $5,000 each to Boston and Philadelphia in a two-hundred-year philanthropic scheme intended to be a poor man's million-dollar gift. He instructed that the money be invested, with one payment to each city at the close of the first hundred years and a final payoff of millions of dollars at the close of the two-hundred-year period. In the meantime, the funds would be lent at 5 percent interest to young married tradesmen, who were under twenty-five and served an apprenticeship. He had received a similar loan himself as a young man.

The plan fell a bit short of his expectations, but it still funded many valuable projects, including the Franklin Technical Institute in Boston and the Franklin Institute science museum in Philadelphia. Thus, the Franklin fortune continued to have an impact on two of the nation's leading cities for many years after his death.

Franklin once said, "I would rather have it said 'he lived usefully' than 'he died rich.' " Franklin was able to do both.

87

Sumner Murray Redstone

(1923–)

The Viceroy of Viacom

Est. wealth: $4.8 billion

In the spring of 1979, Sumner Redstone, then a comfortably successful owner of a chain of movie theaters, was clinging to a third-story ledge at Boston's Copley Plaza Hotel. Flames were racing through the building. Redstone, fifty-six, had crawled out of the window and was now dangling high above the ground. As the fire burned his hands and arms, Redstone refused to let go, counting to ten repeatedly to avoid thinking about the pain.

This was the tenacity and determination that has made him the head of one of the wealthiest and successful communications giants in America. It was this resolve—"My goal is to be number one," he says unequivocally—that built him a $4.8 billion media empire by the time he was seventy-one.

The fire was a turning point for Redstone. After struggling back through painful skin grafts, he began to lay the foundation of his movie and cable empire. At a time when many men were beginning to plan for retirement, Redstone launched his most ambitious and successful career ever.

"Great successes," he told *Forbes* later, "are built on taking the negatives in your life, the challenges and the frustrations, and turning them around. Taking a negative and turning it into a positive. Overcoming hazard. Overcoming danger. Overcoming catastrophe."

Redstone grew up in the movie business. He was born in Boston in 1923, where his father ran a small chain of drive-in theaters. Redstone attended Harvard University and then was recruited by the military during World War II to break codes in Japanese military and diplomatic messages. When he returned, he completed Harvard Law School and practiced as an attorney in Washington.

Twelve years later, he came home to run the his family theater chain. Redstone expanded National Amusements from drive-ins to indoor theaters—pursuing a highly effective strategy of building in densely populated suburbs in the Northeast and Midwest. He also was a pioneer in building multiplex theaters, packing ten to twelve screens into a single site. By 1986, he had built the business into the eighth largest theater chain.

After the fire, however, Redstone took a fresh look at his life and decided he needed a little more adventure than running a theater chain. He not only expanded the theater business, but also began investing in the motion picture industry. In 1986, at sixty-three, he stepped out onto the ledge again—betting the family theater business on a hostile takeover of Viacom, a sleepy cable television company. He didn't know anything about the cable business, and he was not as seasoned as some in the high-stakes game of takeover bids. Yet he put his whole family business and fortune at stake with a bid that would leave his company a dizzying $240 million in debt. As a result of the deal, Viacom was left with a debt and preferred stock of $2.8 billion compared to just $613 million in shareholder equity.

The gamble paid off, because Viacom was just waiting to bloom. Its MTV and Nickelodeon channels would soon become dominant cable networks for young and teenage audiences. By

1994, the two channels would be fixed on the television sets of 260 million homes around the world.

From this base, Redstone then launched an even more daring move—a bitter battle with Barry Diller of QVC for control of Paramount Communications. Once again, Redstone won, making him the second-largest media giant in the country, just behind Time Warner. His holdings now included MTV, Nickelodeon, Showtime, USA Network, Paramount Pictures, Spelling Entertainment, Simon & Schuster, Blockbuster retail stores, Discovery Zone, and hosts of television and cable stations, as well as an even larger chain of movie theaters.

Even after he passed seventy, Redstone showed no signs of slowing down. He is a fierce opponent and negotiator. He shows this same spirit on the tennis court, where he is intensely competitive, playing flat out and screaming and arguing every point—even though he has to strap his racket to a glove because of his burn injury. And he still wakes up in the night in his hotel room. He is not awakened by fear of fire but by the need to find out how Paramount's latest motion pictures have fared at the box office. He phones in on a special line at 2 A.M. to get reports from the front, like a sports junkie waiting for the latest scores.

Redstone's goal is to be number one, and he is always in training, mentally and physically. He runs three miles per day on a treadmill in the morning and often eats a bowl of hot oatmeal for lunch. As a competitor once said, licking his wounds after tangling with the media baron, "He's in this for the game."

88

Capt. Robert Dollar

(1844–1932)

Founded President Lines

Est. wealth: $40 million or more

In 1873, Captain Robert Dollar, the future founder of the largest U.S. shipping line, was $5,000 in debt. He had worked his way up from a "chore boy" in a Canadian lumber camp. He washed dishes, carried firewood, and tended stables for a salary of $6 per month. After a full day of work, he stayed up working on the reading and arithmetic he missed when he had been forced to drop out of school at twelve to help support the family.

By the time he was twenty-two, Dollar was foreman in charge of a camp of forty men. Then he and a partner set out to start their own lumber company in 1872. At first, success seemed assured. One year later, in the financial panic of 1873, the company went under, leaving Dollar $5,000 in the hole.

Dollar spent three years working his way out of debt. He went on to found one of the largest lumber companies in the West, with mills churning out 15 million board feet of lumber. Then he built the biggest shipping business in the Pacific, with two fleets of steamers at the center of coastal travel and trade with the Orient. At the time of his death, the California governor declared that "he had done more during his lifetime to spread the American flag on the high seas than any man in this country."

Dollar was known for his discipline and motivation. He preached moderation in all things, clean living, and the fear of God. He abstained from alcohol (his father had had a drinking problem) and never carried liquor on his Dollar Lines—although the trade was very lucrative for others.

His secret to success? Dollar would later tell young people in lectures that success in his view boiled down to two words: hard work. "Work keeps a man in good health," he used to say. He worked up to the time of his death at eighty-eight.

Dollar moved from success to success. He was fifty-seven before he launched his first ship, and he didn't establish his huge passenger lines until he was in his eighties. He once outlined his life achievements by decade as follows:

     1–10: Helped mother
    10–20: Bought farm for father
    20–30: Rose from chore boy to lumber camp owner
    30–40: Extended lumber business
    40–50: Found new lumber markets
    50–60: Added shipping to lumber business
    60–70: Developed shipping and foreign trade
    70–80: Developed shipping in Far East
      80s: Established greatest American passenger and freight lines

In his seventies, he built the most important trading business between the United States and the Orient. As a pioneer and leader in the China trade, he was loved on both sides of the Pacific, with friends in every port. He was in China during the overthrow of the Manchu government and the establishment of the Republic in 1912, and he worked for peace in the country. He also helped obtain recognition for the new government in the United States. When Li Yuan-hung was named as the new president of China, one of his first acts was to telegram the news to Robert Dollar.

Dollar then moved into the international passenger and freight business with the purchase of seven 10,000-ton passenger steamships from the U.S. government in 1923. Four of the ships were built by the U.S. government at a cost of $2.25 million each during World War I and were sold to Dollar at the end of the war for just $300,000 each. He used the fleet of seven "President" liners (each named for a U.S. president) to establish the first regular round-the-world passenger service. The ships were sent out on a schedule of one every two weeks. He soon had expanded his fleet to forty ships. Dollar's shipping company later became the American President Companies, Ltd., which is the leading firm in trans-Pacific shipping.

Dollar actively pursued and built his passenger and freight business. He had agents across the United States, helping travelers plan their world cruises and shippers plan their world trade. Dollar would tell his agents: "Go out after it hard. And don't take it away from the other fellow. Go after new business all the time. Keep out of the bulk cargo as much as you can. Don't talk tons to me, talk dollars! What we want is high-class freight." When he was nearly eighty, Dollar and his wife circumnavigated the globe to promote his line.

His straightforward approach, commitment to hard work, and vision made him a multimillionaire and took him to the ends of the Earth. As people used to joke, he "made the Dollar go farther than it had ever gone before."

Rich, but Not Rich Enough

Daniel K. Ludwig

(1897–1992)

TANKER TYCOON

Known at one time as the richest man in America, Daniel Ludwig lost part of his $2 billion fortune in investments shortly before his death in 1992. Even if he had kept his wealth at the same level, he would have been outpaced by the growth of the gross national product along with the growth of the fortunes of Bill Gates and others. The "father of the supertanker," Ludwig bought his first boat at age eight—a sunken wreck—for $25. He built a large and powerful fleet of supertankers to become a dominant force in U.S. shipping. He later used his fortune to invest in a wide range of other businesses. He lost a large part of his wealth in a scheme to harvest wood pulp from the Amazon jungle, but retained a fortune of over $1 billion.

Number 89 is Richard Warren Sears, the famous retailer (see page 197).

H. L. Hunt

(1889–1974)

The Wildest of the Wildcatters

Est. wealth: $1 billion or more

In 1930, Haroldson Lafayette Hunt placed a bet on a stretch of unprofitable oil fields in an East Texas field. Oilman C. M. "Dad" Joiner had been drilling there unsuccessfully. He was broke and so far in debt no one would lend him money. No major oil company wanted to risk buying him out. But Hunt offered Joiner $1.34 million for five thousand acres of leases, with only $30,000 in cash up front. Joiner, deep in debt, accepted.

Further drilling turned up one of the biggest oil-producing sections of the East Texas field. H. L. Hunt had won yet another bet, and he was now on his way to building a legendary fortune. Hunt, who won his first oil well in Arkansas in a game of five-card stud, became a master of the high-stakes game of betting on oil leases.

Hunt was one of eight children of an Illinois cattle farmer. He began his career with a $6,000 inheritance from his father, which he invested in a cotton plantation in Arkansas. In 1920, oil was found in El Dorado, Arkansas. Hunt, whose cotton business had been virtually destroyed by a drop in cotton prices, borrowed $50 and headed out to the new oil fields.

Hunt often made his deals without putting up any of his own money. He would ask a farmer how much he wanted to lease his land. Then he would head to town and ask the oil drillers how much they were willing to pay to lease the oil rights on the land. He would pocket the difference between buyer and seller.

Hunt would hedge his bets on oil leases by using a team of informers—oil workers he would pay to let him know if drillings looked promising. When he received a hot tip, he would swoop in and snatch up leases. Hunt also pioneered the use of salt injection wells in East Texas, pumping saltwater into the well to increase production.

By the end of 1923, at the age of thirty-four, he owned forty-four oil wells in Arkansas. A year later, he sold a half-interest in forty of the wells for $600,000. He then expanded his oil holdings in Oklahoma and Louisiana, then to Texas, where he made most of his fortune in the East Texas field. He founded the Hunt Oil Company in 1936.

Even with his informants, Hunt knew the importance of keeping on the good side of Lady Luck. He believed that six-letter words beginning with *P* were lucky. This explains why he named his companies the Panola Pipeline, Penrod Drilling Company, Placid Oil Company, and Parade Gasoline Company.

Another six-letter word beginning with *P* also proved very lucky for Hunt: *profit*. By 1946, his holdings were producing 60,000 barrels per day, and he was drawing in a gross income of $1 million every week. During World War II, Hunt would later assert, his company alone produced more oil for the Allies than the total output from Germany. After World War II, he expanded his operations and was soon drilling about three hundred new wells per year. He opened refineries and service stations, and branched out into the food and pharmaceutical businesses. As if his luck in business was not enough, he also reportedly brought in another $1 million per year through gambling.

Hunt remained in relative obscurity until 1948, when both *Life* and *Fortune* designated Hunt as the richest man in America. He was so obscure at that point that *Fortune* couldn't even come up with a picture of him for its article. *Life* had only a blurry photo snapped on a Dallas street corner.

Hunt used his newfound fame and fortune as a bully pulpit,

becoming an ideologue for the far right. He set up a regular television and radio program, *Facts Forum,* that was ultimately carried by more than three hundred radio stations and twenty television stations across the nation. A strong supporter of Senator Joseph McCarthy, he preached anti-Communism and even racism and anti-Semitism. Ostensibly, the program presented a balance of the far-right and far-left views on topics, but the far-right, or "constructive," view as it was called, was always argued more vigorously and convincingly. After pouring a reported $3.5 million into the project, he pulled the plug in 1956.

Hunt also launched a career as an author. He wrote a novel, *Alpaca,* depicting a utopia—at least for wealthy Texas oil men. In Hunt's mythical land, those who paid the most taxes were given more votes.

Despite his sometimes shy and soft-spoken manner, Hunt was an imposing figure, six feet tall with a face like Herbert Hoover's. He had an oversized replica of Washington's Mount Vernon built for himself near Dallas, in which he reportedly at one time installed a pay phone for guests. He was also known to park his car several blocks from the Dallas skyscraper that housed his company to avoid paying the 50-cent fee for parking.

Hunt had a complex personal life with three often simultaneous but separate families. He was married to Lydia Bunker Hunt from 1914 to 1932. But during a trip to Florida in 1925, he secretly married Frania Tye Hunt, with whom he had four children between 1926 and 1934. Meanwhile, he also had four children with Ruth Ray, a secretary at Hunt Oil Company, between 1943 and 1950. Lydia died in 1955, and two years later Hunt legally married Ruth and adopted their children. In all, Hunt had fourteen children in these three families. His last wife, Ruth, convinced him to give up gambling and join the Baptist Church.

When he died in 1974 at the age of eighty-eight, his estate was appraised at only $55 million, but he had already transferred most of his assets to his children. He had established trust funds for each of his children, beginning in 1935. Because his oil company was a private company, it is hard to estimate its worth, but he was believed to be worth well over $1 billion, and estimates have been as high as $3 billion. Six years after his death, when his family had to mortgage its assets to cover debts, they projected $3.2 billion in assets. Two of Hunt's children from his first family, Bunker and Herbert, had attempted to corner the silver market in 1980, but lost much of their fortune. By 1993, the working assets had been reduced to $10 million, although they reportedly owed $50 million to the IRS. Meanwhile, Ray Lee Hunt, the son of Ruth Ray, took the relatively small part of the company he inherited and built it into an estimated $2 billion fortune through daring oil investments.

Hunt was generally seen as running neck and neck with J. Paul Getty for the title of richest man in America or the world. Getty once conceded the contest, saying, "In terms of extraordinary wealth, there is only one man—H. L. Hunt."

91   92

Jay Van Andel
(1924–   )
Est. wealth: $4.3 billion

Richard Marvin DeVos
(1926–   )
Est. wealth: $4.3 billion

The American Way

Jay Van Andel and Richard DeVos became rich by offering dreams of success. As founders of Amway, they built a committed sales force around the world with an evangelical passion for the American Dream. And they themselves became living examples of the gospel of success they preached. They ranked near the top of the 1995 Forbes 400 list, with wealth of more than $4 billion each. Van Andel and DeVos are known as the "Dutch twins," because they both hail from a Dutch-dominated suburb of Grand Rapids, Michigan. DeVos's father was an electrician. Van Andel's dad owned a car dealership. They attended the same high school in the 1930s, went to the same local college, and both served in the Army Air Corps in World War II.

The partners not only paralleled each other in business, but also in their private lives. They married women from Grand Rapids within a few months and lived next door to each other. They both attended the same church, each had four children, and were active in the Republican party.

After serving in the war, they moved back to Grand Rapids and started a series of businesses—a flight school, and then a drive-in restaurant. In 1948 they sold their air service and bought a thirty-eight-foot schooner. They planned to sail through the West Indies and South America, but neither was an accomplished sailor. In March 1949, they sank the boat off the coast of Cuba, but continued their trip and, when they returned, decided to import goods from the Caribbean. Combining their names, they founded Ja-Ri Corporation in 1949 to sell their products. While looking for other products to sell, they came across a vitamin and mineral supplement called Nutrilite. Van Andel's cousin was looking for sales reps for the product, developed by an entrepreneur who had survived on cooked plants and animal bones in a detention camp in China in the 1920s. The partners signed up as distributors.

After initial success selling the product to retailers, they decided to take it directly to consumers. By 1955 they had built a network of distributors selling the product to customers in homes and offices. Internal strife among the company's leaders, eventually led DeVos and Van Andel to strike out on their own.

Taking their two hundred distributors, they established

Amway in 1959. DeVos and Van Andel initially worked out of their basements and focused on cleaning products. They started out selling a biodegradable cleaner. Soon, they were building a factory to produce it. They ultimately added cosmetics, cookware, and thousands of other products, including name-brand items from Levi Strauss, Coca-Cola, and other top manufacturers.

Their direct-sales approach had been used by Avon, Fuller Brush, and other companies. But their multilevel system of distributorships was an innovation, with sponsors building a network of distributors underneath them (earning bonuses on sales of those they sponsored). This gave individual distributors the possibility of sponsoring large organizations, thus creating large fortunes. By the early 1980s, some successful distributors were earning between $200,000 and $350,000 per year, but the average was about $1,056 in 1995. Although the system has been criticized as pyramid sales, Amway has successfully defended itself against this characterization, including a 1979 investigation by the Federal Trade Commission. The FTC concluded that Amway "is not a pyramid distribution scheme."

Whatever it is called, the system DeVos and Van Andel developed with products they assembled are very effective. By 1995, Amway had more than 2.5 million distributors and estimated retail sales of $6.3 billion. Amway has taken Japan by storm. By 1995, it had some 980,000 salespeople in Japan selling an average of more than $40 of products annually to each and every Japanese family. Amway also has aggressively exported its business to emerging nations, where individuals are receptive to the promise of financial security and success. More than 70 percent of Amway's 1995 sales came from outside the United States.

Amway is more than just a worldwide business. "Amway is a movement to help people help themselves," DeVos told *Forbes* in a 1991 interview. DeVos, a charismatic leader, rallies his distributors with speeches on free enterprise, entrepreneurship, and positive thinking. The message is that distributors can take charge of their lives and realize their dreams. To carry the vision to the troops, each year top Amway distributors sponsor more than two hundred seminars in more than eighty cities in the United States and Canada.

DeVos and Van Andel also have been active in national politics, where their belief in free enterprise is a natural fit with conservative Republicans. They were strong supporters of Ronald Reagan's 1980 and 1984 presidential campaigns, and are also close friends with former President Gerald Ford, and Ford, Reagan and President George Bush have addressed Amway distributors meetings.

Although wealth is one of the driving forces of Amway's distributors, DeVos downplays its personal importance. His goal was building the business. "Getting wealthy was never one of my goals," he said. Yet the "Dutch twins" have built a family empire, with all of their children working for the company and serving on its policy board. As an article in *U.S. News and World Report* observed, "If the heirs keep making the right decisions, and the company continues its strong growth abroad, the DeVos and Van Andel clans could eventually rival rich American families like the Rockefellers and the du Ponts."

93

Henry Phipps

(1839–1930)

The Flywheel of Carnegie's Steel Company

Est. wealth: $60 million

Henry Phipps grew up next door to Andrew Carnegie in Allegheny City, in western Pennsylvania. The two would later become partners in Carnegie's steel business, and Phipps would retire as one of the "Pittsburgh millionaires" with a fortune of over $60 million.

In the beginning, the Carnegies were working for the Phippses. Carnegie's mother took on occasional projects for Phipps's father, a master shoemaker who had emigrated from England. By sewing shoes, Mrs. Carnegie earned the poor family an extra $4 per week. Young Andrew would sometimes assist his mother.

After spending their boyhood together, Phipps and Carnegie went their separate ways. Phipps held a variety of jobs, and eventually went to work for an iron forging and manufacturing business. In 1859 he became a silent partner in Kloman Brothers, a firm that manufactured scales. In 1861 one of Carnegie's associates lent Phipps $800 to buy a one-sixth share in the company, which was renamed Kloman & Phipps. Phipps always was behind the scenes, in the back offices, keeping the books.

Meanwhile, Carnegie was building his own iron business. In 1867 Kloman & Phipps joined with Carnegie's Cyclops Iron Works. Phipps became second in command of the new company, which later became the Union Iron Mills. From that point on, the two friends worked together side by side until they retired in 1901. With Henry Frick, Carnegie and Phipps built Carnegie's steel company into one of the world leaders.

Phipps was a financial genius who was the flywheel of the Carnegie operation. He was a conservative voice in a turbulent industry. He kept the company running smoothly through good times and bad, through panics and progress. He was naturally cautious and a tough financial manager, which helped carry the company through the postwar fluctuations in iron and the transition from producing iron to making steel. His solid management and financial skills provided a needed balance to the ambitious vision of Carnegie.

In 1887, Phipps had established what became known as "the Iron Clad agreement," which provided that if a partner retired from the business, the remaining partners could buy his shares at book value rather than market value. Phipps originally had insisted on this agreement because he was afraid that if Carnegie left the business, the other partners would be unable to buy his shares, and the control of the firm would pass to an outsider.

By 1898, however, Phipps and Frick were anxious to retire. Now the agreement made it impossible to leave without selling his shares at a huge loss. So Phipps and Frick went to Wall Street to find someone who would buy the entire company. They found a group of investors willing to purchase the company for $330 million, but the syndicate ultimately could not raise the funds. When Carnegie found out that the group was led by William Moore, whom he considered a speculator, he was furious at Frick and Phipps. The two men then turned to J. P. Morgan, who put together a group of investors who purchased the company for $480 million. Carnegie Steel became part of Morgan's U.S. Steel.

When Carnegie sold the business to U.S. Steel in 1901, Phipps garnered more than $50 million in profits. Phipps took the "Gospel of Wealth" of his business partner to heart. Like Carnegie, Phipps devoted himself to philanthropy, including creating public baths, playgrounds, and parks. He also set up foundations to fight tuberculosis and mental disease. With a keen interest in medical research, he personally examined studies in the field before making his gifts. He founded important centers for the study of tuberculosis and mental health at the University of Pennsylvania and Johns Hopkins University.

Phipps, who married the daughter of a Pittsburgh manufacturer, had five children. He died in 1930, just before his ninety-first birthday. His heirs quietly built the family fortune, primarily through investments in Bessemer Investments Company, under the skillful leadership of his son John. Bessemer emerged as a major stockholder in several large utilities, as well as U.S. Steel and the International Paper Company.

Laurence Phipps, who retired from Pittsburgh to Colorado when he was thirty-nine, became the nation's richest senator. He was known for his unusual "fox hunts" on his Colorado estate, hunting coyote instead of fox.

In 1957, Mrs. Frederick Guest, one of dozens of heirs to the Phipps fortune, appeared on *Fortune*'s list of the wealthiest Americans, with a fortune estimated at between $200 million and $400 million. In 1995, two of Phipps's grandchildren, Howard Phipps, Jr., and Anne Phipps Sidamon-Eristoff appeared on the *Forbes 400* list with fortunes of at least $375 million each. *Forbes* estimated the total Phipps family share of Bessemer Trust at $3.75 billion in 1995.

94

Lawrence J. Ellison

(1944–   )

A Software Samurai

Est. wealth: $4.2 billion

Larry Ellison may be tired of comparisons to Bill Gates. They both dropped out of college and founded software companies in 1977. They both built companies that would dominate the industry. While Gates has been called the new IBM of personal computing, Ellison is viewed as the Big Blue of corporate computing. Or—as the *Economist* commented—"software's other Bill Gates."

But Gates and Ellison are about as much like identical twins as Arnold Schwarzenegger and Danny Devito. Ellison's fortune is less than a third the size of Gates's and his company revenues are half as big. What he lacks in bulk, Ellison more than makes up for in elegance. While Microsoft's mavens slouch around in T-shirts and jeans,

Ellison is strictly corporate, wearing tailored Grieves & Hawkes suits from London. While the Microsoft mogul lavishes $40 million on a sprawling bigger-is-better mansion, Ellison has constructed a single-story Japanese *daimyo*'s house, with a carp pool and teahouse. While Microsoft is as pedestrian as the mass media in which it advertises, Ellison's company is as lofty as its name: Oracle.

In founding Oracle, Ellison bet on minicomputers and the power of relational databases, which took off as corporations sought to make sense out of an avalanche of data. Oracle data-bases now handle customer service, direct marketing, sales and inventory tracking, and other tasks at thousands of companies.

"I've always been an iconoclast," he told *Business Week* in 1995. "I've gotten into enormous trouble. It cost me dearly in school. It has helped me make out like a bandit in technology where the conventional wisdom changes every five years."

Ellison is somewhat eccentric. He was so impressed with the serenity of Kyoto during a visit to Japan that he built his own Japanese home. His assistant describes how they sometimes start the day by spending forty-five minutes observing the squirrels and ducks in the three-acre garden. Ellison taught himself to play piano and guitar. He also is attracted to the life of the sixteenth-century samurai, men who were cultured enough to write poetry yet fierce enough to kill.

This samurai of software was born in 1944 on the South Side of Chicago, where he was raised by a great-aunt and great-uncle. His unwed mother gave up Ellison in 1945 when he was a year old, and moved to California. She didn't see him again for more than forty-five years, when he hired a private detective to track her down. Ellison was raised by his Russian immigrant relatives, who came to America and took their name from Ellis Island when they arrived in New York.

As a young man, Ellison probably would not have been voted most likely to succeed. He was a bright child but rather unre-markable. Once he took a few spins in the dryer of the local laun-dromat—"laundronauting" as he called it—just for kicks. He then attended the University of Illinois before he was kicked out after he skipped final exams for two semesters in a row. After another year at the University of Chicago, he dropped out for good and got into his turquoise Thunderbird to become a hippie in California. But a funny thing happened on the way to the love-in; he discovered Silicon Valley.

After working as a programmer, Ellison set out on his own. Starting with a $1,200 investment and an additional $400 from a partner in 1977, he founded Oracle. Ellison bet on the shift from mainframes to microcomputers. He also bet on the emerging technology of relational databases, which makes organizing data far easier for businesses. He was right on both counts, as businesses shifted to microcomputers and quickly adopted relational databases to handle information about customers and other data.

By 1990 Ellison was sitting on top of a $1 billion company. The rapid growth, and his own lack of financial training, could have brought the company to the brink of destruction. But he brought in new managers, and the company continued to flourish, growing to $2 billion in revenues by 1994. If his Japanese home reflects the poet side of this samurai, the pair of black high rises that house Oracle's Silicon Valley corporate headquarters reflect the warrior.

Ellison has been married and divorced three times, and has a reputation as a ladies' man. As a friend once commented, "As long as Stanford keeps turning out beautiful twenty-three-year-old women, Larry will keep getting married." He is athletic and articulate, but is sometimes so aloof in his company that employees refer to his appearances as "Elvis sightings."

Ellison spends a lot of time thinking about Gates and his dominance of the software industry. In 1995, they were both squaring off over control of the Internet. Ellison, the warrior, is not content to be No. 2. "We want to be the No. 1 software company in the world," he says unequivocally. That's one more thing he and Gates have in common.

95

Ronald Owen Perelman

(1943–   )

Super-Investor

Est. wealth: $4.2 billion

If Ronald Perelman's Marvel Comics ever came up with a super-hero of investing, they would probably model it after Perelman himself. He has spun a business web that would rival any of Spi-derman's. Perelman's business empire ranges from cosmetics (Revlon) to camping equipment (Coleman) to comics (Marvel) to communications (New World Communications) to banking (First Nationwide) to boating (Boston Whaler). He scooped up a total of more than forty businesses in all, keeping the best of them in MacAndrews & Forbes Holding. Unlike other major investors who work with others' funds, Perelman fully controls the company at the center of a $5 billion empire.

The one connecting thread among this eclectic collection of businesses is Perelman himself. He chooses businesses that he enjoys owning. "I love all the businesses we are in," he told *Business Week* in 1995. "I love coming to work. I would not love making widgets."

This philosophy of investing in what he enjoys made the Consolidated Cigar Company a natural fit for Perelman. He is never far from his trademark six-inch Don Diego cigars, puffing through five per day from sunrise to sunset. As a needlepoint pillow in his office states, "Love Me, Love My Cigar." He loved them so much he bought the company.

Perelman not only puts his funds into the company, he also plays an active role in managing it. He works out of his townhouse, adjacent to the McAndrews & Forbes offices, on East 62nd Street in Manhattan. There is no name on the door, and Perelman and staff of just twenty manage and extend his empire.

Perelman was raised as a dealmaker. His father, Raymond Perelman, a Lithuanian immigrant, built Belmont Industries in Philadelphia. The elder Perelman, a corporate raider himself, bought or built businesses that earned $350 million in revenues in 1987. Raymond is known as a tough trader. For example, in 1993, at age seventy-five, he launched a campaign against Champion Parts, Inc., during which he ousted the CEO and took over the company himself.

At a time when classmates were going to Little League, Ronald Perelman was accompanying his father in big-league investing. They would visit companies the elder Perelman was thinking about acquiring and discuss the pros and cons of the deal on the ride home. By the time he was eleven, Ronald Perelman was attending board meetings and sifting through annual reports. After earning his bachelor's degree and MBA from the Wharton School of the University of Pennsylvania in 1966, the younger Perelman went to work with his father. After more than a decade in his father's business, Perelman asked his father when he would be named president. When his father balked at giving him the title, Perelman established his own firm in New York City.

About all he had to his credit was his dealmaking experience and business contacts. He started with a $1.9 million bank loan he used to buy his first business, a New Jersey jewelry store chain. He acquired a 40 percent stake in the company for $2 million and then sold off most of the company except for the watchmaking business. By efficient restructuring and management, he was able to sell the business for $15 million.

Perelman bought film processor Technicolor for just over $100 million in 1983 and sold it for $625 million. Under his hand, camping equipment maker Coleman expanded from $575 million in sales in 1993 to $950 million in 1995. He built Revlon into the world's largest cosmetics business and revived its tarnished reputation, which had been eroded by stiff competition and a move into drugstores and other mass market outlets. Between 1975 and 1987, when Perelman acquired it, Revlon slipped from first place to below third in the cosmetics industry. Besides his skills in management, Perelman is a shrewd negotiator. Even when he loses, he wins. His bid for Gillette in 1986 didn't result in an acquisition, but he received a $39 million greenmail payment to withdraw his bid.

His success is due in part to his ability to see the gems in tarnished companies. He is skilled at purchasing underdogs, selling the least attractive assets, and putting the cash-rich parts of the business under able managers. He holds on to solid performers, "basic, sound, stable cash-flow generators" and makes them run more efficiently. And, as he told *Fortune* in a 1987 interview, "I am *very* tenacious."

A devout Orthodox Jew, Perelman mixes as naturally with the white-bearded rabbis as with glamorous supermodels and high-powered businessmen. He does no work on Saturday, the Jewish Sabbath. Once when he was trying to woo an executive for his cigar company, he made the unprecedented gesture of showing up at the man's hotel room in New York on a Saturday. Even then, Perelman hadn't shaved, carried no money, and refused breakfast. The executive was so impressed when he found out what an important gesture this was that he later joined the company.

Perelman has been married three times. His first wife, Faith Golding, was the daughter of a wealthy real estate family in Philadelphia. Two years after they divorced in 1983, Perelman married New York gossip columnist Claudia Cohen. After their divorce in 1994, he married his third wife, Patricia Duff, later that year. His oldest son, Steven, one of six children, works at Revlon and is believed to be the heir apparent of the empire. Perelman says only that "I plan to leave my assets to my children, so they should be interested in running them."

96

Peter Chardon Brooks

(1767–1849)

Wealthiest Man in New England

Est. wealth: $1.3 million

Running merchant ships was a perilous occupation, but Peter Chardon Brooks found a way to benefit from the uncertainty. He set up an insurance business in 1789 at the "Bunches of Grapes" tavern in Boston and it proved so successful that he retired at thirty-six with a considerable fortune. He became the wealthiest man in New England.

He started out as one of the poorest. Although Brooks came from a distinguished New England family, his father, the Reverend Edward Brooks, was a poor parish minister in Yarmouth, Maine.

His theology was a bit too radical for the conservative parish, so he took his family back to his ancestral farm in Medford, Massachusetts, two years after Peter Chardon's birth.

They had very little income when his father was alive. His father died when Peter was only fourteen, leaving the family almost destitute. Peter was sent off as an apprentice to a merchant in Boston. After he finished his apprenticeship, he decided on the insurance business.

The last decade of the eighteenth century was a particularly profitable time for American shipping. The turmoil of war in Europe made the world increasingly reliant on American merchants. The uncertain world conditions also created a booming market for insurance. Brooks made enough money in this period, he said later, "to turn any man's head."

After retiring in his mid-thirties, he built a new mansion on the family farm. But the young man grew restless in retirement. His friends convinced him to serve as president of the New England Marine Insurance Company in 1806, the first company in the state to offer insurance for merchant ships. Brooks retired again a few years later. Then, his Federalist friends sent him to the state Senate, where he served from 1806 to 1814. He was sent to the U.S. Constitutional Convention in 1820 and finally to the U.S. House and Senate from 1819 to 1823. His service there, while honorable, was only memorable for his successful opposition to the establishment of lotteries in 1821.

Brooks avoided speculation, preferring moderate but certain returns over high-risk investments in railroads or stocks. He would say, he "preferred to keep in shoal water, not because it was shallow, but because he knew exactly how deep it was. He would occasionally lend his funds to solid, well-run corporations. And he did make an exception to his aversion to land speculation by purchasing property around Cleveland, Ohio. A town in this region was named Chardon, in honor of Brooks.

Another principle that guided his business was to take only moderate interest on his loans. He was said to have never taken more than 6 percent interest on loans and mortgages. He believed that was all the use of capital was worth. To take more would be to steal from the skill, courage, and energy of the borrower. Brooks also lent large sums at below market rates for public projects, and gave generously to a variety of philanthropies. Although he lent his money freely, Brooks himself made it a rule never to borrow.

Brooks lived a balanced life in a time when others were engaged in grasping and wild speculation. As Edward Everett wrote in *Lives of American Merchants*, "Moderation was perhaps the most conspicuous single trait of his character, because [he] practiced [it] under circumstance in which it is most rarely exhibited." His wealth gave him independence, and he was neither "enslaved to its pursuit, nor harassed by putting it at risk."

In his survey of wealthy New Yorkers, Moses Yale Beach (in a listing for Brooks's son, Sydney) called the elder Brooks "the richest man in New England." His estate was assessed at $1.3 million shortly before his death in 1849.

97

Charles W. Post

(1854–1914)
Cereal Czar
Est. wealth: $22 million

In 1891, Charles W. Post, the future king of cereals, was broke and barely alive. He was just thirty-seven. Beset by stomach problems for years, he had suffered a violent attack and fell into a depression. He looked as thin as a skeleton. His career was also in shambles after several business failures. When he came into the famous Battle Creek Sanitarium in Michigan, he had to be pushed in a wheelchair.

At the sanitarium, Post was fed on a diet of health foods and drank a cereal coffee substitute every morning. Under the treatment of the director of the institute, Dr. John Harvey Kellogg, a Seventh-Day Adventist, Post received a meatless diet of nut patties and grain beverages. Post soon gained forty to fifty pounds. Not only that, but he had come up with an idea for a new business.

Post was born in Springfield, Illinois, the son of a grain and farm implement dealer. He joined his father's business before leaving to work as a salesman for a farm machinery firm. In 1880 he became manager of the Springfield Plow Works, but he had to leave his position in 1884 because of poor health. He suffered from severe stomach pain, which may have been caused by a digestive ailment such as colitis or diverticulitis. For the next seven years, he sought a cure for his illness. He moved to Texas and worked in real estate, but his health continued to deteriorate. When he reached Kellogg's sanitarium in 1891, he was at death's door.

When the rejuvenated Post left the Battle Creek sanitarium, he built his own center, La Vita Inn, which offered healing by mental suggestion. In 1894, inspired by his experience at the sanitarium, he created his own cereal coffee—marketed first as Monk's Brew, then as Postum. Through aggressive advertising and extraordinary claims—"Makes Blood Red," proclaimed one ad— Postum soon swept the country.

Post was a master at marketing. Unfettered by medical training, he was able to let his imagination run wild. He created anxiety through stories of a woman who had lost her eyesight drinking coffee, and by creating a disease called "coffee neuralgia." Post sometimes got carried away. In 1910, *Collier's* refused to run his advertisements, stating that their medical claims were overblown. Post fought back, but lost the case in court, where he was fined $50,000. At his height, Post was spending close to $1 million per year on advertising his products.

Bolstered by his success with Postum, the cereal entrepreneur drew upon his sanitarium experiences again to bring out a new cereal called Grape-Nuts. (It looked remarkably like a granola that Dr. Kellogg had served.) It was made from a combination of whole wheat and malted baking powder baked for twenty hours so it was partially digested, much easier on his sensitive stomach. In 1904, Post added Post Toasties corn flakes. By the turn of the century he was netting more than $3 million per year. His factory at Battle Creek covered twenty acres and employed more than 2,500 people, making it the largest in the world.

He was a fierce opponent of unions, and published an antilabor magazine called *The Square Deal*. To keep out the unions, Post also paid some of the highest wages in the nation and built a thousand low-cost homes that were sold to employees.

Post lived in Washington, D.C., with a winter home in Santa Barbara, California, and a 200,000-acre ranch that covered two counties in Texas. He was known for conducting rainmaking experiments on his ranch.

In 1914, at the age of fifty-nine, his health failed again, and he was operated on for appendicitis. The operation was a success, but Post had slipped into a depression and frequently spoke of suicide. The family put him under surveillance and removed all weapons from the house, but they overlooked a hunting rifle at his Santa Barbara home. One afternoon when his wife was out of the house, he put on a business suit, put the rifle into his mouth and pulled the trigger.

Post's $22 million fortune and his control of the company passed to his red-haired only daughter, Marjorie Merriweather Post. From the time she was ten, Post had taken his daughter to board meetings and involved her in every aspect of the firm. He even taught her boxing. "I was always my dad's girl," she would later recall. When he died, she was more than prepared to take over running the company.

Marjorie Merriweather Post became one of the richest and most powerful women in the country. As director of the company, she was as admired in business as she was in society. In 1920, she married Wall Street millionaire E. F. Hutton. He listed the company on the New York Stock Exchange in 1922 and began purchasing fifteen grocery and food manufacturers, including Jell-O, Log Cabin Syrup, Maxwell House Coffee, and Hellman's Mayonnaise. Despite Hutton's objections, Marjorie also succeeded in pushing through a $22 million purchase of a frozen food company run by Clarence Birdseye. In 1929, this large conglomerate was renamed General Foods Corporation.

In 1927, Post and Hutton built Mar-a-Lago, a 114-room, 17-acre estate that stretched from sea to lake in Palm Beach, at a cost of $8 million. She and Hutton spent most of the Great Depression partying in Palm Beach, or eating caviar as they sailed around the world on their 316-foot yacht. They were known for their extravagant parties that included the governor of Rome, Mary Pickford, Errol Flynn, George Bernard Shaw, Will Rogers, and other prominent guests. Post remained the queen of high society despite four turbulent and scandalous marriages. (She divorced Hutton when she caught him making love to a Mar-a-Lago chambermaid.) Post lived as close to royalty as any American. When Norway's Queen saw Post's yacht, the queen commented, "Why, you live like a queen, don't you?" Despite her extravagant tastes, Post increased the family fortune to more than $150 million by her death in 1973. She left most of her fortune to her three daughters, who include actress Dina Merrill.

Rich, but Not Rich Enough

Will K. Kellogg

(1860–1951)

HEALTHY PROFITS

The Kelloggs—who gave Post his inspiration—eventually became one of Post's most fierce rivals. They had a slow and difficult start of it. Will K. Kellogg, brother of the doctor who treated Post, was frustrated because Dr. Kellogg refused to allow aggressive advertising and expansion of the business. The doctor objected to advertising, forcing Will to sell their cereals through health magazines. Finally, the impatient Will broke away from his brother. He then began building a business that would become one of the leaders in the cereal industry. By the time Kellogg died in 1951, he had built a highly successful company and a personal fortune of about $50 million—still not enough at that late date to earn him a spot among the wealthiest Americans.

98

Samuel I. Newhouse

(1895–1979)

Paper Tiger

Est. wealth: $1.5 billion

When Samuel I. Newhouse was seventeen, he worked as clerk for city magistrate Hyman Lazarus in Bayonne, New Jersey, earning just $2 per week. Lazarus had just taken control of 51 percent of the failing *Bayonne Times* as payment for a bad debt.

"Sammy," he told Newhouse, "go down and take care of the paper until we can get rid of it."

A succession of managers had tried and failed to revive the struggling paper. Newhouse, the oldest of eight children of poor Jewish immigrants, had quit school at thirteen to help support his family. He was a go-getter, and he wasn't about to set up a hospice for a dying newspaper. He began his new assignment with the characteristic energy and creativity he applied to every task in his life.

Lazarus was surprised when his young clerk came back to report that the paper was running in the black. The paper had lost money during most of its existence, but Newhouse worked with local merchants to plan advertising campaigns for the newspaper. His creative approaches and attention brought in advertising to the failing newspaper.

Thus began a career of turning around losing newspapers, and the foundation for S. I. Newhouse's vast media holdings. By the time of his death in 1979, Newhouse controlled an empire that included thirty-one newspapers, seven magazines, six television stations, five radio stations, and twenty cable systems. It was drawing in revenues of $750 million.

After rescuing the *Bayonne Times*, Newhouse negotiated with the magistrate for a percentage of the profits for the paper. Newhouse, an aspiring lawyer, passed the bar at twenty-one and promptly lost his first case. By then he was drawing in $30,000 per year from his 25 percent share of the profits of the *Bayonne Times*. At twenty-one, he used his earnings to purchase the struggling *Staten Island Advance* in 1922, for $98,000. He turned it around and then used those earnings for his next purchase. Soon he had bootstrapped his way up to a string of more than two dozen successful papers stretching from the *Newark Star-Ledger* to the *Portland Oregonian*, with a combined circulation of three million. He also owned such prominent magazines as *Vogue, Glamour, House & Garden*, and *Mademoiselle*. (He acquired *Vogue* and the other Conde Nast publications just in time to present them to his wife, Mitzi, on their thirty-fifth wedding anniversary in 1959.) His cable business ultimately served 175,000 customers. Shortly before his death, he made the largest newspaper purchase in American history, paying more than $300 million for a chain of newspapers in Michigan.

Forbes estimated that his empire was worth well over a billion dollars by the time of his death in 1979, making it perhaps the most valuable private company in the nation. He had kept absolute control of his holdings and had virtually no debt.

He was no Citizen Kane. Despite the reach of his holdings, Newhouse did not use his editorial muscle to promote his own ideas. Instead he ran this loosely linked empire as a collection of local enterprises, giving near total editorial control to the leaders of the separate businesses. "I'm not interested in molding the nation's opinion," he once said. He wanted his newspapers to become self-reliant. As a result, some leaned toward Republicans, others favored Democrats, like Newhouse himself. His hands-off editorial policy drew praise for its democracy, but critics called him an absentee owner. Because of his policy of picking up poor performers, he was also called a journalistic ragpicker.

While he gave his properties editorial license, he certainly wasn't a hands-off manager. He knew every detail of their business operations. He could recite circulation and ad revenues for any given time, for any part of his sprawling media empire. He believed the surest way to ensure the journalistic freedom of a paper was to put it on a firm financial footing. He was an expert at modernizing the papers and making them more efficient. He spent much of his time traveling the country and touring his businesses.

For a man in the middle of so much media, Newhouse kept a surprisingly low profile. He lived simply and operated his empire out of a battered briefcase. He avoided speaking engagements and routinely ignored requests for information from *Who's Who in America*.

The business also kept his family employed, with various Newhouse relatives running different parts of the business. At the center were his two sons, Donald and S.I. Jr., who took over the business after their father's death. Donald continued to run the newspapers and cable television holdings in the same quiet, unobtrusive style as his father. S.I., two years older and more rigorous and hard driving, took a very different approach to running the family's more than sixty magazines and book publishing operations. Keeping a close eye on circulation and profits, he didn't hesitate to topple icons to improve performance. He shocked the publishing world when he forced the resignation of William Shawn, editor of *The New Yorker* for thirty-five years. He also fired Grace Mirabella, the respected editor of *Vogue* for seventeen years, who heard about her dismissal through a call from a reporter. Finally, he forced the resignation of Robert Bernstein, who had been president of Random House for twenty-three years, taking over from founder Bennett Cerf. These and other moves infuriated authors, editors, magazine staffers, and readers, but the companies continued to perform well under S.I. Newhouse's fierce hand. In addition to the two brothers, more than two dozen other

Newhouses work in the family business. As magazine entrepreneur Paul Diamandis commented in 1990, "The only certainty about what will happen to the company is that, whoever runs it, the boss's family name will be the same." By 1995, Donald and S.I. were listed as sharing an $8.4 billion fortune, placing them near the top of the *Forbes* 400 list.

99

William Wrigley, Jr.
(1861–1932)
Double the Flavor, Double the Fortune
Est. wealth: $34 million

William Wrigley had included chewing gum with his baking powder as an incentive for customers to purchase his product. It turned out that the customers were more interested in the premium than the product. So Wrigley became a gum maker.

Wrigley had been selling since he was ten. His father was a soap maker in Philadelphia, and William would spend Saturdays walking the streets with a basket of soap, hawking his father's wares. It was much more interesting than school, so at eleven, William ran off to New York with a friend to make their fortunes in sales. After a few weeks of peddling newspapers, he returned home to work in his father's soap factory. By thirteen, he was a soap salesman traveling around the city and the country.

At twenty-nine, he set out on his own for Chicago, where he established a business with his cousin. First they made soap, then baking powder. Wrigley had made such clever use of premiums—from gum to lamps to clocks and even accident insurance—that his sales boomed. But when he found customers wanted more of the chewing gum he included as a premium, he decided to change businesses.

For nearly the first two decades that he was in the gum business, Wrigley didn't even manufacture his own gum. He contracted out the work to Zeno Manufacturing Company, a gum maker. In 1911, he took over the manufacturer, establishing the William Wrigley, Jr. Company.

Wrigley had developed "Wrigley's Spearmint Gum" in 1893, but the new flavor was slow to catch on. In 1907, Wrigley launched a massive advertising campaign, running up a $280,000 advertising tab that year. His approach to advertising was, "Tell 'em quick and tell 'em often." Within two years of launching the campaign, Wrigley's spearmint gum sold more than a $1 million worth per year. By 1910, it had become the top-selling gum in America.

His simple but effective advertising made chewing gum and the white packages of Wrigley's spearmint gum part of American life. In 1915, he took the unprecedented step of sending a free sample of his gum to every single person listed in U.S. telephone books. It was perhaps the first use of free direct-mail samples to sell products. He also set up a mile-long sign near Atlantic City that consisted of huge replicas of his familiar gum boxes, interspersed with slogans such as "The Flavor Lasts."

Then, proving that he could walk and chew gum at the same time, Wrigley took his product around the world. Before his death in 1932, he was advertising in thirty languages and selling $75 million worth of gum per year. He had factories in Chicago, New York, Toronto, London, and Sydney.

A baseball fanatic, Wrigley used to enjoy giving out cigars for home runs while sitting in the stands in Chicago, watching the Cubs play. With his fortune, he bought a controlling interest in the Chicago Cubs, then the Los Angeles Baseball Club, and finally a Reading, Pennsylvania, Internationals team. He also invested in resorts, tropical birds, mines, and hotels. Among his acquisitions was Santa Catalina Island, which he bought in 1919 and developed into one of the nation's leading resorts.

Shortly after William Wrigley's death in 1932 at the age of seventy, the value of the family's holdings in the company was estimated at $34 million. The family continued to control both the company and much of its stock. William's only son, Philip K. Wrigley, took over from his father in 1925. He held the price of a package of the gum to a nickel until 1971, even though rivals had boosted their prices to a dime a pack. He remained president and CEO until 1961 and served on the board until his death in 1977. He was followed by his son, William Wrigley. The family also continued to hold 35 percent of the company's stock, worth more than $300 million in 1983. By 1995, *Forbes* estimated the family fortune at $1.5 billion.

David Packard

(1912–1996)

The H-P Way

Est. wealth: $3.7 billion

David Packard and Bill Hewlett started their electronics business in a rented garage in California and ended up in the Fortune 500. When Packard died on March 26, 1996, at the age of eighty-three, the company he and Hewlett had founded had more than a hundred thousand employees and revenues of $31 billion.

The son of a prosperous Colorado lawyer, David Packard attended public schools and then majored in electrical engineering at Stanford University. Lanky and athletic, he was a track star and also earned letters in football and basketball. At Stanford, he met his future partner, Bill Hewlett, a fellow engineering student with a genius for electricity and radio. After graduating from Stanford in 1934, Packard went to work for General Electric in Schenectady, New York. Hewlett earned his master's degree from MIT, before returning to California in 1936.

Their Stanford engineering professor, Frederick Terman, arranged for work and fellowships to bring the two young men back to California. Terman, who recognized the talent of his bright young assistants and the growing potential of technology firms, urged Packard and Hewlett to start their own business.

In 1938, they started the company in a rented garage in Palo Alto, which later became known as "The Birthplace of Silicon Valley." Putting together $538 in capital, they bought a secondhand Sears press and baked the glazing on their instrument panels in Packard's kitchen oven. They were initially a company in search of a product. Their first products included an electronic harmonica tuner, a bowling alley fault indicator, and even an automatic urinal flusher.

Their first successful product was an audio oscillator, which generated signals that could be used to test sound quality. They whimsically priced it at just $54.40, in honor of the "Fifty-Four Forty or Fight" slogan from the fight for the Pacific Northwest. Their nearest competitor was selling the same machine for $400. One of their first big orders came from Walt Disney Co., which ordered eight Hewlett-Packard oscillators for its movie *Fantasia*. In 1939 the partners needed to name the company, and they flipped a coin to determine whose name should go first. Bill Hewlett won.

By the end of that year, they had moved out of the garage with revenues of more than $5,000 per year. With Terman's encouragement, they built a plant in Stanford's industrial park— becoming one of the first of more than a thousand firms to settle in what would become known as Silicon Valley. At the start of World War II, they had seventeen employees and $100,000 in annual sales. Because Hewlett was called into service during the war, Packard was left to run the company on his own. By 1946, with intense demand for technology for the war, the company had $2 million in sales and two hundred employees.

With the end of the war, however, government orders dropped off, and the company was forced to halve its workforce. By 1950, the partners had brought the company's sales and workforce up to their former level, now producing more than three hundred products. The company had diversified into heart monitors, atomic clocks, and computers.

In 1969, with company sales of over $280 million per year, Packard was called to Washington to serve as deputy secretary of defense. His appointment was controversial, so he was forced to place his $300 million in Hewlett-Packard stock in a blind charitable trust to avoid a possible conflict of interest. (In fact, government contracts fell during Packard's three years in Washington.)

With one of the finest groups of scientists and engineers in Silicon Valley, Hewlett-Packard turned out a string of successful products. In 1972, H-P introduced its HP-35 scientific calculator, which became an instant leader in calculators among students and engineers. It also virtually put an end to the slide rule, and brought H-P, which had primarily handled corporate contracts, into the mass market. Also in 1972, H-P entered minicomputers, and after a slow start, became a leader in computer manufacturing.

The company became one of the most admired and successful companies in America. Besides its financial results, Packard and Hewlett created a unique corporate environment. The partners developed a set of principles known as "the H-P Way," reflecting a corporate morality that included deep respect and concern for employees, as well as refraining from long-term borrowing and not entering any business they did not truly understand. H-P's employee innovations included a promise never to lay off employees and a generous profit-sharing plan. During recessions, the company scaled back on hours to avoid layoffs.

In 1978, Hewlett and Packard left the active management of the company and became partners in a new venture together—an Idaho cattle ranch. Their cattle were marked with an H-P brand. Packard also advised President Reagan on defense and other issues as part of Reagan's "kitchen cabinet."

By October 1995, *Forbes* estimated Packard's fortune at $3.7 billion. Hewlett was slightly behind his partner with $2.7 billion. The two partners gave Stanford more than $300 million, most of it in anonymous gifts, and funded an electrical engineering building to honor their former mentor, Professor Terman.

Packard donated more than $1 billion during his lifetime, including a $40 million gift to found the Monterey Bay Aquarium. His David and Lucille Packard Foundation had dispersed more than $480 million in gifts by the time of his death. He bequeathed his $4.3 billion share of H-P stock to his family foundation, making it one of the richest in the nation, with more than $7 billion in holdings.

Packard was opinionated and sometimes crusty, but he was always very humble about his achievements. As he told employees in 1993 when he stepped down as H-P chairman, "You shouldn't gloat about anything you've done; you ought to keep going and try to find something better to do."

Afterword: Who Are the Wealthy 100?

These portraits offer a view of the diverse panorama of American wealth—from the merchants and landowners of the Revolution to the robber baron industrialists of the turn of the century to the whiz kids of Silicon Valley. The only rule for creating an American fortune is that there are no rules. Fortunes are not made by simple recipes, but there are some common characteristics of these individuals and their empires.

Most of the Wealthy 100 found their fortunes on the frontiers. It is there, rather than the clear and well-worn paths, where wealth is discovered or created. Some, like Elias Hasket Derby and other New England merchants, made perilous sea journeys to trade with China. Some, like William Andrews Clark and the Silver Kings, found wealth on the geographic frontiers of the mining camps of Montana or Nevada. Others, like James J. Hill or William Aspinwall, cut across unbroken territory to build the railroads or span the isthmus of Panama. Some built wealth by extending the frontiers of knowledge or invention—creating automobiles, aluminum, software, or computers. Some also pushed the limits of moral frontiers, stretching law and ethics in pursuit of fortunes. On each of these frontiers, they recognized opportunities. They drove forward brashly into these territories, for they knew wealth is not found by following the herd, but rather by finding a new direction.

Some of the great fortunes came from invention, but invention alone was not enough, as Eli Whitney, Charles Goodyear, and others learned. The Wealthy 100 often rode to success on a new innovation—the sewing machine, the automobile, the spinning mill, the personal computer—but many were not inventors. They were, instead, able to turn the inventions into commercial successes. It is clearly not enough to create the better mousetrap. The key is to find a way to capture the value generated from the invention—to get the world to beat a path to your door. This was the genius of marketing. Nowhere is it more apparent than in the story of Charles W. Post, who appeared to draw much of his early inspiration from his visit to the sanitarium run by the Kelloggs, and then beat them to the punch in taking healthy cereals and beverages to market.

Once the frontiers are broken, when the footpaths become superhighways, the opportunities to create great wealth no longer existed. Once the cities such as New York, Cincinnati, or Chicago grew up, the opportunity was gone for an Astor, a Longworth, or a Field to buy farmland that would become the downtown. So, with each succeeding generation, old frontiers are civilized and new areas have to be found to conquer.

One characteristic almost all of the individuals in this book share is driving ambition. Sometimes this ambition was just to accumulate as much money as possible. At other times, it was directed toward accumulating power or building a successful enterprise. But it was this ambition and audacity that allowed them to pursue their goals and to survive the inevitable failures on the road to success. Also, this ambition allowed them to trample rivals, exploit employees, and ransack national treasuries.

They had extraordinary determination. Nowhere is this seen more vividly than in the story of Frank Woolworth. He suffered failure after failure as a salesmen in retail stores. He couldn't even hold down a decent job. He was discouraged and broken. Yet he rebounded to create the five-and-ten and found one of the most successful retail chains in the nation. Then there is Samuel Colt, a talented inventor, whose concept of a revolver was turned down time and again by the military. But he didn't let go of the idea, and his six-shooter, with the encouragement of the Texas Rangers, became the standard issue in the West. This determination in the face of setbacks is a quality seen in almost all of the Wealthy 100.

Driving ambition was often linked to a broad vision or a daring plan. Some of the plans were nefarious, such as Jay Gould's scheme to corner the silver market or Rockefeller's plan to consolidate the oil business into his own hands. Others were just bold. Robert Dollar saw a worldwide shipping line, Edward Clark saw a sewing machine in every home, and Bill Gates envisioned personal computers transforming life and work.

One might think that these visionary, ambitious individuals would be loners, and a few were. But many of these fortunes were the result of effective collaborations. There were, of course, financial backers. There also were organizations that included a balance of personalities to realize the vision of the founder.

It is intriguing how many of the fortunes are the result of a combination of talents. Brothers such as the Mellons or the Dodges were like Siamese twins, living and working together, reading each other's thoughts. There also were the vinegar and water combinations such as the bohemian Isaac Singer and button-down Edward Clark, or the lyrical Richard Sears and the practical Julius Rosenwald. There were quartets of partners such as the Silver Kings in Nevada or the Big Four railway builders in California, with each member contributing a distinct capability. Sometimes it was the chemistry of diametrically opposed characters that reacted to produce great wealth.

Some, like Andrew Carnegie, established even broader organizations—organizations that combined many talented individuals and produced many great fortunes. As Carnegie commented, his greatest talent was surrounding himself with "men far cleverer than himself." Loyal lieutenants such as Henry Frick and Henry Phipps earned a place among the wealthiest Americans for their services.

Others, like J. P. Morgan, built institutions that have far lasted their founders. These companies continue to grow, and are a source of wealth and employment to this day.

The only woman on this list is Hetty Green, who played the man's game of Wall Street investment, building a $10 million inheritance into $100 million. Because of the way this list was defined, with a bias against inheritance, it is natural that there should not be extraordinarily wealthy women on it. Many women play a prominent role in the stories of these fortunes—Marjorie Merriweather Post, the Astors, Vanderbilts, and others. But, throughout most of American history, women did not have the opportunity to accumulate wealth at all. Even today, their opportunities are often less than those of men, with very few women other than inheritors at the top of the *Forbes* 400.

This situation is slowly changing, and will do so even more rapidly as women entrepreneurs continue to expand their firms. Oprah Winfrey and other women are beginning to move into the ranks of the wealthiest Americans based on their own fortunes.

WHERE THEIR MONEY CAME FROM AND WHERE IT WENT

Half or more of the members of the list started out with nothing or almost nothing. Rockefeller, Vanderbilt, Astor, Girard, and Carnegie—the first five—all were born to families of modest means, and some immigrated to the United States with little more than the clothes on their backs. One, Stephen Van Rensselaer, gives us a glimpse of a different kind of old-style American wealth, with huge land grants from Europe that were given away at the start of the nation. Other members of the Wealthy 100, such as Howard Hughes, inherited millions of dollars, but then built their fortunes larger.

Some lived in splendor, others held on to every cent. Remember that Nicholas Longworth dressed so shabbily that when he stopped to mop his brow on a hot Cincinnati street, a passerby dropped a quarter into his outstretched hat. (Longworth replied with good humor that it was the easiest quarter he had ever earned.) Hetty Green used to carry stale sandwiches in the capacious pockets of her black dress, a dress that had turned a greenish color from neglect. Russell Sage pilfered fans and other small items from his Western Union board meetings, which he attended punctually to receive his free lunch.

Others built extraordinary pleasure domes—fabulous marble mansions that lined Fifth Avenue, ornate carriages, beach homes, and private railway cars. William Randolph Hearst managed to spend an estimated $15 million per year. Others indulged in horse racing, yachting, and other hobbies. Some were as visible as the Vanderbilts, and others as secretive as Howard Hughes.

Many—either directly or through their heirs—demonstrated generosity commensurate with their fortunes. The names of the founders of these great fortunes are also the names of some of the most prominent foundations in the world—the Carnegie Foundation, the Ford Foundation, and Packard Foundation, among others. Some of the Wealthy 100 contributed to charity after their deaths, in spite of themselves—thus there is even a Russell Sage Foundation, named for a notorious tightwad who was uninterested in philanthropy.

For many families, the great wealth was not a blessing but a curse. The Singers, the Dodges, the Gettys, the Dukes, and others suffered from the burden of being born into wealth. They also struggled with the often challenging personalities of the men who built their fortunes. Some couldn't get rid of the family fortune fast enough, while others carefully managed and built it.

WHERE WILL THE NEXT WEALTHY 100 COME FROM?

The next great American fortunes will likely be derived from some of the same combinations of vision and ambition as in the past. But the details will be different. There will be some new technology that will launch its owner into the financial stratosphere, as the fortunes of Bill Gates and Larry Ellison were made in the past. There will be new opportunities for future Warren Buffetts, investors who can read opportunities in the market and capitalize on them. Every time one frontier closes, a new frontier opens up. And every new frontier offers the possibility of a new American fortune. The question is not whether these fortunes will be created, but rather by whom?

NOTES

p. xvi   *"Citizens may be equals"*: Lundberg, Ferdinand. *America's 60 Families.* New York: Citadel Press, 1946, p. 7.

p. xvi   *Philadelphia survey:* Myers, Gustavus. *History of the Great American Fortunes* (Vol. I). Chicago: Charles H. Kerr, 1911, p. 195.

p. xvi   Fortune *magazine estimate:* Smith, Richard Austin. "The Fifty-Million-Dollar Man," *Fortune.* November 1957, p. 176.

p. xvii   *133,400 millionaires in the U.S.:* Thorndike, Joseph J., Jr. *The Very Rich: A History of Wealth.* New York: American Heritage, 1976, p. 6.

p. xvii   *3.2 million households of $1 million plus:* Hacker, Andrew. "The Upper Tail," *New York Times Magazine.* November 19, 1995, p. 71.

p. xvii   *Edward Koch quote:* Koch, Edward. "Commodore Cornelius Vanderbilt's 200th Birthday and Service of Commemoration," May 27, 1994, New York City.

p. xx   *"If you can count your money"*: Hewins, Ralph. *The Richest American.* New York: E.P. Dutton, 1960, p. 352.

p. 4   *Rockefeller estate estimate:* Lundberg, Ferdinand. *The Rockefeller Syndrome.* Secaucus, N.J: Lyle Stuart, 1975, p. 10.

p. 6   *"This modern Croesus"*: Redmond, George F. *Financial Giants of America* (Vol. I). Boston: The Stratford Company, 1922, p. 18.

p. 8   *"an enduring institution"*: Collier, Peter, and David Horowitz. *The Rockefellers: An American Dynasty.* New York: Holt, Rinehart and Winston, 1976, p. 6.

p. 12   *Vanderbilt letter:* Josephson, Matthew. *The Robber Barons: The Great American Capitalists.* New York: Harcourt, Brace & World, 1934, p. 15.

p. 14   *"I have a large family"*: Vanderbilt, Arthur T. *Fortune's Children: The Fall of the House of Vanderbilt.* New York: William Morrow, 1989, p. 24.

p. 14   *Cigar smoking story:* ibid, p. 26.

p. 16   *"not one millionaire among them.":* ibid.

p. 17   *1925 Guggenheim and Du Pont estimates:* Lundberg. *America's 60 Families,* op. cit., p. 25.

p. 17   *Pierre S. Du Pont estate:* Winkler, John Kennedy. *The Du Pont Dynasty.* New York: Reynald & Hitchcock, 1935.

p. 17   *Record divorces:* Thorndike, op. cit., p. 85.

p. 17   *Simon Guggenheim estimate:* Tebbel, John. *The Inheritors: A Study of America's Great Fortunes and What Happened to Them.* New York: G.P. Putnam's Sons, 1962, p. 269.

p. 19   *"clothed the city people of two continents"*: Chamberlain, John. *The Enterprising Americans: A Business History of the United States.* Institute for Christian Economics: Tyler, Tex.: 1961, p. 83.

p. 19 *no fortune "within approachable distance of his":* Myers, *op. cit.*, p. 194.

p. 22 *"buy every foot of Manhattan Island":* Churchill, Allen. *The Splendor Seekers: An Informal Glimpse of America's Multimillionaire Spenders— Members of the $50,000,000 Club.* New York: Grosset & Dunlap, 1974, p. 5.

p. 23 *undisputed social Mecca":* Sinclair, David. *Dynasty: The Astors and Their Times.* New York: Beaufort Books, 1984, p. 11.

p. 26 *"richest man in America":* Groner, Alex, ed. *The American Heritage History of American Business & Industry.* New York: American Heritage Publishing, 1972, p. 67.

p. 27 *"ugly ducking":* Myers, *op. cit.*, p. 83.

p. 28 *"may have rivaled J. P. Morgan":* Fisher, Kenneth L. *100 Minds That Made the Market.* Woodside, Calif.: Business Classics, 1993, p. 22.

p. 32 *"wagered everything he possessed":* Dictionary of American Biography, p. 502.

p. 39 *an area larger than the state of Wisconsin:* Smith, Arthur D. Howden. *Men Who Run America: A Study of the Capitalistic System and Its Trends Based on Thirty Case Histories.* New York: Bobbs-Merrill, 1936, p. 72.

p. 42 *"only man who ever swindled Vanderbilt":* ibid., p. 32.

p. 44 *"Mephistopheles of Wall Street:* Hoyt, Edwin P. *The Goulds: A Social History.* New York: Weybright and Talley, 1969, p. 328.

p. 45 *"a paltry $1 million":* Swanberg, W. A. *Jim Fisk: The Career of an Improbable Rascal.* New York: Charles Scribner's Sons, 1959, p. 281.

p. 48 *manor hall . . . preserved:* Van Rensselaer, Philip. *Rich Was Better.* New York: Wynwood Press, 1990, p. 135.

p. 50 *"You have no home":* Weisberger, Bernard. "The Forgotten Four Hundred: Chicago's First Millionaires," *American Heritage.* November 1987, p. 42.

p. 56 *Henry Ford story:* Thomas, Henry, and Dana Lee Thomas. *Living Biographies of Famous Americans.* Garden City, N.Y.: Blue Ribbon Books, 1946, pp. 305–306.

p. 59 *"No inventor probably has been so harassed":* Myers, *op. cit.*, p. 135.

p. 63 *"an anonymous figure":* Tebbel, *op. cit.*, p. 16.

p. 63 *Estimate of Mellon wealth in 1937:* Koskoff, David E. *The Mellons.* New York: Thomas Y. Crowell, 1978.

p. 64 *Gave away $310 million:* Allen, Michael Patrick. *The Founding Fortunes.* New York: E. P. Dutton, 1987.

p. 67 *"hootchy-kootchy girls danced by the lake":* Walton, Sam. *Sam Walton: Made in America.* New York: Doubleday, 1992, p. 1.

p. 82 *Troy & Schenactady line deal:* Sarnoff, Paul. *Russell Sage: The Money King.* New York: Ivan Obolensky, 1965, p. 62.

p. 92 *"would rather battle than eat":* Smith, A., *op. cit.*, p. 222.

p. 93 *"Once he determined upon an object":* Redmond, *op. cit.*, p. 18.

p. 94 *"jump in with both feet":* Churchill, *op. cit.*, p. 98.

p. 99 *"Flew the Jolly Roger":* Lundberg. *America's 60 Families, op. cit.*, p. 5.

p. 99 *"God made the world in 4004 B.C.":* Jennings, Walter Wilson, *20 Giants of American Business.* New York: Exposition Press, 1953, p. 194.

p. 99 *"his very great power and truthfulness":* ibid., p. 197.

p. 100 *"bought them at the wholesale rate":* ibid., p. 172.

p. 102 *J. P. Morgan, Jr., had to sell paintings:* Redmond, *op. cit.*, p. 62.

p. 103 *"we are an institution"* Redmond, *op. cit.*, p. 61.

p. 107 *"see him in hell":* Schriener, Samuel Agnew. *Henry Clay Frick: The Gospel of Greed.* New York: St. Martin's Press, 1995, p. ix.

p. 107 *"success simply calls for hard work":* Forbes, B. C. *Men Who Are Making America.* New York: B. C. Forbes, 1917, p. 133.

pp. 107–8	*"first large-scale union buster":* Schriener, *op. cit.,* p. 289.
p. 109	*"only time separated him":* ibid., p. 267.
p. 116	*"truest and best man that ever lived":* Latta, Estelle. *Controversial Mark Hopkins.* New York: Greenberg, 1953, p. 96.
p. 118	*"what an empty existence":* Tebbel, *op. cit.,* p. 158.
p. 122	*"more a beggar than a millionaire":* Myers, *op. cit.,* p. 256.
p. 124	*"I do not love the money":* Weisenberger, *op. cit.,* p. 37.
p. 125	*"The world is a worse place":* Forbes, *op. cit.,* p. 5
p. 128	*"Even as a kid":* Kirkpatrick, David. "Over the Horizon With Paul Allen," *Fortune.* July 11, 1994, p. 75.
p. 131	*"In short, I'm a fan":* Gates, William. "Gates on Buffett," *Fortune.* February 5, 1996. [Originally published by the *Harvard Business Review,* January/February 1996. From "What I Learned From Warren Buffett," by Bill Gates. Copyright © 1995 Microsoft Company. (All Rights Reserved.)
p. 135	*"ideally complemented":* Brandon, Ruth. *A Capitalist Romance: Singer and the Sewing Machine.* Philadelphia: J. B. Lippincott, 1977, p. 87.
p. 139	*"richest and most detested woman in America":* Lewis, Arthur H. *The Day They Shook the Plum Tree.* New York: Harcourt, Brace & World, 1963, p. 8.
p. 170	*"mayors are his office boys":* Fisher, *op. cit.,* p. 138.
p. 171	*"$20 million to the Roman Catholic Church:* Lundberg. *America's 60 Families, op. cit.,* p. 29.
p. 185	*"her ailing husband":* Mansfield, Stephanie. *The Richest Girl in the World.* New York: G. P. Putnam's Sons, 1992.
p. 186	*"the greatest that has ever been":* Myers, *op. cit.,* p. 58.
p. 187	*"investments in real estate":* ibid., p. 58.
p. 201	*"That's our name":* American Dynasties Today, Homewood, Ill.: Dow Jones-Irwin, p. 70.
p. 203	*"even the rankest Socialist":* Forbes, *op. cit.,* p. 18
p. 206	*Washington's land holdings:* Myers, *op. cit.,* p. 43.
p. 207	*"persistent gathering of public contributions":* ibid., p. 43.
p. 214	*"It is my aim":* Hernon, Peter, and Terry Ganey. *Under the Influence: The Unauthorized Story of the Anheuser-Busch Dynasty.* New York: Simon & Schuster, 1991, p. 13.
p. 214	*"P. T. Barnum, Buffalo Bill":* ibid., p. 19.
p. 215	*Busch estate:* ibid., p. 87.
p. 222	*Value of Pullman estate:* Leyendecker, Liston E. *Palace Car Prince.* Colorado: University Press of Colorado, 1992, p. 259.
p. 225	*"We are building":* "Robert Wood Johnson, 74, Dies; Chairman of Johnson & Johnson," *New York Times,* January 31, 1968, p. 41.
p. 226	*"to ignore the conditions":* ibid.
p. 226	*Johnson Foundation details:* Allen, *op. cit.,* p. 345.
p. 228	*Dodge fortune:* Latham, Caroline. "Where's Mommy?" *Forbes.* October 23, 1995, p. 87.
p. 230	*"wealth is a curse":* Latham, Caroline, and David Agresta. *Dodge Dynasty: The Car and the Family That Rocked Detroit.* San Diego: Harcourt Brace Jovanovich, 1989, p. 5.
p. 231	*"a sparrow to an eagle":* Marcus, George E. *Lives in Trust: The Fortunes of Dynastic Families in Late Twentieth Century America.* Boulder, Col.: Westview Press, 1992, p. 244.
p. 232	*Getty estate figure:* Lenzner, Robert. *The Great Getty.* New York: Crown Publishers, 1985, p. 220.
p. 232	*"I just fleeced":* ibid., p. 50.

p. 247 *"However inferior in wealth":* Sobel, Robert, and David B. Sicilia. *The Entrepreneur: An American Adventure.* Boston: Houghton Mifflin, 1986, p. 152.

p. 249 *"He had given millions":* Myers, *op. cit.,* p. 133.

p. 251 *"second only to Morgan":* Forbes, *op. cit.,* p. 368.

p. 253 *Whitney's physical description:* Churchill, *op. cit.,* p. 135.

p. 254 *"I am done with politics":* Swanberg, W. A. *Whitney Father, Whitney Heiress.* New York: Charles Scribner's Sons, 1980, p. 82.

p. 255 *"had gratified every ambition":* ibid., p. 1.

p. 260 *"The reaping machine":* Jennings, *op. cit.,* p. 29.

p. 261 *McCormick's wealth:* Darby, Edwin. *The Fortune Builders.* New York: Doubleday, 1986, p. 240.

p. 262 *Deere's wealth:* Clark, Neil M. *John Deere: He Gave to the World the Steel Plow.* Moline, Ill. Privately printed 1937.

p. 265 *"large body of money":* "Tycoons," *Time.* March 5, 1956, p. 102.

p. 265 *"No one but Mr. Davis":* "People of the Week," *U.S. News & World Report.* August 16, 1957, p. 14.

p. 269 *"as a man without spot":* Hunt, Freeman. *Lives of American Merchants.* New York: Hunt's Merchants' Magazine, 1856, p. 101.

p. 279 *Hughes's estate:* Barlett, Donald L., and James B. Steele. *Empire: The Life, Legend, and Madness of Howard Hughes.* New York: W. W. Norton, 1979, p. 584.

p. 279 *"If he had invested":* ibid., p. 622.

p. 290 *Slater's wealth:* Tucker, Barbara M. *Samuel Slater and the Origins of the American Textile Industry, 1790–1860.* Ithaca, N.Y.: Cornell University Press, 1984, p. 190.

p. 293 *Belmont's obituary:* Black, David. *The King of Fifth Avenue: The Fortunes of August Belmont.* New York: Dial Press, 1981, p. 723.

p. 293 *Belmont's estate:* ibid.

p. 293 *"Where had the money gone?":* Tebbel, *op. cit.,* p. 150.

p. 295 *"did not come from manufacture":* Myers, *op. cit.,* p. 43.

p. 298 *"Great successes":* Lenzner, Robert, and Marla Matzer. "Late Bloomer," *Forbes.* October 17, 1994, p. 44.

p. 299 *"He's in this for the game":* Therrien, Lois. "Sumner Redstone's Idea of a Good Time Is Hardnosed Bargaining," *Business Week,* October 20, 1986, p. 77.

p. 307 *Bunker and Herbert Hunt's finances: Forbes.* October 18, 1993, p. 65.

p. 308 *Ray Lee Hunt's fortune: Forbes.* October 16, 1995, p. 128.

p. 311 *"Amway is more":* Klebnikov, Paul. "The Power of Positive Inspiration," *Forbes.* December 9, 1991, p. 245.

p. 312 *"If the heirs keep making":* Grant, Linda. "How Amway's Two Founders Cleaned Up," *U.S. News & World Report.* October 31, 1994, p. 77.

p. 317 *"I've always been an iconoclast":* Brandt, Richard. "Can Larry Beat Bill?" *Business Week.* May 15, 1995, p. 94.

p. 318 *"As long as Stanford":* ibid.

p. 321 *"I plan to leave":* Spiro, Leah Nathans. "The Operator," *Business Week.* August 21, 1995, p. 60.

p. 324 *"enslaved to its pursuit":* Hunt, *op. cit.,* p. 180.

p. 332 *"The only certainty":* Whitaker, Leslie. "A Search for Glitz," *Time.* June 4, 1990, p. 77.

p. 335 *Wrigley company stock's worth:* Allen, *op. cit.,* p. 391.

p. 339 *"You shouldn't gloat":* Hamilton, Joan O'C. "David Packard: Silicon Valley's Class Act," *Business Week.* April 8, 1996, p. 42.

SELECT BIBLIOGRAPHY

Allen, Michael Patrick. *The Founding Fortunes.* New York: E. P. Dutton, 1987.

Beach, Moses Yale. *The Wealth and Biography of the Wealthy Citizens of the City of New York.* New York: Sun, 1846.

Black, David. *The King of Fifth Avenue: The Fortunes of August Belmont.* New York: Dial Press, 1981.

Brandon, Ruth. *A Capitalist Romance: Singer and the Sewing Machine.* Philadelphia: J. B. Lippincott Company, 1977.

Browder, Clifford. *The Money Game in Old New York.* Lexington, Ky.: University Press of Kentucky, 1986.

Churchill, Allen. *The Splendor Seekers: An Informal Glimpse of America's Multimillionaire Spenders—Members of the $50,000,000 Club.* New York: Grosset & Dunlap, 1974.

Corey, Lewis. *The House of Morgan.* New York: G. Foward Watt, 1930.

Darby, Edwin, *The Fortune Builders.* New York: Doubleday & Co., 1986.

Diamond, Sigmund. *The Reputation of the American Businessman.* New York: Harper Colophon Books, 1966.

Fisher, Kenneth L. *100 Minds That Made the Market,* Woodside, Calif.: Business Classics, 1993.

Forbes, B. C. *Men Who Are Making America.* New York: B. C. Forbes Publishing Company, 1917.

Groner, Alex, ed. *The American Heritage History of American Business & Industry.* New York: American Heritage Publishing Co., 1972.

Hernon, Peter, and Terry Ganey. *Under the Influence: The Unauthorized Story of the Anheuser-Busch Dynasty.* New York: Simon & Schuster, 1991.

Higham, Charles. *Howard Hughes, The Secret Life.* New York: G. P. Putnam's Sons, 1993.

Hirsch, Mark D. *William C. Whitney: Modern Warwick.* New York: Dodd, Mead & Company, 1948.

Hunt, Freeman. *Lives of the American Merchants.* New York: Hunts' Merchants' Magazine, 1855.

Ingham, John. *Biographical Dictionary of American Business Leaders.* New York: Greenwood Press, 1983.

Ingham, John N., and Lynne B. Feldman. *Contemporary Business Leaders: A Biographical Dictionary.* New York: Greenwood Press, 1990.

Jennings, Walter Wilson, *20 Giants of American Business.* New York: Exposition Press, 1953.

Johnson, Rossiter, ed. *The Biographical Dictionary of America.* Boston: American Biographical Society, 1906.

Josephson, Matthew. *The Robber Barons: The Great American Capitalists.* New York: Harcourt, Brace & World, 1934.

Koskoff, David E. *The Mellons.* New York: Thomas Y. Crowell, 1978.

Latta, Estelle. *Controversial Mark Hopkins,* New York: Greenberg, 1953.

Lewis, Arthur H. *The Day They Shook the Plum Tree.* New York: Harcourt, Brace & World, 1963.

Lewis, Oscar. *The Silver Kings.* New York: Alfred A. Knopf, 1947.

Lundberg, Ferdinand. *America's 60 Families.* New York: Citadel Press, 1946.

———. *The Rockefeller Syndrome.* Secaucus, N.J.: Lyle Stuart, 1975.

O'Connor, Harvey. *The Guggenheims.* New York: Covici Friede, 1937.

Marcus, George E. *Lives in Trust: The Fortunes of Dynastic Families in Late Twentieth-Century America.* Boulder, Col.: Westview Press, 1992.

Myers, Gustavus. *History of the Great American Fortunes.* Chicago: Charles H. Kerr, 1911.

Pessen, Edward. *Riches, Class, and Power Before the Civil War.* Lexington, Mass.: D. C. Health and Company, 1973.

Redmond, George F. *Financial Giants of America* (Vols. I & II). Boston: The Stratford Company, 1922.

Richards, William C. *The Last Billionaire.* New York: Charles Scribner's Sons, 1948.

Sarnoff, Paul. *Russell Sage: The Money King.* New York: Ivan Obolensky, 1965.

Smith, Arthur D. Howden. *Men Who Run America: A Study of the Capitalistic System and Its Trends Based on Thirty Case Histories.* New York: The Bobbs-Merrill Company, 1936.

Sparkes, Boyden. *The Witch of Wall Street: Hetty Green.* New York: Doubleday, 1935.

Swanberg, W. A. *Citizen Hearst.* New York: Charles Scribner's Sons, 1961.

———. *Whitney Father, Whitney Heiress.* New York: Charles Scribner's Sons, 1980.

Tebbel, John. *The Inheritors: A Study of America's Great Fortunes and What Happened to Them.* New York: G. P. Putnam's Sons, 1962.

Thorndike, Joseph J., Jr. *The Very Rich: A History of Wealth.* New York: American Heritage, 1976.

Thorpe, James. *Henry Edwards Huntington: A Biography.* Berkeley: University of California Press, 1994.

Vanderbilt, Arthur T. *Fortune's Children: The Fall of the House of Vanderbilt.* New York: William Morrow, 1989.

Van Rensselaer, Philip. *Rich was Better.* New York: Wynwood Press, 1990.

Walton, Sam. *Sam Walton: Made in America.* New York: Doubleday, 1992.

Weiss, Murray, and Bill Hoffman. *Palm Beach Babylon.* New York: Birch Lane Press, 1992.

Winkler, John Kennedy. *The Du Pont Dynasty.* New York: Reynald & Hitchcock, 1935.

PICTURE ACKNOWLEDGMENTS

Illustrations for *The Wealthy 100* were obtained through the courtesy of the following institutions.

The Alan Mason Chesney Medical Archives of the Johns Hopkins Medical
    Institutions: Johns Hopkins, Henry Phipps
Amway Corp.: Jay Van Andel, Richard Marvin DeVos,
Archive Photos: Philip Danforth Armour, John Jacob Astor, Jean Paul Getty, John
    Werner Kluge, Thomas Handasyd Perkins, Thomas Fortune Ryan, Russell Sage,
    Samuel Slater, William Thaw
The Boston Athenaeum: Peter Chardon Brooks
Brown Brothers: John I. Blair, Adolphus Busch, James Buchanan Duke, Hetty
    Green, Jay Gould, George Hearst, John W. Mackay, John Pierpont Morgan,
    Col. Oliver Payne, George Pullman, William Rockefeller, Henry Huddleston
    Rogers, Alexander Turney Stewart, Cornelius Vanderbilt, Peter A. Widener
Campbell Soup Company: John T. Dorrance
Carnegie Mellon University: Andrew Carnegie, Andrew Mellon
Citibank: Moses Taylor, James Stillman
Culver Pictures: Anthony N. Brady
Detroit Public Library, National Automotive History Collection: John Francis
    Dodge, Horace Elgin Dodge
Ford Motor Company: Henry Ford
Frank & Marie-Therese Wood Print Collections: William Aspinwall
Frick Art & Historical Center Archives: Henry C. Frick
Girard College Collection: Stephen Girard (photo of portrait by Bass Otis)
Hewlett-Packard Company: David Packard
Johnson & Johnson: Robert Wood Johnson, Jr.
Kraft Foods, Inc.: Charles W. Post
Liaison International: Ronald Owen Perelman
Marshall Field Archives: Marshall Field
Merck & Co., Inc: William Weightman
Monterey County Parks: Claus Spreckels
New York Historical Society: Edward Stephen Harkness, Daniel Willis James
New York State Historical Association, Cooperstown: Stephen Van Rensselaer
Paul Allen Group © Kathleen King: Paul G. Allen
Peabody Essex Museum, Salem, Mass.: Elias Hasket Derby, George Peabody, Israel
    Thorndike
Ohio Historical Society: John W. Garrett, Nicholas Longworth
Oracle Corp.: Lawrence J. Ellison
Salomon Brothers Inc.: Warren Buffett

INDEX